Disability and Religious Diversity

Disability and Religious Diversity
Cross-Cultural and Interreligious Perspectives

Edited by
Darla Schumm and Michael Stoltzfus

palgrave
macmillan

DISABILITY AND RELIGIOUS DIVERSITY
Copyright © Darla Schumm and Michael Stoltzfus, 2011.

First published in 2011 by
PALGRAVE MACMILLAN®
in the United States—a division of St. Martin's Press LLC,
175 Fifth Avenue, New York, NY 10010.

Where this book is distributed in the UK, Europe and the rest of the world,
this is by Palgrave Macmillan, a division of Macmillan Publishers Limited,
registered in England, company number 785998, of Houndmills,
Basingstoke, Hampshire RG21 6XS.

Palgrave Macmillan is the global academic imprint of the above companies
and has companies and representatives throughout the world.

Palgrave® and Macmillan® are registered trademarks in the United States,
the United Kingdom, Europe and other countries.

ISBN: 978–0–230–11973–4

Library of Congress Cataloging-in-Publication Data

Disability and religious diversity : cross-cultural and interreligious
perspectives / edited by Darla Schumm and Michael Stoltzfus.
    p. cm.
ISBN 978–0–230–11973–4 (hardback)
    1. Disabilities—Religious aspects. 2. Chronic diseases—Religious
aspects. 3. Human body—Religious aspects. I. Schumm, Darla Y.
(Darla Yvonne) II. Stoltzfus, Michael, 1965–

BL65.B63D57 2011
200.87—dc22   2011014233

A catalogue record of the book is available from the British Library.

Design by Newgen Imaging Systems (P) Ltd., Chennai, India.

First edition: October 2011

10 9 8 7 6 5 4 3 2 1

Printed in the United States of America.

For Rebecca, William, Jonathan, and Henry

Contents

Acknowledgments

All books have collaborative elements, but this book and its companion volume, *Disability in Judaism, Christianity, and Islam: Sacred Texts, Historical Traditions, and Social Analysis* truly reflect collaboration on many levels. We thank all those who gave their time and talents and contributed chapters to the book. We had a vision for the book that was realized only through the contributions of Maysaa Bazna, Lynne Bejoian, Aimee Burke Valeras, Priscilla Gilman, Lavonna L. Lovern, Jeff McNair, Jo Pearson, Molly Quinn, Erynn Rowan Laurie, and Abigail Schindler.

Palgrave Macmillan graciously reviewed our original manuscript and recommended that we divide it into two separate volumes. Editor Burke Gerstenschlager and Editorial Assistant Kaylan Connally deftly guided us through the process of preparing two manuscripts for publication. We are grateful to the editorial board of Palgrave Macmillan for their willingness to bring issues of religion and disability to the forefront and publish these books.

Most of what we do would not be possible without the love and support of our families. We thank our parents, Glenn and Geneva Stoltzfus and Clare and Katie Ann Schumm, for their constant care, encouragement, and nurture. Our spouses and children Rebecca Green, William Stoltzfus, Jonathan Harris, and Henry Schumm provide daily inspiration and encouragement and receive our deep gratitude for sustaining us from the beginning to the end of the project.

We thank Elizabeth Smoak, a student assistant at Hollins University, for her help with many details in the editing process. Finally, we are profoundly grateful for the immense contribution that Lindsay L. Gray made to the project. She logged countless hours of proofreading, editing, formatting, and then doing it all over, again and again. Lindsay oversaw many of the details involved in compiling and publishing two edited volumes. She kept us on track, and without her work we could have never brought the project to its successful completion.

Editors' Introduction

Michael Stoltzfus and Darla Schumm

*D*isability and Religious Diversity: Cross-Cultural and Interreligious *Perspectives* and the companion volume titled *Disability in Judaism, Christianity, and Islam: Sacred Texts, Historical Traditions, and Social Analysis* (also published by Palgrave Macmillan) examine how distinctive religions of the world represent, understand, theologize, theorize, and respond to disability and/or chronic illness. It is widely recognized that religious teachings and practices help to establish cultural standards for what is deemed "normal" human physical and mental behavior and in establishing a moral order for the fit and healthy body and mind. Religion, in its multiple manifestations, plays a critical role in determining how disability is understood and how persons with disabilities are treated or mistreated in a given historical-cultural context. The existent literature exploring intersections between religion and disability typically focuses on a single religious tradition or cultural context, often prioritizing a Judeo-Christian approach. In response to the challenges and opportunities posed by a postmodern, pluralistic, global world, our goal in both books is to promote interdisciplinary, cross-cultural, and interreligious conversations regarding disability and religious diversity. All multicultural education and literature must address the issues of how to balance the particularity of cultural or religious identity with openness to learning from our neighbors who are different. The interplay of the opening and boundary-setting dimensions of religious life is of crucial importance to the flourishing of multicultural societies in general and to the growing field of disability studies in particular.

This book and its companion volume began with the editors' desire to create a resource that investigates issues in disability studies from the perspective of religious pluralism. The response to our open call for papers that address interreligious and cross-cultural perspectives on topics relevant to disability studies produced too much for one volume to contain. After Palgrave Macmillan's gracious offer to publish the collection in two volumes, we were left with the rather daunting task of how to organize and divide the chapters between volumes. When the review process was complete, about half of the remaining chapters addressed disability studies within the frameworks of Judaism, Christianity, or Islam. We therefore decided to dedicate one book largely to these traditions. The religious traditions that explore disability or chronic illness in this volume include Baha'i, Celtic Pagan, Wiccan, Native American, Daoist, as well as narrative and comparative pieces that incorporate Catholic and Protestant Christianity, Buddhism, and Islam. While we have tried to organize the divergent body of work presented here in some orderly fashion, we are left more in hope than certainty that the chapters are both fluid and balanced.

The contributors in both books employ a wide variety of methodological and theoretical approaches including ethnographic, historical, cultural, or textual analysis, personal narrative, theological/philosophical investigation, and interreligious comparative analysis. In addition, the authors incorporate literature and theoretical perspectives from the growing field of disability studies. Both books explore the intersections between religion and disability, give voice to scholars and practitioners of many of the world's rich and varied religious traditions, actively engage the field of disability studies, and reflect multicultural and interreligious attitudes and perspectives. The chapters present creative, critical, and practical insights and conversations among and between differing religious traditions concerning issues relating to disability. Both of the editors and multiple contributors approach their scholarship from the perspective of living with some form of disability or chronic illness.

Disability and Religion: Beyond Definitions

The chapters in this volume do not represent a uniform approach to defining or responding to disability or religion; nor do they present a monolithic experience of disability or religion. Diversity, not uniformity, is the mark of both religion and disability. One reason that disability studies are so rich, varied, and interesting is because "disability" defies definition. There are porous boundaries between disability and apparent health. More significantly, disability cuts across all races, classes, genders, ethnicities, nationalities, religions, and generations because it can potentially happen to anyone because anyone may become disabled. For example, in 2000, it was estimated that some

64 million or 20 percent of Americans have one or more physical or intellectual disabilities or chronic illnesses and that number is increasing as the population ages (Davis 2002; Harrington n.d.). This makes people with disabilities the largest and most diverse minority group in the United States. Similar statistics are likely representative of the world population as a whole.

Who are disabled people? The response to this question is far from self-evident. People with disabilities have more differences than similarities. Disabling conditions can include intellectual, physical, and/or psychological issues. For example, blindness, paralysis, multiple sclerosis, deafness, and intellectual differences may produce similar social issues involving marginality and stigma, but they generate vastly different functionalities. Individuals with similar disabilities may differ significantly in impairment or difficulty. Furthermore, disabilities can be progressive or static, acquired or congenital, episodic or chronic, remittent or persistent. The social experience of a person who becomes disabled as an adult might differ significantly from that of a person with a congenital disability. Finally, chronic disabilities such as paralysis or blindness differ significantly from chronic illnesses such as Lupus, Crohn's disease, or rheumatoid arthritis. While the chronically disabled body is often all too visible in its impairment, the chronically ill body is often all too invisible in its pain and discomfort. These dissimilarities make a broad definition of people with disabilities difficult, if not impossible.

In addition to these articulated differences, the very notion of disability as a concept, comprising a wide range of cognitive, physical, sensory, and psychological states of being, is understood quite differently in varying religious communities and even within those communities. The very notion of disability as a cultural concept may be unfamiliar to a range of communities; in fact, some languages do not have a word for disability. The limiting and fragmented ways that religious, medical, and cultural traditions conceptualize disability, and the struggle against such conceptualization, is a major theme addressed in multiple chapters throughout this book.

As with disability, religious practice and belief systems are beyond cognitive confinement, systematic summation, or categorical definition. Religious traditions, meanings, transformations, practices, texts, symbols, rituals, prayers, meditations, and approaches to transcendence are nearly as numerous and diverse as grains of sand on the seashore. The world has always had immense religious plurality but in the past three or four decades the ever- transforming geographical, linguistic, ethnic, and cultural boundaries have occurred on an unprecedented scale. We live in a developing global civilization made up of many religions and cultures interconnected by mass media, international corporations, international transportation, the Internet, not to mention the local context of family, neighbors, colleagues, community, and friends. No longer can any person, country, religion, or academic discipline be an island. Today everyone is the next-door neighbor and spiritual neighbor of everyone else. A commitment to religious freedom is leading people of many faiths to embrace and respect a wide range of diverse religious expressions, and a commitment to religious practice is leading people of many faiths to recognize and acknowledge the worth and dignity of all human bodies, whether they be abled or disabled.

How do different religious traditions explain and respond to disability or chronic illness? The response to this question is also far from self-evident. Religious practices are ever-changing, and there is great diversity and variation within each religious tradition, making it impossible to give definitive answers to specific questions such as "What is the explanation or response to disability within a specific religious community?" Indeed, such broad questions may not be the best place to begin an inquiry into our topic as they tend to cultivate monolithic theoretical responses to pluralistic practical issues. While the themes of disability as punishment for sin or moral failure, disability as a lesson for learning or growth, or disability as a gift or test from God do appear in diverse religious traditions, it is not accurate to suggest that religious traditions have a uniform approach to defining or responding to disability. Most of the contributors in this volume endorse the position that religious life is based in and confirmed by human experience, specifically the human experience of living with some form of disabling condition. Religious expression is viewed as a practical application for living in the world in the midst of the human capacities for joy and pain, hope and despair, explanation and mystery, uniformity and complexity, humility and selfishness, commitment and estrangement, exhilaration and disappointment.

Recurring Themes in Disability Studies: Normalcy, Bodies, and Margins

The disabled body retains symbolic power that is embedded in cultural structures of meaning affiliated with what is deemed "normal" human functionality. Lennard Davis (1995) has argued that the term "normal" was invented 150 years ago via the advent of mathematical statistics; with these developments came the idea of the "average citizen," an exclusionary category that marginalizes the disabled. This means that people who struggle with disabilities and/or chronic illnesses struggle not only with physical and intellectual health issues but also often with the cultural exclusion that goes along with having an "abnormal" body. Susan Wendell (1996) convincingly demonstrates how the disabled body is often rejected in many contemporary cultural milieus that tend toward obsession with images of the perfect body. Disabled bodies confront people with illness, pain, and difficulty that many would rather remain hidden. Nancy Eiesland (1994) writes: "The difficulty for people with disabilities has two parts really—living our ordinary but difficult lives, and changing structures, beliefs, and attitudes that prevent us from living ordinarily" (p. 13). Many cultures view pain and illness as abnormal episodic problems to be ignored or quickly overcome, rather than ordinary elements of the human condition from which we might learn and grow.

The growing field of disability studies develops as a response to prior culturally prescribed meanings or models of disability and disability issues. A brief overview of some of the typical categories used to contextualize disability helps to integrate the diverse perspectives on religion and disability presented in this book. In an effort to minimize abnormality and explain disability, social-scientific models tend to label individual bodies with descriptive terms such as sick or healthy, abnormal or normal, disabled or abled. In spite of the vast diversity associated with disabling human conditions, efforts to define those with disabilities abound. Medical, religious, and social models are common examples used as conceptual categories.

Medical models of disability tend to emphasize individual deficits or impairments and stress a narrative focusing on diagnosis, treatment, and cure. A person is not whole, not really able, unless he or she is "cured" or moved closer to an abled, well, "norm." Normal human bodies eventually get better; the bone mends, the pain subsides, the scar heals. This model often ignores important issues associated with chronic conditions that have no established medical protocols for their cure, and often fails to incorporate issues associated with social exclusion or social accommodation (Garland-Thomson 2005; Kleinman 1988; Longmore and Umansky 2001; Reynolds 2008; Sidell 1997). According to the medical model, the disabled body is a defective body that requires repair through medical procedures. Like all people, those with disabilities and/or chronic illnesses desire access to quality medical care. However, the medical model perpetuates the misnomer that the root problem of disability lies in the disabled individual body rather than in the social-religious forces that may marginalize and stigmatize persons with disabilities.

While religious attitudes and responses to disability are anything but monolithic, it is not uncommon for religious models to connect disability with individual spiritual deficiency. There is a persistent tendency to associate disability with suffering, and well-meaning people from multiple religious traditions often struggle to offer religious explanations and religious solutions to the "problem" (Reynolds 2008; Simundson 2001). For people with disabilities, such explanations can lead to spiritual anxiety in the private sphere and alienation from religious association in the public sphere. Isolated from the public sphere for physical or intellectual abnormality or difference, such persons likewise find themselves singled out through religious interpretations of that difference, interpretations that might generate stigmatization.

In contrast to the medical and religious models that tend to associate disability with individual impairment or suffering that requires treatment, solution, or explanation, the social model of disability tries to normalize impaired bodies and minds in order to contextualize oppressive social and historical conditions. Many in the disabled population argue that economic hardships, inaccessible environments, and prejudicial social attitudes pose greater difficulty than the actual disability although this is certainly not always the case (Davis 2002; Garland-Thomson 2005; Linton 1998; Wendell 1996). Nonetheless, the integration of disability as a natural form of embodiment and a normal element of social awareness empowers disability activists and theorists to destabilize oppressive interpretations and rethink inflexible categories. As physical and/or psychological outsiders, disabled people offer a valuable critique of a world that nondisabled people take for granted, thereby opening new vistas for creative transformation in the interpersonal and social dimensions of our collective lives.

An important way that the growing field of disability studies is enhancing the exploration of our human condition is by recognizing it as an interdisciplinary and multidimensional field. Increasingly, disability studies invite people not to isolate disability as an individual medical or religious pathology but instead to integrate the dynamic connections of disability across many fields of analysis including health care, legal, psychological, economic, religious, literary, artistic, social, historical, and other perspectives. This book can be viewed as one small part of an ongoing effort to expand our horizons of availability by incorporating cross-cultural narratives and interreligious perspectives regarding disability and religious diversity.

Organizational Format and Section Divisions

The organization of this book reflects the type of interreligious and cross-cultural dialogue we hope to model and inspire. This book is loosely divided into three sections: (1) Religion, Narrative Identity, and Disability; (2) Religion, Accessibility, and Disability; and (3) Interreligious and Cross-Cultural Comparisons of Disability. Each section is prefaced by a brief introduction that highlights key themes and provides synopses of the chapters that follow. It is important to note that while each chapter is distinctive and stands on its own as an academic, literary, and creative work, broad themes run throughout each section and between sections. Religion and disability are the themes that navigate broad topics associated with narrative, access, and comparative analysis.

Religion, Narrative Identity, and Disability

As insinuated earlier in the Introduction, professional "experts" have tended to try to label and categorize the experience of those who live with disabling conditions. These attempts have resulted in a scarcity of firsthand information regarding the goals, feelings, and self-definitions of disabled persons. However, alongside the changes in legislation and public dispositions inspired by the disability rights movement have come changes in the very language and methods used to describe disability. People with disabilities are not content to be defined by others and have begun to name themselves, tell their own stories, and identify their own desires and ambitions. Autobiography, ethnography, and other forms of narrative story telling empower people living with disabilities through communicating their own reality.

The four chapters in Section 1 of the book incorporate a narrative approach to the exploration of the intersection of religion and disability. One chapter results from academic interviews of people living with a chronic illness in the United States, incorporating Catholic stories and themes. Two chapters are autobiographical, written by two women living with chronically debilitating disabilities; one chapter incorporates Baha'i and Christian spiritual perspectives while the other integrates Celtic Pagan stories and analysis. Neither author assumes familiarity with Baha'i or Celtic Pagan traditions. Rather, both writers weave a double narrative merging the stories of their own spiritual traditions with their personal stories of chronic pain and renewal, alienation and healing.

Religion, Accessibility, and Disability

In Section 2, narratives and stories continue to be an important part of the analysis as they are integrated with the ongoing struggle for full access to social and religious integration. Accessibility has become a rallying cry among people with disabilities, and the body is often the focal point of struggle for political and social access. In challenging society's definitions of disabled bodies as flawed and incapable, people with disabilities have refused to have their bodies be discriminated against in employment, be restricted from public buildings, be isolated from educational opportunities, and be refused access to medical care or legal protection. But access, as we use the term here, goes beyond issues of institutional accommodation and physical modification to include issues of attitudinal orientation and participatory availability. There is a notable difference between physical accessibility and socioreligious integration, between formal protection under the law and the advent of community, friendships, and group belongingness. When religious affiliations treat the disabled as they treat the abled, as multidimensional people with diverse spiritual and dispositional needs, then these affiliations extend a gesture of accessibility that is as important as architectural accommodation.

The four chapters in Section 2 address diverse themes pertinent to accessibility and disability in Christian, Daoist, Wiccan, and Native American religious traditions. Authors investigate how physical and mental disabilities affect access to participation in religious rituals, how physical accommodation of people with disabilities is often not matched by social integration in secular or religious groups, how many Native Americans continue to be denied access to basic medical or disability care, and how Daoist themes and symbols integrate new vistas for thinking about disability and chronic illness.

Interreligious and Cross-Cultural Comparisons of Disability

Exploring how different religious and cultural perspectives distinguish and respond to the full spectrum of ability is critically important to disability studies. Central to the writing and editing of this book is the desire to examine how different religious traditions and cultural communities respond to disability and chronic illness. What can we learn about ourselves by opening to the perspectives of other modes of thought and action? Cultures and religious practices are continually transforming. One way to investigate the perpetual shift in religious and cultural discourse as it relates to disability studies is to offer cross-cultural and interreligious analysis and comparative perspectives. The authors in the final section explore the connections between suffering, healing, and disability within Buddhism, Christianity, and Islam and consider some of the similarities and differences that exist between Native American and Western cultural concepts of health and ability. The chapters in Section 3 of the book highlight the significance of critical reflection on taken-for-granted cultural practices and imagine new possibilities for interreligious and cross-cultural communication.

Hopes and Intentions

It is our hope that this book and the companion volume *Disability in Judaism, Christianity, and Islam: Sacred Texts, Historical Traditions, and Social Analysis* will appeal to a broad audience including members of the disabled community, scholars and students from many disciplines, healthcare professionals, social service professionals, and religious practitioners from multiple traditions. We believe that these books can function as useful tools for college and university courses and as resources for more general audiences interested in the intersection of religion and disability. The books might also help people expand what is sometimes a narrow professional and/or personal frame of reference for viewing and responding to both disability and religion.

The chapters in these edited volumes begin to fill a significant gap in both academic and popular literature in the area of religion and disability. Currently, there is no available text focused on consideration of disability and chronic illness across a variety of religious traditions. While numerous books, journals, and articles have been written about religion and disability, most of these texts and articles focus on the history, literature, and practices of a single religious tradition. Furthermore, the vast majority of available scholarship focuses on various elements of the Christian tradition. There are a few articles about disability and religion from non-Christian perspectives in the *Journal of Religion, Disability, and Health* and in *Disability Studies Quarterly*. However, we are not familiar with any resources that include a single source of essays and perspectives from multiple and varied religious traditions and their interpretation of disability, nor any that explore issues related to comparative religion. Our hope is that these books will begin a long and fruitful conversation among and between those interested in the relationship of religious diversity and disability.

Given the vast and pervasive role that disability and religion play in human experience, the chapters included in these volumes portray varied and complex perspectives of disability and religion that are by no means exhaustive. Consensus regarding the experience of disability or the understanding of how religious traditions should conceptualize disability is not the goal of this project. Rather, our intention is to foster interreligious and cross-cultural dialogue about religion and disability and to cultivate innovative ways to respond to the expanding fields of both disability studies and religious studies.

References

Davis, L. (1995). *Enforcing Normalcy: Disability, Deafness, and the Body.* New York, NY: Verso.

Davis, L. (2002). *Bending over Backwards: Disability, Dismodernism & Other Difficult Positions.* New York, NY: New York University Press.

Eiesland, N. (1994). *The Disabled God: Toward a Liberatory Theology of Disability.* Nashvile, TN: Abingdon Press.

Garland-Thomson, R. (2005). Feminist disability studies. *Signs: Journal of Women in Culture and Society 30*(2), 1558–1587.

Harrington, C. (n.d.). Disability Statistics Center. Retrieved from http://dsc.ucsf.edu/main.php

Kleinman, A. (1988). *The Illness Narratives.* New York, NY: Basic Books.

Linton, S. (1998). *Claiming Disability: Knowledge and Identity.* New York, NY: New York University Press.

Longmore, P., & Umansky, L. (Eds.). (2001). *The New Disability History: American Perspectives.* New York, NY: New York University Press.

Reynolds, T. (2008). *Vulnerable Communion: A Theology of Disability and Hospitality.* Grand Rapids, MI: Brazos Press.

Sidell, N. L. (1997). Adult adjustment to chronic illness: A review of the literature. *Health & Social Work 22*, 5–11.

Simundson, D. J. (2001). *Faith under Fire: How the Bible Speaks to Us in Times of Suffering.* Lima, OH: Academic Renewal Press.

Wendell, S. (1996). *The Rejected Body: Feminist Philosophical Reflections on Disability.* New York, NY: Routledge.

SECTION 1

Religion, Narrative Identity, and Disability

The power of story to cultivate creative transformation in people's lives has long been recognized by religious traditions. A narrative approach to learning is founded on the assumption that our understanding of both religious experience and disability experience is powerfully shaped by the kind of story that we think we are in and the role that we see ourselves playing in that story.

As disabled people across the globe begin to play a more prominent public role in every avenue of life, they are increasingly expressing the power of their own voices and are not content to have their experiences dictated by professional experts or social convention. The narratives offered in this section depict how various religious traditions inspire the human qualities of hope, humility, struggle, commitment, and love in the individual lives of those living with diverse disabling conditions. The lessons that religious traditions teach are not restricted to scriptures, creeds, or rituals but create practical ways of living in the midst of complex cultural sensitivities and dynamic human relationships. The process of reading religious narratives or disability narratives does not mean that everyone will agree with the perspectives presented, but it does provide the opportunity for people to appreciate what gives purpose to the religious lives of people from different traditions and to demonstrate respect for them as equal members of the human family.

Aimee Burke Valeras opens Section 1 with two powerful stories that utilize a narrative research approach to highlight the experience of hidden disability in the lives of children and young adults. The narratives explore two hidden disabilities in particular, juvenile rheumatoid arthritis and celiac disease. These stories make no effort to hide the personal and social hurdles that come when living with chronic illness; and these stories recognize no limits to the capacity of young people to find life meaningful in the midst of pain and difficulty. Narrative description is utilized to highlight how religion, gender, and culture influence the integration of chronic illness into personal identity and social relationships. Valeras prefaces her riveting stories by introducing the advantages associated with using a narrative research methodology in exploring the complex interaction of religious identity with chronic disability in the lives of children.

In Chapter 2, Priscilla Gilman allows readers to witness her harrowing and inspiring journey to unite chronic illness and spiritual transformation by sharing her experiences in both the Baha'i and Christian traditions. After years of commitment to building the Kingdom of God on earth as a practicing Baha'i, Gilman found herself immobilized by fatigue and pain, even though no specific disease could be diagnosed. She struggled to find a way to unite her spirit and body with the teachings of the Baha'i tradition even as her body could do little or no physical activity for long periods of time. While continuing to celebrate many elements of Baha'i praxis, Gilman's journey involves a return to the left-behind Christianity of her youth with a new perspective on the radical affirmation of our bodily lives in the teaching of the incarnation. Gilman yearns for a religious view where disability is neither the exception nor the norm, but the universal human reality into which the divine enters, broken and whole, so that the human body, broken and whole, might become divine.

Gilman's critical engagement with Baha'i tradition and constructive suggestions for how Baha'i religious understanding might change how the human body is interpreted, particularly the chronically ill body, are offered in a spirit of love and respect. We believe that this narrative will provide inspiration for many who find themselves immobilized by chronic fatigue and pain and will cultivate compassion in all who read it.

In Chapter 3, Erynn Rowan Laurie combines a detailed synopsis of "mad" figures affiliated with Celtic myth with her personal experience of posttraumatic stress disorder and chronic depression in an essay/narrative where spirituality and madness intersect with creativity in potentially expressive and healing ways. Celtic myth is rife with male and female figures who abandon society after battle, trauma, or being cursed, with symptoms that, in modern terms, resemble such emotional and psychological disabilities as schizophrenia, paranoia, and depression. After long sojourns in the wilderness, these figures were perceived as part animal, transgendered, growing feathers or fur instead of clothing. Yet, they are also closely and intricately linked to visionary states, prophesy, music, and poetry. Laurie demonstrates how these stories and images are incorporated into modern Celtic Pagan spiritualities by individuals coping with psychological and emotional disorders as a way to bring art and healing together within the context of a spiritual path.

CHAPTER 1

God's Will? How Two Young Latina Catholic Women Negotiate a Hidden Disability Identity

Aimee Burke Valeras

Introduction

A *hidden disability* is a physical medical condition that is unapparent to the unknowing observer. The following essays explore the identity processes of two young women with the hidden disabilities juvenile rheumatoid arthritis and celiac disease. These stories were obtained using a narrative research methodology. In the data representation, vivid narrative depiction is used to understand how culture, religion, gender, and accepted social norms influence adaptation and integration of a hidden disability into one's personal identity.

Human beings create stories to make meaning of their experiences, dreams, discoveries, troubles, courage, love, and loss. Symbols, images, language, and icons are used to tell our stories in ways that instruct, guide, comfort, chasten, or surprise. By sharing stories, we connect with each other, overcoming the polarization of difference (Saleebey 2006). Utilizing a narrative research approach enables access to and presentation of a distinct perspective of disability and what it means to be impaired or disabled, which may clash with how disability is usually constructed and recorded (Siebers 2004; Thomas 1999).

Narrative Research Methodology

Our identities are our narratives. Such an evolving, fluid, contextual identity is therefore best understood through story. I solicited the participants' "stories" through a face-to-face two-hour interview, which was tape-recorded with permission. Conversations were guided with nine questions, prompting the unfolding of the participants' "story," initiated with the question, "Tell me about what your life has been like living with (specific condition), from the beginning." Asking only general open-ended questions, such as this one, prompted storied answers from the participants, allowing them control over the direction of the narrative they shared (Polkinghorne 1995). These stories reveal how participants' selves are crafted, offering me a window into their constructed "disabled" or "nondisabled" identity (Barone 2000).

The names used in the stories are all pseudonyms, and all identifying information has been altered slightly to ensure participant anonymity. Soon after the first interview, participants received a copy of the complete transcript and had the opportunity to add or delete any aspects of their narrative. I communicated face to face with participants after they read the transcript to inquire about their reactions to reading the transcript and their response to my preliminary understanding of specific motifs that were emerging through the data collection and analysis process. In this way, the two women joined with me in the construction of the results. Together we tried to answer the questions, "How does an unapparent medical condition affect identity?" and "How are self-disclosure decisions negotiated?" In this process, the participants and I together embraced the multiplying questions that emerged through discovering similarities and uniqueness within the experience of hidden disability.

By assembling the elements of participants' descriptions into a single vivid narrative, I attempt to draw the reader into the individuals' lived experience as an alternative reality (Barone and Eisner 1997; Polkinghorne 1995). Representing the data in this way offers the reader the opportunity to vicariously participate in a virtual world that had previously been private and inaccessible. This "empathetic witnessing" of a different kind of life inspires a dialogue between the reader and the text, invoking an understanding of why and how a person acts as he or she does (Barone and Eisner 1997; Coulter 1999; Docherty and McColl 2003).

Narrative construction is utilized to transform actions, events, and happenings into one descriptive explanatory story, emphasizing unique differences across cases (Polkinghorne 1995). My goal of writing narrative constructions, thus, is to lead thought from case to case rather than from case to generalization (Charon 1993; Polkinghorne 1995). Narrative construction reveals the particular to hint at multiple universal truths (Polkinghorne 1995). Enabling the reader to focus on the particular characteristics of a "character's" actions illuminates the difference and diversity of human behavior, allowing for the understanding of human action as an outcome of both previous experiences and proposed purposes (Polkinghorne 1995).

The narrative constructions are written using *thick description*, a vivid portrayal of the ordinariness of the routine experiences of participants' lives. This grounds the narrative in a particular context, making it accessible to audiences beyond academia (Barone and Eisner 1997). As the researcher/writer, I relinquish control over how the text will be read, interpreted, and understood when the reader fills in the gaps in the story (Barone 2000). The reader makes meaning of the significant events in participants' personal stories and the absences therein, both of which illuminate the construction of identity (Woodward 2002). Readers, thus, are actively involved with the construction of the knowledge yielded from the research (Docherty and McColl 2003).

The poignant and riveting narratives of these two young Catholic Latina women in the United States are portrayed in such a way that the reader can vicariously experience and understand how their religious foundation helps, and also hinders, them in markedly different ways, as they embark on a journey to find meaning in their disability. By identifying as protagonists in a narrative, defining their own reality, shaping a new identity, and naming history, the participants might "come to voice" (hooks 1994), liberating their silenced and unheard stories silenced (Clandinin and Connelly, 2000).

Stations of Victoria

The deeper that sorrow carves into your being, the more joy you can contain. Is not the cup that holds your wine the very cup that was burned in the potter's oven? And is not the lute that soothes your spirit, the very wood that was hollowed with knives?

—Kahlil Gibran (1923)

The Prophet

The sun was creeping through the window shades over her bed rousing her from sleep. She tried to move, and pain seared through her body. She screamed. Her voice echoed through the house, bringing her mother and father running. Her father tried to pick her up. She screamed. Her entire body was wracked with pain. Her parents looked at each other, their eyes communicating worry in a silent adult language. Through her tears, she caught her sister's wide brown eye as she peered through the crack in the almost-closed doorway. There was devastation in her face.

She was five years old, a year older than Victoria, but somehow they knew. They just knew. Victoria's childhood was over.

* * *

Everything was white. Her father stood up and pulled a colorless curtain around her bed in an attempt to shut out the sporadic yelps coming from somewhere off in the distance. The machines around her whirred and beeped. The swollen redness around the needle in her hand stood in sharp contrast to the whiteness of the bed sheets, the curtain, the walls. She was scared.

Her father brought his face close to hers. She could smell his smell. It comforted her. He swept his finger across her forward, pushing her hair away from her eyes.

"*Mijita*," he whispered, "You're going to be okay."

Tears welled up in his eyes. He reached for her and her tiny hand disappeared in his strong clasp. The tears spilling down his cheeks told her that something was wrong.

"You're going to be okay, Victoria," he repeated. She believed him.

A shrill voice came from just outside the thin screen, "Knock, knock." Her father jerked upright, straightening his posture and smoothing his shirt. A blond head poked through a sliver in the curtain and announced that her blood was needed for tests. Blood? Tests? She looked up at her father as he nodded to her stiffly.

"Is it going to hurt?"

"No. It is not going to hurt. You're going to be okay," he said as the nurse materialized into their small white space with glass vials. She didn't cry. She wanted to show her father that she can be strong. She wanted him to believe himself when he said that she will be okay. The blond woman concentrated on the dark red liquid filling up vial after vial, and Victoria sat there in unyielding silence. She didn't cry.

* * *

After two weeks of white coats, clipboards, nurses, needles, blood, tests, Victoria was allowed to go home to her sisters, her dolls, her dance shoes. It was the same perfectly pink bedroom, but it felt different. She was in the bathroom in the hallway. Her mother knelt down and gingerly lifted her off the toilet seat. She stood unsteadily in front of her mother as she tenderly pulled up the Strawberry Shortcake underwear and corduroy pants.

"*No!*" her father's frame suddenly filled the doorway. "You will *not* do that for her." He spoke in a firm stern voice. "She can do it."

Her mother hastily got to her feet. She suddenly seemed small next to his commanding presence. His voice rose, "We will *not* do things for her. If we do, she will end up crippled. We can't have that. She needs to do everything on her own."

Each night while her body slept, her joints petrified. The early morning sunshine carried with it unbearable pain. Her sisters held their hands to their ears to muffle the sound of her reverberating anguish. It took two hours every morning to bend her solidified arms and legs. As her mother struggled against her cemented joints, Victoria looked pleadingly up into her maternal chocolate eyes. Her mother's eyes were a mirror of her own—filled with pain.

*   *   *

Victoria's mother stood in the doorway of her daughters' bedroom and listened to the sounds of their rhythmic breathing. She savored these dark hours of the night when her child was at peace. She dreaded the morning. Every ounce of her motherly instinct wanted to allow Victoria to stay in bed, to keep her from the horrible experience of moving.

Her husband came behind her and slid his arms around her midsection. He held her and, as if he had read her mind, whispered, "It is what we have to do, *mi amor.*" He lifted her chin and wiped her tears. He did not like to see her cry. "We will *not* have her in a wheelchair."

She turned away and walked over to the portrait of Virgin Mary. She looked up at this savior, this role model. Mother Mary's pure painted eyes seemed to connect with hers.

"You had to watch your child suffer and you were courageous. You were heroic. I must follow your example," she spoke silently to the portrait. She resolved to be stronger, for Victoria. If she wasn't strong as a parent, how would her baby daughter be able to stay strong?

*   *   *

It was Easter Sunday. Victoria and her two sisters, Estrella and Maya, all wore matching frilly pink dresses covered in lace and beaded flowers. Their long dark hair flowed in big curls from carefully combed ponytails. They stood admiring each other while their mother fiddled with the camera. Victoria, the middle child, stood in between her sisters posing. Her mother held the camera to her face and called out "Smile, girls!" She watched through the lens, waiting for the perfect moment to snap the shot. Estrella and Maya were flashing their best smiles, but Victoria's face seemed frozen.

"Victoria, smile!" Her mother raised the camera again, ready to click. Through the lens, she could see Victoria bearing her teeth, but her face held an expression that far from resembled a smile. Exasperated, her mother admonished her, "Victoria, *smile*! What's wrong with you?"

Victoria raised her hand with pink-polished nails, to her face and felt her cheeks. "I'm trying to smile, Mom. I can't."

* * *

They arrived early for the Easter Mass. Her mother and sisters scurried over to the rapidly filling pews. Her father took Victoria by the hand, and they slowly made their way around the perimeter of the church walls. The sun filtered through the vibrant stained-glass windows casting a rainbow of colors on the white tiles. On the walls hung 14 three-dimensional illustrations—the Stations of the Cross. Victoria stared up wide-eyed at the depictions of the scenes before her: Jesus being condemned to death, Jesus being crucified on the cross, Jesus's body being buried in a tomb. And she knew the end of the story: Jesus was resurrected.

Each Easter, she made her way through the series of images of Jesus's journey. The portrayal remained the same year after year, but as Victoria grew older, she appreciated it slightly differently. She realized that Jesus suffered for the salvation of his people. *I suffer too*, she thought, *I can benefit from my own suffering the way we benefit from Jesus suffering.* She grew through experiencing the Stations of the Cross.

"I can do this," she thought to herself. "Every step is hard, but I have my faith and I have my family. Every little step literally is hard and painful, but I can do it. I have a cross I bear. I have this cross, but because I have my faith, it's so much easier to walk."

Rosalina's Broken Bread

A pastel garden emerged three-dimensionally from the white frosting canvas, surrounding perfectly rounded cursive penmanship. Rosalina marveled at the artwork. Birthday cakes: round, oval, square, rectangular, shaped like ballerina slippers, footballs, the countenances of cartoon characters. They were the center of attention at every party.

"Happy birthday to you! Happy birthday to you..." a chorus of sticky fingers and runny noses gathered around the cake, chanting together.

"Here's your piece, Rosa!"

Rosalina declined by shyly shaking her head. She was never tempted to put even a spoonful of the celebratory food in her mouth. She had learned her lesson years ago when her sister peeled the chocolate layer of frosting off her Hostess cupcake and generously offered it to her. The tiny pieces of cake stuck to the frosting left her doubled over in stomach pains and retching for hours. No, she would never sneak even a bite. In her mind, cake was poison.

"You're not going to have cake? But it's a birthday party! Everybody gets a piece of birthday cake!" The birthday boy's mother held a plate out to her.

Using her fingers and the palm of her hand to represent the inside of her intestines, she explained, "My intestines are lined with villae and they flatten if I eat something wrong, like wheat or gluten. I can't absorb it." This was the best way to process and explain the complex medical concepts that she learned at the National Celiac Conference last October.

"What?" all the kids shrieked, "Rosalina has fingers in her stomach! Rosa's weird!"

*   *   *

The hallways of the middle school were packed with commotion after lunch hour. On her way to her locker, she caught girls giving her sidelong looks and hiding their whispers behind their hands. She flushed with self-consciousness, subtly looking herself over. Did her clothes match? Was there toilet paper sticking out of her jeans? Did her thick black hair spring into frizzies? Was there food stuck in her braces? She ducked into the nearest bathroom and checked herself over. She pushed open the door, about to conclude that her paranoia must have been in her head, when she heard it: "Rosalina's *anorexic!*"

"She *is?*"

"Watch her at lunch. She doesn't eat hardly anything. She never eats junk food!"

"That's true, I did notice that!"

"And look how skinny she is..."

At the Spring Fling that weekend, instead of joining in the excitement of who was wearing what and who was dancing together, she made a point of deliberately parading through the food-lined tables, picking out the most unwholesome fattening foods. She took her plate piled high with candy, chocolate, and greasy chips and marched by her classmates.

*   *   *

The eating disorder accusation followed Rosalina into high school. It seemed that eating was the center of every situation that she found herself in. She paid careful attention to how other people declined the offer of food.

"Oh, I just ate. Thanks anyways!"

How simple for them, she thought, and she would test it out.

"Just a little bit, Rosalina."

"Just try a bite."

"I made it myself. I would be insulted if you won't just try it."

Maintaining obstinate refusal was sure to produce the inevitable allegation: "You're awfully thin," which evolved into, "Do you have an eating disorder? Are you anorexic?"

"Actually, I would get really sick if I ate this!" She would finally respond in exasperation. She had to launch into a long-winded explanation of celiac disease just to refuse a small bite of what was being offered. She thought once it was out there, celiac disease not an eating disorder, the scrutiny of her eating habits would be dropped. But instead, a harsher tone of condemnation followed.

"Oh. That's why you're skinnier than me."

School lunches were the worst period of self-consciousness. She felt as though she needed to carefully conceal her meal.

"What a tiny sandwich you're eating," someone would inevitably observe, as though it were offensive. Rosalina glanced at her sandwich and sighed. This one slice of gluten-free bread, a quarter the size of a regular slice of bread, has almost 200 calories in it. But what's the point in explaining her disease again? Or defending her diet? Her explanations went unacknowledged.

"I wish I had that disease because then I would be as skinny as you," her friends would say, with an undertone of blame in their voices.

"Isn't it lucky that you have an excuse not to eat this food!" they declared as they dove into a box of pizza with everything on it. She looked at them, wondering if they have any understanding of how restrictive a strict gluten-free diet is. She wanted to scream, "You have a choice!" She felt as though they faulted *her* for not being happy with *their* bodies. At that moment she wondered what it would be like to be protected by a layer of fat. Being overweight would shield her from these reproachful comments.

*   *   *

As the plane circled Seattle toward its descent, Rosalina grabbed her mother's arm to point out the Space Needle amid the intervening water and land. They were on their annual trip, excited to rejoin the large group of parents and children affected by celiac disease, whom they now considered friends. Rosalina looked around for Bobby as their mothers excitedly caught up.

"He's not here, Rosalina. He's gone off the diet," Bobby's mother told her.

"*What?*" Rosalina's jaw dropped and she at once understood for the first time how her mother felt when her uncle, a recovering alcoholic, started drinking again. "What do you mean he's not on the diet?"

His mother sighed heavily. "It's because of his friends, the peer pressure," she explained. "We were hoping you could talk to him." His mother was in the midst of anguish and helplessness, as her son toggled between dependence and independence. Every night they see him curled up in a fetal position, heaving, enveloped in pain. But they don't see the ridicule that he faces for not sharing a hamburger or buffalo wings or pizza, for drinking only "girly drinks," for refusing beer.

* * *

Rosalina's fingers tapped the steering wheel and her head bobbed as she sang aloud to the music blaring on the car radio. The scenery whizzed by in a blur as she accelerated south on the highway, armed with cookbooks, educational pamphlets, and a list of stores and restaurants that cater to the gluten-free diet. She was still reeling elatedly from the knowledge that her two aunts were diagnosed with celiac disease.

Rosalina had looked around her at every celiac conference and noticed that she and her mother were always the only Latinas. The literature reported it as a disease traceable to European roots. Her aunts' diagnosis was like the missing piece of the puzzle, having triggered exposure of the fact that a great-grandparent was of European ancestry. Rosalina anticipated connecting, for the first time, with another person as both a Mexican and a celiac.

The smell of fresh handmade tortillas wafted down the driveway as Rosalina approached the house. Inside, a lunchtime feast was going on: arms reaching, forks scraping against plates, mouths chewing, everybody talking at once. Her aunt spotted her and gestured her to a seat.

"Rosa, make yourself a plate!"

Rosalina looked around, confused. Her aunts were eating the tortillas, the chimichangas, the enchiladas, the tamales, the beans. "*Tia*, you know I can't eat that food. I thought you couldn't either."

The sounds of the feast halted. Her cousins looked from their mothers to her. Her aunt stood, "Rosa, you thought I would stop eating this food? This food is our culture. This is what we do when we are together. Now go on, make yourself a plate."

Rosalina slumped into a chair, talking distractedly with her cousins while they ate. Later, with fading enthusiasm, she offered the reading material that she brought to her aunts. They took it, but with a look that didn't promise that it would be read. Rosalina finally burst out, "I don't get it! Don't you get sick? Doesn't the food make you ill?"

They described the drive from her house to theirs after every family gathering. During the one-hour drive, they would have to stop on the highway to throw up. They never once made it home without having to pull over. Their bosses threatened to fire them if they missed one more day of work because of "stomach issues," and so they went to work and spent hours in the bathroom. Yes, they answered her with their stories, we get sick. "But it is God's will. This is the way it's supposed to be."

"It's not God's will!" Rosalina exploded, "It's physiological! Your body can't digest wheat or gluten because you have a disease. It is as simple as that. Eating it all the time can cause intestinal damage. You could get cancer from this!"

"Oh, Rosa, that is such an American way to think about it! You cannot just point to science. The Bible tells us that breaking bread is how we participate in Christ's body; it is how we are bonded to one another. If I get cancer, then it is His will. It is my fate."

*　*　*

The day started out cloudy but ended up being perfect weather for her friend's outdoor wedding. Rosalina fished through her purse for her license as she waited for the smartly dressed man in front of her to finish ordering drinks. He turned around with a cocky smile and handed her a colorful concoction. Before taking it, she asked him what it was.

"It's one of my favorite mixed drinks. Just try it," he told her.

"Uh," she hesitated, "I can only drink rum. Is there anything other than Bacardi in it?"

"You only drink rum? Right." He wandered off muttering "*Snob!*" under his breath.

She rolled her eyes and ordered her own drink as he wandered off.

She sat down at her assigned table just as a caterer set a dish in front of her. The plate was a collage of colors. The fresh steamed vegetables looked tempting, but questionable, being on the same plate as a sauce-dripping meat and rice pilaf. Rosalina had decided not to call the caterers ahead of time for a special meal, so as not to draw attention to herself among a table of people she had just met. As everyone dug in, she joined in the idle conversation while painstakingly cutting up all of the food into miniscule pieces. She casually and gradually mixed the food around on her plate to make it appear as though she were making a dent. As the caterers collected the finished plates, she let out a sigh of relief. No one seemed to notice.

*   *   *

One of her coworkers ordered Italian food for everyone. The mouth-watering smells of oregano and garlic wafted through the office drawing an immediate crowd. As Rosalina passed the open door, her coworkers beckoned her in. She attempted to refuse the offered plate of pasta.

"No, thank you," she smiled, looking down at the platter that smelled so delicious but would be toxic to her system.

"Rosa, you have to have a plate! It's from Georgio's—the best Italian in town!"

She looked around at the expectant faces, all eyes watching her. "Well, sure. I'll take a plate, but I have to get back to work," she gave in. Her coworker gave her a big smile as she handed her the dish. On her way down the hallway, she glanced around to make sure that no one was looking, and she dropped the full plate into the trash barrel.

Conclusion

When we tell our story, we make meaning of our experiences, express-ing fluid, changing, and adapting identities. Articulating our personal narratives is a way of seeking unity, coherence, and diversity of identity, if only temporarily (Woodward 2002). The very act of creating, tell-ing, revising, and retelling our story enables us to discover, know, and reveal ourselves. In effect, our identities are located within emplotted stories and our narratives *are* our identities (Lieblich, Tuval-Mashiach, and Zilber, 1998; Polkinghorne 1991; Riessman,2003). It is through these narratives that we come to know, understand, and make sense of the world and who we are (Somers 1994). Identity becomes a mediator between the personal, private world and the public space within cul-tural and social relationships (Scott-Hill 2004). Persons with a hidden disability morph their identity depending on the social and contextual pressures by highlighting or suppressing various aspects of who they are, like chameleons, maintaining multiple identities simultaneously (Darling 2003).

Like Victoria and Rosalina, many persons with a hidden disability discover an identity that enables living not "either/or" but "both/and." They learn how to maximize their unique strengths toward adaptation while acknowledging and allowing for the struggles that accompany disability. Take Victoria, for example; she is a living optical illusion and breaker of assumptions. She sits comfortably with a snug turquoise T-shirt that spells "Latina" across her chest asserting an ethnic and cultural identity that her light skin belies. Internal imaging of her joints reveals bone degeneration that her healthy appearance contradicts. An intense look into her deep brown eyes reflects a soul far elder than her youthful appearance. Her experience of hidden disability is bound in both suffering and adversity *and* the discovery of strengths and passions that might have otherwise remained unknown. The unquestionable resiliency of these individuals stands out across their stories, urging us to question how we conceptualize persons with a hidden disability.

References

Barone, T. (2000). *Aesthetics, Politics, and Educational Inquiry: Essays and Examples*. New York, NY: Peter Lang.

Barone, T., & Eisner, E. (1997). Arts-based educational research. In R. M. Jaeger (Ed.), *Complementary Methods for Research in Education*, 2nd ed. (pp. 75–116). Washington, DC: American Educational Research Association.

Charon, R. (1993). The narrative road to empathy. In H. M. Spiro (Ed.), *Empathy and the Practice of Medicine: Beyond Pills and the Scalpel* (pp. 147–159). New Haven, CT: Yale University Press.

Clandinin, D. J., & Connelly, F. M. (2000). *Narrative Inquiry*. San Francisco, CA: Jossey-Bass.

Coulter, D. (1999). The epic and the novel: Dialogism and teacher research. *Educational Researcher 28*, 4–13.

Darling, R. B. (2003). Toward a model of changing disability identities: A proposed typology and research agenda. *Disability & Society 18*, 881–895.

Docherty, D., & McColl, M. A. (2003). Illness stories: Themes emerging through narrative. *Social Work in Health Care 37*, 19–39.

Gibran, K. (1923). *The Prophet*. New York, NY: Alfred A. Knopf, Inc.

hooks, b. (1994). Narratives of struggle. In P. Mariani (Ed.), *Critical Fictions: The Politics of Imaginative Writing* (pp. 53–61). Seattle, WA: Bay Press.

Lieblich, A., Tuval-Mashiach, R., & Zilber, T. (1998). *Narrative Research: Reading, Analysis, and Interpretation*. London: Sage.

Polkinghorne, D. (1991). Narrative and self-concept. *Journal of Narrative and Life History 1*, 135–154.

Polkinghorne, D. (1995). Narrative configuration as qualitative analysis. In J. Hatch & R. Wisniewski (Eds.), *Life History and Narrative* (pp. 5–25). London: Falmer Press.

Riessman, C. K. (2003). Performing identities in illness narrative: Masculinity and multiple sclerosis. *Qualitative Research 3*, 5–33.

Saleebey, D. (2006). The strengths perspective: Possibilities and problems. In D. Saleebey (Ed.), *The Strengths Perspective in Social Work Practice*, 4th ed. (pp. 279–301). Boston, MA: Allyn & Bacon.

Scott-Hill, M. (2004). Impairment, difference and 'identity', In J. Swain, S. French, C. Barnes, & C. Thomas (Eds.), *Disabling Barriers—Enabling Environments* (pp. 87–93). London: Sage .

Siebers, T. (2004). Disability as masquerade. *Literature & Medicine 23*, 1–22.

Somers, M. (1994). The narrative construction of identity: A relational and network approach. *Theory and Society 23*, 605–649.

Thomas, C. (1999). Narrative identity and the disabled self. In M. Corker & S. French (Eds.), *Disability Discourse* (pp. 47–56). Philadelphia, PA: Open University Press.

Woodward, K. (2002). *Understanding Identity*. London: Arnold.

CHAPTER 2

Whatever the Sacrifice: Illness and Authority in the Baha'i Faith

Priscilla Gilman

Writing from Bed

I woke up this morning feeling horrible. There's nothing unusual in that; I feel horrible every day. The variation is in how horrible, how much of the time, in how many ways, with what diminishment of functionality.

I date my illness to 33 years ago, when I was about five. I woke up feeling sick and fainted on the way to tell my mother. I opened my eyes to her hovering face and asked, "Where am I?" Until college I bore privately, for the most part, my increasing fatigue and my difficulty with sustained standing or sitting. Midway through college, however, the disease—whatever it is—took over. I have no encompassing diagnosis. Without medication my resting heart rate is 120 beats per minute and races faster if I sit, stand, move, think, or feel. Also, my blood pressure runs high but plummets to nothing useful when I am upright. They call these dysfunctions of my autonomic nervous system *postural orthostatic tachycardia syndrome* and *neurally mediated hypotension*. But these are just fancy names for symptoms. They don't explain anything.

Medication enables some function, but still I have fatigue, headaches and motion sensitivity, pain everywhere, difficulty concentrating, sick emptiness in my limbs, and a kaleidoscopic array of other somatic unpleasantnesses. Although my hands and arms look normal I can use them little. I write by dictation. My husband, Larry, must do all the earning, driving, shopping, cooking, dishes, laundry, and house chores.

I have spent years barely able to move, but I can now futz around the house. I take a five-minute walk once a week, most weeks.

"People with disabilities are not sick," cautions Thomas Reynolds in *Vulnerable Communion* (2008: 37). Actually, a lot of us are. I've been thinking of writing to him to say as much, but I haven't had the energy. If I don't even have the energy to find Thomas Reynolds's e-mail address, honestly—try not to panic—how am I going to write this chapter? Why do I get myself into these binds? Why do I even try to do anything? I can't change the story, because I can't keep up, can't make deadlines, can't run my body on schedule.

The Illness Wins

Reynolds also writes, "There is a wider horizon in which all persons in their uniqueness and vulnerability coexist within the enfolding presence of a gracious God. This horizon is our shared humanity, a fragile and contingent humanity that God is present to, suffers with, and transforms" (2008: 43). I believe, despite my panic. Actually, the end of his sentence reads "transforms by embracing in Jesus Christ." I believe that part too, but I just had to cut it off. My fragile contingent humanity is embarrassed by most things Christian, including me—and Jesus.

As I said, I woke up this morning feeling horrible. I've been feeling more horrible in recent weeks than I was in the few months before, but not as horrible as a year ago, and more or less horrible than many other points in memory. I *could* write, dammit, if I wasn't so sick, if I could sit at my desk, look at my notes, throw myself with zealous abandon at the task. But I am sick, and I have to write from where I am.

I'm lying in bed. I'm weak. I'm floating today, when I'm not panicking, drifting around in my thoughts. To my left, through two tall panes of glass, I see the last light of day diffused against solid clouds. Closer I see the silhouettes of mostly bare tree branches—only the oaks still have their ruddy crisp leaves. It's the last day of October. Larry is clanking in the kitchen making beef stew, filling the house with good smells.

I've been wretched, exhausted, hypersensitive to noises, hurting all over. I'm having a hard time remembering what I was going to write—something about the tales I've told and the tales I've been told, the different stories that have defined my relationship to others, to community, to God, to my body and my illness, to the constraints and pleasures of my life. Working with ideas from philosopher Charles Taylor, Reynolds (2008) writes, "We only become selves insofar as we define how things have significance for us, and this implies the presence of others." He says we become "authors of our actions" in community, within shared frameworks of meaning. Communities need "integrative focus as they encounter novel circumstances and understand them to be meaningful. This focus, according to Taylor, is created and maintained by stories and narratives..." (2008: 54).

I'm not quite thinking about those things yet; I'm only drifting in that direction, hoping that my head will bump gently into something relevant. Then I'll start talking into my digital voice recorder and summon in imagination my younger, more mobile, still-active, ambitious self.

New Faith: 1989–1992

Smitten I am when those first words of this novel faith reach my ears. It is my eighteenth birthday. "Why did your family leave Iran?" someone asks my guest at our dinner table. Religious persecution of the Baha'i Faith, she says. "What is the Baha'i Faith?" is the next question. Baha'is believe, she says, that God has sent a succession of messengers through human history to guide and teach humanity—Moses, Jesus, Mohammed, Krishna, Buddha, Zoroaster—and that the messenger, or manifestation of God, for our time is Bahá'u'lláh, a nineteenth-century Iranian nobleman and the founder of the Baha'i Faith, whose teachings are intended to bring about the time of peace promised in all faiths.

I have grown up a passionate atheist in a family well stocked with agnostics; however, a year as an exchange student living with a Muslim family in Indonesia has softened me to religion, even left me feeling that I might someday believe. I do not know what has provoked me to invite Maryam, a year behind me in high school, to be my sole friend at this dinner—I barely know her. But I sit looking around the table this evening, tingling like I have just found the Lost Ark and wondering why nobody else looks to feel anything more than mild interest.

Underneath the table are many feet, 16 at least I would guess, including my two, well clad in some neat little ankle-high boots. My feet are useful, painless, willing and able, easily ignored. They do their job—what else is there to think about? I walk to and from school, up and down stairs and mountains. I bike and swim and run. And those feet never complain. Even so with the whole of my body. Mostly. Underneath my absolutely-taken-as-the-order-of-the-universe functionality is a private worry, something that only occasionally registers consciously. I can't build strength like my peers...at the end of the school day I'm desperate to lie down...I almost fainted a few times...so many things like that...Is something wrong with me?

Within a few months of that dinner I became a Baha'i, through the simple act of saying that I want to and signing a card. By doing so I agree to abide by Baha'i law and be faithful to the Baha'i Covenant, which obligates each Baha'i to follow absolutely, in matters concerning the Faith, the current head appointed by the former (Baha'i International Community 2010). I thus pledge obedience, without quite realizing it, to a succession of authorities: Bahá'u'lláh, the Blessed Beauty, revealer of the word of God for this day; 'Abdu'l-Bahá, his son, the Master, center of the Covenant; Shoghi Effendi, 'Abdu'l-Bahá's grandson, the Guardian; and the Universal House of Justice (UHJ), an elected body of nine men.

Maryam hands me a copy that spring of the annual letter from the UHJ to the Baha'is of the world: "Having ended a year of momentous achievements, we stand at the threshold of the last decade of this radiant twentieth century facing an immediate future of immense challenges and dazzling prospects" (UHJ 1990). The ambition excites me. "The order brought by Bahá'u'lláh is intended to guide the progress and resolve the problems of society" (UHJ 1990). Being an action-oriented, world-saving kind of gal, I'm all right with that. Solve the world's problems? Let's do it! End racism and war, establish gender equality, eliminate poverty and extreme wealth, as the Baha'is proclaim? Awesome!

We are well matched, me and this faith, if only I can get over my distaste for God, worship, obedience, and being known as religious. I start squirming as soon as I sign up. I want that card back, but I can't muster the courage to ask for it. So I stay. I stay because, though embarrassed and afraid, I am falling in love.

I arrive at college expecting an ecstasy of friendship with the other Baha'i students and whole-hearted collaboration in world-transforming action. I find that the two other Baha'is, not new to the Faith, are taking sabbaticals from the passion that is fresh on me. My first year is one of longing, contemplative hunger, and much interior inquiry. I organize a Baha'i club, largely alone.

As I work to fulfill Baha'i laws and study Baha'i writings, my religious ambivalence turns to eagerness. I read Shoghi Effendi's 1944 book *God Passes By*, on the dramatic history of the Baha'i Faith. It tells the story of the Báb, forerunner of Bahá'u'lláh, who stirred up a scene in nineteenth-century Iran with his claim to be the Promised One of Islam, the Qa'im. I want to be like his followers, the Bábís, who, as the story is told, died in great numbers defending their faith. They were the Dawnbreakers. We, the Baha'is, are their spiritual descendants. But I have no horse to ride around on or sword to wield in life-defending drama, and I have no Muslim veil to rip from my face or simply refuse to wear, no society of holy men to shock by such a deed. The governments of the United States of America and the state of New Hampshire do not care what my religion is, and really, nobody else does either.

What I have is a local community, the sweet, regular meetings of the Baha'i club, and my largely fruitless attempts to attract interest to the Faith. "May you continue, through your selfless deeds in His service, to be blessed from the inexhaustible treasury of His love and tender care" (UHJ 1991). But what comes to me by my deeds is not enough. It doesn't satisfy.

I sit with my hunger in solitude. By my second year, I am praying, meditating, and reading Baha'i writings three to four hours a day. I am an anomaly in Animal House (my college was the model for the movie). The Short Obligatory Prayer, once difficult for me to say at all, now feels too slight. I turn to the Medium Obligatory Prayer—longer, more choreographed, more ritual. Three times a day, I prop open my prayer book by the bathroom sink and wash my hands as I say, "Strengthen my hand, O my God, that it may take hold of Thy Book with such steadfastness that the hosts of the world shall have no power over it..." And while washing my face, I say: "I have turned my face unto Thee, O my Lord; illumine it with the light of Thy countenance..." Finally, I say that succinct statement of the story that is increasingly shaping my consciousness:

> Blessing and peace, salutation and glory, rest upon Thy loved ones, whom the changes and chances of the world have not deterred from turning unto Thee, and who have given their all in the hope of obtaining that which is with Thee. (Bahá'u'lláh 1992: 98–100)

Unlike most of my fellow students, I sleep all night and often during the day, often in public. I *have* to lie down. I know all the best couches, patches of lawn, and carpeted floors on campus. Halfway through yoga classes, I assume the Corpse Pose and don't stir until everyone is leaving. I maneuver to take only two classes at a time. I walk, bike, and swim as regularly as I can manage, thinking that exercise will resuscitate me. At the end of my second year, I ask a fellow art student, as we exit the studio, if he feels incredibly tired after class. He doesn't look incredibly tired—none of them do. They are all bounding off to their next engagements, while I am getting horizontal as soon as I can. He looks at me like I am speaking in an accent that he's never heard. "No, not really," he says, and bounds off.

Unconsciously I hold, at least partially, an instrumental view of my body, and I find much reinforcement for it in my Baha'i life. "You should not neglect your health, but consider it the means which enables you to serve," reads a letter dated November 23, 1945, written on behalf of Shoghi Effendi to an individual Baha'i (*Extracts,* item 65). "It—the body—is like a horse which carries the personality and the spirit and as such should be well cared for so it can do its work!" The letter goes on to advise caring for the body and forcing oneself to rest. Well, I am trying to care for my body. I am. The central authorities of the Faith affirm this necessity. I never meet a Baha'i who doesn't say, "The body is the temple of the soul." I know Baha'i scripture praises medicine. I know Baha'is are obliged to consult a physician in times of illness.

Yet I have little specific to tell a doctor; I don't think of myself as sick, and these affirmations of the body are like outposts in sand, standing and failing against greater powers of tide and current: The narratives of Baha'i and Bábí history, the words of Bahá'u'lláh and 'Abdu'l-Bahá, Shoghi Effendi's books and letters, the communications of the UHJ and the National Spiritual Assembly—these sources together make a chorus calling incessantly for dramatic service and fresh sacrifice. They praise individuals who give their lives over to "the Cause" as tireless and indefatigable, and they press the urgency of action.

Each April, the UHJ addresses the Baha'is of the world from Mount Carmel in Israel. We read their words as we remember Bahá'u'lláh declaring his mission while his followers mound roses around him in a garden on the edge of Baghdad. It is the nine-day festival of Ridván. We elect our governing bodies (local and national "spiritual assemblies" annually, the UHJ every five years). We celebrate the founding of our faith. And, through the words of the House, we remember the year just past and look to the year to come. Their letters tell us our story.

From the peak of triumph of the Six Year Plan now ended, we come to the threshold of the Holy Year, now begun...we can do no less than invite you all to take pause to enter into this period of reflection, this time of reconsecration, this stage of preparation for tasks yet to be done, heights yet to be attained, splendours yet to be unveiled. For if we look back at one hundred years of an unexampled history of unremitting progress, we also look forward to many centuries of unfolding fulfillment of divine purpose—fulfillment, which as experience has shown, is incrementally realized through the systematic advances of Plans and the wondrous leaps and thrusts of epochs...This is a time for recommitment to the Covenant, for rededication to duty, for revitalizing the energy for teaching, the "most meritorious of all deeds"...(UHJ 1992)

I did not learn when I first encountered the Baha'i Faith that the overriding preoccupation of the contemporary community is to massively increase its membership. In Baha'i terminology, sharing the Baha'i message and seeking new converts is "teaching" and the ever-expected, much-coveted, massive influx of people is "entry by troops." Through multiyear Plans—they are capitalized—the House directs the community toward specific goals of expansion and development. We must save the world from its troubles, and the one and only way to end hunger, war, racism, sexism, economic disparity, environmental destruction, you name it, is to draw lots and lots and lots more bodies and souls into the Baha'i system.

Our numbers are as yet too small to effect an adequate demonstration of the potentialities inherent in the administrative system we are building, and the efficacy of this system will not be fully appreciated without a vast expansion of our membership....Since the Administrative Order is designed to be a pattern for future society, the visibility of such a pattern will be a signal of hope to those who despair. (UHJ 1990)

I am discomfited as this becomes gradually clear to me. I want direct effort toward social change. Yet, I want to share what I love. I don't want to be alone. I too long for hordes of Baha'is and drool over any reports of such ecstasies of expansion. I believe we are making a new, right order. In this great story of salvation realized, I want a place. I want to be one of those who have "given their all." The need is on me. The hunger. The longing. The desire. For what? I don't know. Something of God. Something I don't have. Something I have to earn. Something I have to give everything to get.

I turn my feet away from campus, out into the world.

Travel and Change: 1992–2000

I set out for Indonesia thinking I can readily find where to pin the tail on humanity. I'm no freak there; everyone is religious. There's little pressure among Baha'is to teach the Faith, as its legal status is tenuous. I work with Baha'i youth and children, doing what I love. We are transforming ourselves through our everyday lives, our spiritual disciplines, and our life in community. We are making the world we want. For five months I teach meditation, drama, and consultation. We study Baha'i writings, play games, translate songs, perform for the community. Everything I know or can do is useful and needed there. I give it all. And then I collapse.

> Our appeal for immediate, redoubled and sustained action on all aspects of the Plan is addressed primarily to the individual believer... The goals of the Three Year Plan will not be easily won, but they must be magnificently achieved, whatever the sacrifice. (UHJ 1993)

I come back from Indonesia spun all round, ready to fall down, with no idea where the donkey or the tail or the wall or the floor or the party or anything has gone. I sleep 15 hours a day and nurse abdominal pain and extreme lethargy when awake. An infectious disease specialist sees me for five minutes and prescribes antibiotics for a presumed parasite. It is the first of several courses. The diarrhea improves but does not resolve. I revive enough to return to classes, the Baha'i Club, and the—now much greater—struggle to keep up.

Where has my desire to pray gone? I am dry inside. Yet I do my part. I hold regular gatherings for prayer and devotion in my apartment. I host "firesides," informal meetings about the Baha'i Faith, and invite my friends. I plan activities and sleepovers for the Baha'i kids in the area. I serve briefly on a local spiritual assembly. I help organize Baha'i events at my college and attend regularly our club's weekly devotional meetings.

> Beyond the need to win our goals, humanity's current plight summons us to redoubled action. The cloud of despair hanging over the fortunes of a deranged world is the very harbinger of the spring rain that can quench the spiritual and material thirst of every people. It has only to be seeded through constant and confident acts of teaching... As we send you this message, clearly before us is a vision of untold victories waiting to be seized. (UHJ 1995)

In my second year back in school, I continue to see doctors, get tests. One morning I faint. I am having blood drawn and go out on the last tube. The tech and the doctor think it is nothing unusual, but I feel like my brain has been thrown against a masonry wall. When a nurse insists I am fine and must sit up, I vomit. Just for you, honey. Finally, my betrothed scoops me up, metaphorically speaking, and deposits me gently on a couch at home, where I lie awake, unmoving, for the rest of the day.

I graduate from college, marry, move to Chicago, start graduate school. The day before our wedding Larry and I try to climb a small mountain together. Partway up I feel sudden light-headedness, and desperate fatigue in my limbs drops me to the ground. I cry in exasperation. We lie on the mountainside and look up at the sky and clouds. Larry says, this is good, we're together.

At our wedding, we say the Baha'i marriage vow, *We will all, verily, abide by the will of God,* and exchange rings (Bahá'u'lláh 1992: 105). Larry has to lick his finger to slide his on.

I enter the department of Performance Studies at Northwestern University. I want to study the way collaborative, community-based theatre and other forms of performance can facilitate social change. I'm particularly interested in religious communities, particularly my own.

The Chicago Baha'i community is bigger than any I've known. I feel very much the outsider, but faithfully attend Feast—the gathering of Baha'is every 19 days—to overcome the unfamiliarity. Much of our consultation at Feast is on what more we should be doing, what more we could be doing, and what more we are failing to do. Everybody is very busy, yet nothing much is happening.

As humanity is tossed and tormented by the ravages inflicted upon it by a civilization gone out of control, let us keep our heads and hearts focused on the divine tasks set before us. For amid this turmoil opportunities will abound that must be exploited... "for enlisting fresh recruits in the ever-swelling army of His followers." (UHJ 1996, quoting Shoghi Effendi).

One lap around the calendar for a master's, and then I'm in for the PhD. Fatigue is constant. I can just manage classes. I squat when others stand. I fidget, lean over, cross my legs, or pull my feet up into my chair. I don't know why, I just do. How I feel can turn in an instant: wretched headaches, extreme sensitivity to motion in my field of vision, wooziness, leaden emptiness in my limbs. A sudden change can immobilize me for days. I lie on the couch, silent and still, waiting for the passage of hours to put the demon back in the box.

For a class I develop a performance on the life of an early African American Baha'i, Louis Gregory, and on the Baha'i vision of race unity. It's a fool's undertaking—a white woman performing alone the life of a Black man. But somehow I'm tricksie, and it works.

The Baha'i fast, from sunrise to sunset March 2 to 21, begins just before my show. I love the Fast. I should not be fasting, but I do not know that I should not be fasting. Baha'i law exempts those who are sick. But I don't *know* that I am sick. I have no diagnosis, no named disease. Besides, exemption *feels* like exclusion. I don't want an exemption. We do these things to become closer to God. If I don't fast, what then?

One afternoon at home, something happens, something very bad, something (is it possible?) in my brain. I *must* have food and drink. I break the fast. I do not recover. I never do. Everything is worse.

I make arrangements to keep my fellowship for a term while taking no classes. I drag myself painfully through the work assigned to me. I live each day to make it back to bed. I lose my fear of death.

> The opportunity offered by the brief span of time before the century ends is precious beyond all telling. Only a united and sustained effort by the friends everywhere to advance the process of entry by troops can befit such a historic moment. Responsibilities urgent and inescapable press upon every institution, every member of a community striving towards its God-promised destiny. As there is only a short period in which to achieve a great deal, no time must be spared, no opportunity lost. (UHJ 1997)

After a succession of useless and traumatic appointments with doctors at the student health service, we travel to see a cardiologist my husband knows. He verifies through testing that gravity, not my need, is dictating where my blood goes. If I maintain an upright position, my heart races and blood pools in my lower limbs until my blood pressure plummets, sometimes causing a loss of consciousness but much more often a sudden and dramatic worsening of my symptoms. We expect diagnosis to bring effective management with drugs. It doesn't.

I take leave from school. I spend months motionless and horizontal, staring into space or at a piece of furniture for hours. Fatigue consumes me. My head swims. Food crises are frequent. "I need something *now*," I say, and Larry jumps to the kitchen. Many days I must sip liquid food before I can get out of bed. I manage to read some, but computing lying down brings rapid pain. I am trapped. My mind monitors every sensation to catch the signs and avoid crashes. I can hardly sit or stand. When I must stand, I march in place to return blood to my heart. Yet too-vigorous movement will also trigger a drop in pressure. I can walk, though, and by God I'm going to do it. I can walk. I walk every other day, regardless of the weather, regardless of how I feel. I walk.

> [T]he mind of the alert follower of the Blessed Beauty must undoubtedly be astir with anxious questions as to what part he or she will play in these few fleeting years... To ensure a soul-satisfying answer, one thing

above all else is necessary: to act, to act now, and to continue to act. (UHJ 1998)

I hate my feet. I think of cutting them off. The legs, too—lop the lousy things *off.* I want to be able to *do* things. If I can't function because the blood is pooling in my legs, what good are they to me? A lot, of course, but I'm desperate.

I learn slowly, over months, to reduce crashes. I manage a little better. I still feel sick all the time, hurt all over, have to lie down everywhere I go. But I do go out, and I do do things. I audit a class. I go back to making art. I even show my work and start building an exhibition résumé. I regularly attend Feast and organize a gospel choir. For some time I think I will finish the PhD. I continue my research on Black sacred music and the Baha'i community. But I'm not going back to school. The more I do the sicker I feel, the more I hurt. I adjust my expectations, carry on, and cope. Will. Determination. Persistence. I'm one of the *good* sick people.

The choir work is difficult. "We are one human family," Baha'is like to say, but we are a dysfunctional family, I want to add. And the Baha'i community is no exception. We produce and distribute statements and videos on the Baha'i vision of race unity, but we are not talking honestly about the particular workings of race in our own community. There is an abundance of resistance and ignorance. Yet there are many people who remain faithful anyway. Bless them. We make a joyful noise, and people love it.

The days pass swiftly as the twinkle of a star. Make your mark now, at this crucial turning point of a juncture, the like of which shall never return. Make that mark in deeds that will ensure for you celestial blessings—guarantee for you, for the entire race, a future beyond any earthly reckoning. (UHJ 1999)

I am eroding even as I persist. More and more I am outside the Baha'i story of salvific busy-ness. Do dodododo. Urgent urgent. Deeds ensure blessings. I hope and try to keep doing. I also stand at Feast and say we need to do less. I hear a quiet gasp from a local spiritual assembly member as she turns to look at me, panicked. "And show up for each other more," I add.

I draw a little every day, though my arms ache, and I have trouble holding myself up. One day my thumb hurts afterwards and doesn't stop hurting. It burns. It feels angry. I ice it and use my other hand. My other thumb starts hurting. Then my hands. The pain feels malicious, almost evil. It spreads to my arms and shoulders.

If I can't use my hands, I'll walk more, I decide. Soon, however, I throw up one day while walking. Then I throw up all the time. Everything triggers the reflex: fatigue, anxiety, hunger, toothpaste. Food hardly helps. I am hungry always. Next my feet fall into pain, my knees, hips, upper and lower back. I retreat, the pain abates; I return to function, the pain returns.

I lose the ability to drive and spend much time unable to leave our apartment. One day when I am doing a bit better, I see yet another useless doctor, then take the train from her office in Evanston to Wilmette. After walking recklessly a long way along the shore of Lake Michigan, I climb the many steps to the lace-domed auditorium of the Baha'i House of Worship.

Sitting there, I think of how I have said my obligatory prayer, fasted, said *Alláh'u'Abhá* 95 times a day, read the writings, memorized prayers, contributed to Baha'i funds, run a college Baha'i club, gone short-term pioneering, tried to teach the Faith, married according to Baha'i law. Obedience cannot sustain me anymore, and promised future total resolution of the world's problems doesn't make my actual life worth living. Bahá'u'lláh writes in *The Hidden Words*, "Turn thy sight unto thyself, that thou mayest find me standing within thee, mighty, powerful, and self-subsisting" (1988c: 12–13). Within myself I find weakness, need, dependence, despair. He also writes, "Love me that I may love thee. If thou lovest me not, my love can in no wise reach thee" (1988c: 11). I can't find that love in me. I have tried mightily to cultivate it, and it isn't there. Not for Bahá'u'lláh. For God? I don't know. Does God love me?

All my most important beliefs, I realize, I can have without being a Baha'i. Yet the thought of leaving the Faith feels like stepping out of the small circle of light. Sitting alone in the silence, under the gold letters of the name of God, I read in a small blue book:

> Oh Lord of loving-kindness! We stray about Thy dwelling, longing to behold Thy beauty, and loving all Thy ways. We are hapless, lowly, and of small account.... Whatever we are, still are we Thine, and what we speak and hear is praise of Thee, and it is Thy face we seek, Thy path we follow. ('Abdu'l-Bahá 1982a: 6)

Two Years Later: 2002

Our inescapable task is to exploit the current turmoil, without fear or hesitation, for the purpose of spreading and demonstrating the transformational virtue of the one Message that can secure the peace of the world . . . Unhampered by any doubts, unhindered by any obstacles, press on, then, with the Plan in hand. (UHJ 2002)

We live in Vermont now. I lie on my back all day. I sit to eat and drink. I walk to the bathroom, to the table, back to the bed. I hold onto walls and furniture as I move. I cannot carry anything, think of anything, speak, or listen while I walk. I must concentrate to make steps. Sounds and vibrations hurt. I cannot be near the washing machine when it's running. Larry's footfalls strain my mind; he learns to walk lightly, move carefully. Dressing and undressing are slow and precarious. I cannot stand barefoot. Even in the shower I wear shoes. Reaching for the soap feels dangerous, like I might fall over any moment. When I finish there's a rough sea in my head, and I sit on my stool by the sink to catch my breath. I'm stubborn and afraid and desperate. I don't want to be where I am.

A man I pay to come to the house teaches me how to live with pain. His name actually is Payne. He tells a story about the need to reckon with where one is, however difficult:

> "Imagine you are coming to my house, you call me for directions, and I say, 'I need to know where you're coming from.' And you say, 'I don't care where I'm coming from, I just want to get there.' And I say, 'I can't tell you how to get here, unless I know where you are.'"

He says there is no self, only the ever-changing flow of sensory experience, thoughts, and feelings. Then he asks me questions to expand my awareness beyond the pain, starting with, "What are you noticing?" followed by "What are you noticing now?" and "Now, what are you noticing?" I'm noticing Larry's typing in the room above, the bare rafters in the ceiling, the sensation of breath in my nose. When we are done I feel calm.

I go every other day to a warm pool for relief from the press of my body against the bed, the chair, the floor. Much is difficult there—the concrete floor, the shower handles, the locker locks, the toilet paper dispensers, the steps into and out of the pool, the woman who thinks I need cheering up, the people who think I need a stranger to manage my crisis. In the car we place a cushion under my feet. Every bump and turn and stop and start is painful. To spare me, Larry drives as smoothly as he can. A few times in the summer I sit in our yard for ten minutes, traversing the 15 feet from the door to a well-cushioned wire chair. I hold Larry's arm on the uneven ground. Once there I remove my shoes and socks to place my bare soles on the grass and weeds. In bed at night I lie on my back as in the day, only socks covering my feet. Even a sheet is a painful weight. My dreams are violent. Each morning my situation is still shocking.

"The body isn't what really matters," a Baha'i friend says. The words are meant to comfort me, like, you still have what really matters.

> That a sick person showeth signs of weakness is due to the hindrances that interpose themselves between his soul and his body, for the soul itself remaineth unaffected by any bodily ailments.... (Bahá'u'lláh 1976: 154)

What I have is a life taken over by the needs, limits, and suffering of a body that doesn't really matter. I want to find another story in the Baha'i Faith, but I find this one most where I look. By now I'm familiar with it anyway, I've heard and lived it countless ways these 12 years as a Baha'i.

> He was sorry to hear you have been ill, and urges you to cooperate fully with your doctors in order to regain your health as soon as possible and be free to serve the Cause. (Letter written on behalf of Shoghi Effendi: *Extracts*, 2010, number 78)

My doctors have no idea what is awry with me. I finally have medications to help control my blood pressure and heart rate, but the underlying problem is worse. At times I feel I may lose my mind. In my world, what you do is who you are. I cannot do anything. I am hardly a person. One Baha'i friend says I've done wonderful things; another tells me how a prominent Baha'i studied the Faith deeply while he was sick, preparing him for greater service when he recovered. Service is what you do—when you are well. I am not well. I am getting worse. I am falling farther and farther outside the story. So what if I did good things in the past? So what if I may do good things in the future, *if* I recover? I'm alive now. How do I survive *now?*

> [E]very malady afflicting the body of man is an impediment that preventeth the soul from manifesting its inherent might and power. When it leaveth the body, however, it will evince such ascendancy, and reveal such influence as no force on earth can equal. Every pure, every refined and sanctified soul will be endowed with tremendous power, and shall rejoice with exceeding gladness. (Bahá'u'lláh 1976: 154)

Is this pain, need, vulnerability, dependence, and loss just obstruction, my life a long waiting and enduring till I die and my soul ascends with power and glory?

> If healing is right for the patient, it will certainly be granted; but for some ailing persons, healing would only be the cause of other ills, and therefore wisdom doth not permit an affirmative answer to the prayer. ('Abdu'l-Bahá 1982a: 161–162)

Is this illness the wisely ordained lesser of two evils? Or is it "the way to self improvement" (*Extracts*, 2010, number 49, Shoghi Effendi)—useful, a test, a lesson, something for my benefit? "All calamities and afflictions have been created for man so that he may spurn this mortal world..." ('Abdu'l-Bahá 1982a: 239)

There is another story in my imagination, one of which I was more ignorant than I realized until I started stepping regularly into a little church in Maine, where we summered during our Chicago years. What was a Baha'i doing in church? Living the oneness of religion, I said in my heart—a fundamental principle of the Faith. But church got into me. There, every Sunday and Wednesday people ate and drank grace, and the story about God was emphatically physical. This God floated upside down in his own urine before squeezing through a woman's pain, into someone's hands. His body mattered. Looking at 'Abdu'l-Bahá's words in *Some Answered Questions* on Christian subjects, I find in every case a dephysicalizing—the sacraments, the miracles, the resurrection, all interpreted away:

> [W]here it is said that the blind received sight, the signification is that he obtained the true perception; where it is said a deaf man received hearing, the meaning is that he acquired spiritual and heavenly hearing....All [the Divine Manifestations'] states, Their conditions, Their acts, the things They have established, Their teachings, Their expressions, Their parables and their instructions have a spiritual and divine signification, and have no connection with material things. ('Abdu'l-Bahá 1982b: 102, 103)

In Church, and later from some Christian writers, I hear instead of a fecund materiality:

> During a meal with his disciples he [Jesus] takes off all his clothes, wraps a towel around his loins, pours water into a basin, and begins

to wash the disciples feet, wiping their feet with a towel which he was using to cover himself. That's a crazy story to tell to illustrate the love of God...How could God be so immodest and insensible, to not only become incarnate in the world, to chase after us in this way, but to expose his loins as he washes the disciples feet? To suffer and die naked on a cross? (Blue 2004: 101)

Chase after us? I've been trying to work my way *to* God. Giving all to obtain my hopes. Pouring out my heart till it's empty. "Love me that I may love thee." Deeds for blessings. Now I have nothing left to give except my need and my broken body.

But in this Christian story, a broken body is at the center of everything. My body isn't holding me back from participating: my body is on the altar.

Now what am I noticing? Grace, here in this hard life, where God is kneeling to wash my feet.

Temple, Tool, Obstacle, Servant

What we need is not the notion of a world that ought to be but the capacity to see the dimension of grace irradiating the world that *is*. (Wolfe 2009: 5)

Conversion narratives are tricky. Too often the tellers take negative experiences as the Truth of the faith (or absence of faith) they've come from, and positive experiences as the Truth of whatever they've turned to. I hope I do not do either. What the Baha'i Faith might become is not narrowly delimited by what it has been. And I can easily imagine somebody struggling in a Christian community with ideas of the body as sinful, inherently evil, and corrupting, or with being told that the continuance of their illness or disability is a result of inadequate faith. I can easily imagine such a person finding the Baha'i Faith and, through it, freedom and happiness in an accepting, eminently reasonable community. In fact, I'd be surprised if it hadn't happened. There is certainly enough ugliness in Christian tradition and communities to set someone on that journey. Christianity needs its good critics and has them. The Baha'i Faith needs good critics too—and hasn't had many. The particular difficulty of writing about the Baha'i Faith, the body, disability, and chronic illness is that almost everything that needs to be said remains to be said.

In my experience, the most common metaphor for the body in Baha'i oral discourse is as a temple of the soul or spirit. Surprisingly, primary sources for this are few and slight. One of these is a letter written on behalf of Shoghi Effendi, March 22, 1957, "The spirit has no more connection with the body after it departs, but, as the body was once the temple of the spirit, the Baha'is are taught that it must be treated with respect" (*Extracts*, number 82). This establishes the principle of respect, but does not explain the metaphor. Does it mean the body is the place where the spirit worships God? Or is the individual spirit the god of the bodily temple?

Whatever else he might mean, here Shoghi Effendi declares divisibility or dualism, an ordinal relationship between one entity, the soul or spirit, and another, the body. In other Baha'i writings, I find this dualism explicit and emphatic.

> Therefore, it is evident that this spirit is different from the body, and that the bird is different from the cage, and that the power and penetration of the spirit is stronger without the intermediary of the body. Now, if the instrument is abandoned, the possessor of the instrument continues to act. For example, if the pen is abandoned or broken, the writer remains living and present; if a house is ruined, the owner is alive and existing. ('Abdu'l-Bahá 1982b: 228)

This dualism readily supports an egalitarian understanding of human life: no matter the physical impairment, the person has an unimpaired spirit. We can trust in that, live in that, and so value them or ourselves equally. 'Abdu'l-Bahá, echoing Bahá'u'lláh (1976: 154), makes this clear in the next paragraph. Speaking of how the body may become tired or ill, blind or deaf, and how limbs may become paralyzed, and the like, he concludes that "the body may have all the imperfections. Nevertheless, the spirit in its original state, in its own spiritual perception, will be eternal and perpetual; it neither finds imperfection nor will it become crippled" ('Abdu'l-Bahá 1982b: 229).

However, while this approach rejects one ground for devaluing people with disabilities and illness—a one-to-one correspondence between physical and spiritual conditions—it adopts another. This becomes apparent in 'Abdu'l-Bahá's next sentence: "But when the body is wholly subjected to disease and misfortune, it is deprived of the bounty of the spirit, like a mirror which, when it becomes broken or dirty or dusty, cannot reflect the rays of the sun nor any longer show its bounties" ('Abdu'l-Bahá 1982b: 229). Thus, while disability is not seen as reflecting any spiritual imperfections—as he says elsewhere, "Defects in the body or its members do not imply defects in the spirit" ('Abdu'l-Bahá 1982c: 259)—health and ability, the implied opposites of "disease and misfortune," are associated with the reflection of the spirit in the world.

I can imagine these ideas giving comfort to a healthy person as he or she contemplates illness or other forms of impairment as an external observer. I can even imagine someone with minor or moderate impairment finding some affirmation in this scheme. But how is a person living every day with severe impairment of illness to respond? With a wistful longing for death, beyond which, "unaffected by any bodily ailments," their soul will manifest "its inherent might and power...and shall rejoice with exceeding gladness" (Bahá'u'lláh 1976: 154)?

In the passage quoted earlier, 'Abdu'l-Bahá uses a number of body metaphors to emphasize the distinctness of body and spirit. The first three are cage, pen, and house, all inanimate objects, all disposable. The body is like a tool that may be abandoned without ill effect to its owner. Let's be specific, though. In lived truth, if we can abandon our bodies it is only in death. A bird doesn't *need* a cage, a writer *can* pick up another pen, and there are always other houses on the market, if you've got the money, but what happens if, in life, your one and only pen has no ink and your cage or house is a windowless cell? If we seek hope in a life lived with illness, the metaphors fail. 'Abdu'l-Bahá's next metaphor compounds this trouble: in life, when subjected to illness, the body becomes a dirty mirror. When healthy, the body is a useful tool; when diseased, an impediment. When the body is dead, the spirit is free.

In Shoghi Effendi's letter quoted above, the body is a beast of burden "like a horse"; its health, what allows one to serve (*Extracts*, number 65). Serving the Cause is what one does when one is healthy and active: "cooperate fully with your doctors in order to regain your health as soon as possible and be free to serve the Cause" (*Extracts*, number 78). Illness thus not only prevents the reflection of one's spirit in the world but also prevents one from serving the Cause. Add to this the emphasis on activity reiterated annually by the UHJ in its Riḍván letters. In its narrative of community identity and purpose, the body is the implied servant, perhaps even an expendable one: "The goals...must be magnificently achieved, whatever the sacrifice" (UHJ 1993).

In Baha'i terms, my body was neither a good tool nor a good servant, but a formidable obstacle and a crumbling temple. Where was the goodness in a life taken over by the needs of such a body? The reply might be made: The question is ill-posed. Each must do as they are able, and whatever one can do will be accepted by God. My crisis, however, was not about whether my tiny efforts (if any) were acceptable, but about whether my life *as a whole*—left behind by the community, marching with bright banners into the Future—was meaningful.

It is helpful but insufficient to read the body/spirit dualism in 'Abdu'l-Bahá's and Bahá'u'lláh's writings as intended to affirm the absolute value of the person regardless of the bodily condition. We cannot live well by hidden value alone, particularly when communal understanding of meaningful participation in the shared story is defined by able-bodiedness, as in the writings of Shoghi Effendi and the UHJ. Serving the Cause is what you do when you are healthy and involves much action—often "redoubled" (UHJ 1993, 1995).

As I've pondered these words on body and spirit, cage and bird, horse and rider, dirt and light, imperfection and might, I've started to wonder: Where is God in this story? One metaphor I favor for my body is a wilderness: fragile, endangered, full of life. It's just a metaphor, but I think of it sometimes when I'm lying in bed, tracking sensations through the complex interior of my flesh. Interestingly, Bahá'u'lláh uses the same metaphor for our world, from which, I would note, our bodies are not separable. In saying the Long Obligatory Prayer, an individual Baha'i beseeches God by "Thy footsteps in this wilderness, and by the words, 'Here am I. Here am I' which Thy chosen Ones have uttered in this immensity" (Bahá'u'lláh 1992). Although the words "Here am I" are attributed in the prayer to the manifestations of God ("Thy chosen Ones"), the supplicant says them too. I read here an encounter between the supplicant and God. Perhaps all I can discern are God's footsteps; nevertheless, here am I, here am I, witnessing to them, offering myself. Influenced now by the Eucharistic rite, I see this as one of the fundamental acts of faith, offering to God what belongs to God. "Whatever we are, still are we Thine" ('Abdu'l-Bahá 1982a: 6).

Bahá'í mysticism will not resolve all the issues I've raised, but it may be a beginning. In *The Hidden Words*, Bahá'u'lláh writes, as revealer of God's word, "My grace to thee is plenteous, it cannot be veiled. My love has made in thee its home, it cannot be concealed. My light is manifest to thee, it cannot be obscured" (Bahá'u'lláh 1988c: 14). Does illness obstruct the light of the individual spirit? 'Abdu'l-Bahá, as already quoted, says so (1982b: 229), though these aren't my terms. But there is another light, Bahá'u'lláh says, that "cannot be obscured," a love in us that "cannot be concealed."

Where does that leave the body? Is this plenteous grace only for our souls, this love not at home in our bodies, this other, divine light also unreflected in diseased flesh? In distinguishing body from soul, Bahá'u'lláh emphasizes the soul's "inherent might and power," "undiminished" by the weakness of disease. Similar vocabulary is often applied by Bahá'u'lláh to God, "the Almighty...the All-Powerful" (Bahá'u'lláh, The Báb, & 'Abdu'l-Bahá 1985: 120), who may be perceived within oneself, "mighty, powerful" (1988c: 12–13), recalling the originally Hebrew notion of humans as made in God's image. The soul is powerful and mighty because God is powerful and mighty. 'Abdu'l-Bahá elaborates the contrast of weak body and mighty soul: "The body may have all the imperfections" while the spirit "neither finds any imperfection, nor will it become crippled" (1982b: 229). The ideal here is power, might, perfection. Any deviation from the socially agreed-upon norm of health and bodily completeness is seen only as a defect or imperfection. But then healthy bodies resemble the divine more closely, and the "crippled" ones are farther from the divine by definition. How can the sick or disabled, at least, not experience that as a problem—as I did?

Perhaps we need another likeness of God—a likeness not founded solely in power and "perfection." Baha'u'llah says, "Nature in its essence is the embodiment of My Name, the Maker, the Creator. Its manifestations are diversified by varying causes, and in this diversity there are signs for men of discernment" (Bahá'u'lláh 1988a: 142). Are not our bodies, with all their "imperfections," part of Nature and thus, in "essence," also embodying of God's "Name"? Can a particularly Baha'i theology rooted in such texts support perception of God's "Name" in the broken body, as well as in the conventionally whole one?

Such a Baha'i theology might have affinities with some existing Christian theology. In his 1992 article in *Theology Today*, "The Disabled God," Burton Cooper writes, "from a christological perspective, God's perfection, God's goodness, God's identity are so far from transcending the suffering of the world that they participate deeply and unavoidably in that very suffering" (Cooper 1992: 3).

The life-situations and subjective experiences of people with disabilities are diverse; it is important not to simplistically equate disability with suffering. However, all our bodies come apart in the end, and in this way we share, across all that may divide us, a common vulnerability. And I don't think Cooper is saying God *only* experiences our suffering. God also participates deeply in our naps and finger painting. "It is our total personality, formed by a history of our experiences and activities, that enters into and participates in God's eternal life" (Cooper 1992: 181). In my case, I have no problem speaking of suffering in relation to my illness. There may be two or three people in the world who would not experience flesh-ripping pain as a form of suffering, but I am not one. I can at this time keep my body out of that state, but at a great cost in functionality. Could my body reflect the divine in Baha'i theology, or is it too dirty a mirror? I think the answer depends first on another question, suggested here by Cooper's words: Is God's love a suffering love? Cooper answers in the affirmative:

> Without compassion toward a suffering other, we neither communicate love nor become a vehicle of redemptive power toward the sufferer. In the view of God I am outlining, this is as true for God as it is for us. Whitehead calls God "the suffering companion who understands," meaning, among other things, that even (or especially) divine understanding presupposes suffering with the other. God could not be God without suffering because those who do not experience the suffering of the other do not understand the reality of the other. The converse is also true: Those who suffer the suffering of the other confirm the reality of the world of the other. (Cooper 1992: 5)

Here is an attempt to cast these concerns in Baha'i language. The Long Healing Prayer of Bahá'u'lláh addresses God by many names, but most recurrently as "the Abiding One" (Bahá'u'lláh The Báb, & 'Abdu'l Bahá 1985: 91–99). The word "abiding" is several-valued in English; which meanings apply here? Is God "abiding" in the sense of unaffected, steady-state, nothing bothers this guy? Or is God "abiding" as in with us, through all, suffering our pain, celebrating our joy? The question can be stated more succinctly: is *God* vulnerable, or merely permanent? I believe the answer is *vulnerable*, but I do not speak as a Baha'i anymore.

My search for primary sources for the body-as-temple metaphor took me to the writings of the Báb, the forerunner of Bahá'u'lláh, who also has in the Bahá'í Faith the status of a manifestation of God, a perfect reflection of the divine. "As this physical frame is the throne of the inner temple, whatever occurs to the former is felt by the latter. In reality that which takes delight in joy or is saddened by pain is the inner temple" (Báb 2006: 95). The Báb's statement is a confusing tangle of metaphors: we don't usually attribute feelings to temples, and we don't put them on thrones. He doesn't specify the "inner temple" as the spirit or soul, but this is implied by the temple's distinctness from the body and its survival after death. In context, it is clear that the experiences of the soul or "inner temple" are directly linked to what happens to the body *even after death*—which is why a dead body must be "preserved to the extent possible, so that nothing that causeth repugnance may be experienced" (Báb 2006: 95).

The passage in its entirety appears to be the source for Shoghi Effendi's statement, quoted above, referencing the body as temple of the soul (*Extracts*, number 82). Both passages justify particular care for the body after death in terms of the relationship between body and spirit, but the terms are rearranged and altered. In apparent contradiction to the statements of Bahá'u'lláh, 'Abdu'l-Bahá, and Shoghi Effendi, the Báb emphasizes the connectedness or intimacy of body and spirit. Far from being unaffected by the body, the inner temple (spirit) "feels" what occurs to the "throne" (body); for example, the inner temple is "saddened by pain." Does this intimacy, read in conjunction within Bahá'u'lláh's language about finding God "standing within" the human (Báb 1988c: 12–13), offer another ideal of the divine—God as intimately concerned with, even vulnerable to, our embodied lives, rather than defined overwhelmingly in terms of "power"?

Baha'is pray with the words of Bahá'u'lláh: "whatever I behold I readily discover that it maketh Thee known unto me" (Bahá'u'lláh 1987: 272). If Baha'i theology can support a God of suffering love such as I have suggested, then it is possible to perceive not only (as Bahá'u'lláh says in the next few lines of the prayer) the glory of God in the sky, the bounty of God in the earth, the majesty of God in the sea, and the omnipotence of God in the mountains but also the vulnerability of God in our bodies. Especially as they break.

Listen

As the many implications of the concept of the unity of mankind, enunciated more than a century ago by Bahá'u'lláh, take hold in the world at large, Baha'is believe that the obligation, both moral and utilitarian, to insure the full integration of the disabled and the disadvantaged into society will be increasingly recognized, and that the enormous resources now dissipated on war and economic conflict will be channeled into turning this obligation into reality. (National Spiritual Assembly of the Bahá'ís of the United Kingdom 2000)

Thus reads the final paragraph of "A Baha'i Perspective on Disability," from the website of the Baha'i Community of the United Kingdom, the only substantial contemporary statement on disability by a Baha'i community or institution that I was able to find. Kudos to them for producing it. It's a good start. But, take a close look.

It says that when the whole world acknowledges people with disabilities as part of humanity in a future of perfect peace and economic tranquility, then we will get what we deserve—full inclusion. Rather, whoever is alive will get it. For us, now, too bad. And what is the Baha'i community of the United Kingdom doing right now, besides writing this statement? The full text contains no specific information on *that* subject. The need for change is acknowledged but left nonspecific, externalized to "society," and put off to the future.

The Baha'i Faith often announces its intent to build a just and inclusive social order whose unity reflects the familial relationship of all humanity. However, generic affirmations of the oneness of humanity don't mean anything unless the principle is lived out through true inclusion in the particular workings of community.

If the Baha'i Faith is going to speak meaningfully with and to people living with chronic illness and other disabilities, it must value and serve us as present people in the fullness of our actual lives. The Baha'i community of the United Kingdom may be admirably mindful of common accommodations. But no matter how many elevators and ramps are installed, sign language interpreters are hired, home visits are made, if the story a community tells about the goodness of life and collective work in the world is founded on the assumption of able-bodiedness and makes exceptions to accommodate people with disabilities, that community is being helpful, but not inclusive. You must let our particular lives challenge your understanding of humanity, including your own, and transform community ideas and practices. This may not cost much money, but may challenge dearer treasure.

I became a Baha'i eager to join a community committed to understanding injustice in ourselves and in our institutions and social structures, and to renewing those structures based on justice and equality. This is what unity and the oneness of humanity meant to me. However, I found that the primary approach promoted by the UHJ is to seek mass conversion to the Baha'i Faith, the belief being that it is by incorporation into the Baha'i system that people will be transformed and a new structure raised up. The new, just structure is that specified by Bahá'u'lláh and elaborated by his successors. The foundation of this structure is the Covenant. "As the Word of God as revealed by Bahá'u'lláh is the source and impetus of the oneness of mankind, so the Covenant He has established is the organizing principle for its realization" (Bahá'í International Community 2010). That is, the oneness of humanity is to be realized not *primarily* through social action informed by self-examination and dialogue with others, but by obeying the Covenant in ever-growing numbers.

That is the narrative: We don't need to develop a program. We already have a program, *the* program.

> The Covenant is the most remarkable feature of His [Bahá'u'lláh's] Revelation, for it is designed, unlike any religious system of the past, to preserve the unity of all humanity through the organic workings of a social order based on spiritual principles. (Bahá'í International Community 2010)

The UHJ, the contemporary authority on this narrative, renews it annually in its Ridván letters. But what if a person finds that his or her life makes a poor fit with this narrative, or encounters other substantial problems in the community?

In June 2000, Peter Khan, then a member of the UHJ, gave a speech to New Zealand Baha'is in which he said that the most pressing need for Baha'is today is to develop a "heightened sense of spiritual consciousness" (Khan 2000: 7). He said that this is done by carrying out the various religious observances prescribed by Bahá'u'lláh. Then he said that

> the spiritual perspective leads one to accept the station of the manifestation of God and to accept that He doeth whatsoever He willeth, to accept unquestioningly that since Bahá'u'lláh said so, it must be right even if I don't see the reason for it. (Khan 2000: 8)

This is the basis, he said, for following all the laws, and for accepting the succession of authority and the idea of infallibility at the center of the Baha'i Faith, which in the present day means "that this group of nine individuals"—the men of the UHJ—"who gather in the holy land several times every week and deliberate and make their decisions, that their decisions are divinely guided by the Báb and Bahá'u'lláh and are free from error." He also talked about people like me:

> In your community you may be aware of the fact that people are drifting away from the Faith. Why? Because they have neglected that sense of heightened spiritual consciousness. They're becoming bitter, they're becoming disillusioned, they're becoming frustrated, they're giving up on the Baha'i community—not because there's anything wrong with the Baha'i community or the Baha'i Faith, because they have failed in their primary duty as Baha'is to develop this sense of heightened spiritual consciousness. (Khan 2000: 7)

That is, people who are frustrated with the community or drift away are spiritual failures—they have failed to develop "heightened spiritual consciousness," which, in Khan's terms, is synonymous with accepting the Covenant's succession of infallible authorities. To criticize is to fail in the Covenant. The modeling of this blanket judgment by such a prominent Baha'i is a tiny sample of how social control is exercised in the Baha'i Faith. (Here's another: if I were still a Baha'i, I would have to submit this paper to the Baha'i national headquarters of my country for prepublication review.) For more in-depth analysis of obstacles to critical speech within the Baha'i community, see the writings of Cole (1998, 2002) and Bacquet (2001, 2006).

At what cost are attempts to examine dysfunctions of the community and of Baha'i institutions put down as contrary to the Covenant, the essence of unity? The Baha'i Faith will not, in fact, be inclusive of diverse, embodied lives while the community allows so little challenge. The promised social transformation will remain largely an abstract good, proclaimed to the public and promised to Baha'is as the future fruit of their sacrificial action.

Again I ask, where is God in this story? In Baha'i terms, we perceive God through the persons and words of the Báb and Bahá'u'lláh; we obey God in heeding the writings and actions of 'Abdu'l-Bahá, Shoghi Effendi, and the UHJ. We seek God in private prayer and meditation, in shared worship and devotion. We serve God by serving humanity.

But I add one more place—God is in the lives and voices of those excluded from the story.

Listen. Listen.

References

'Abdu'l-Bahá (1982a). *Selections from the Writings of 'Abdu'l-Bahá*. A Committee at the Baha'i World Center & Marzieh Gail (Trans.). Southampton, UK: Camelot Press. (Original work published 1978).

'Abdu'l-Bahá (1982b). *Some Answered Questions*. Wilmette, IL: Bahá'í Publishing Trust. (Original work published 1908).

'Abdu'l-Bahá (1982c). *The Promulgation of Universal Peace*. Wilmette, IL: Bahá'í Publishing Trust. (Original work published in two volumes, 1922 and 1925).

Báb, Ali Muhammad Shiraz [The Báb] (2006). *Selections from the Writings of the Báb*. Wilmette, IL: Bahá'í Publishing Trust. (Original work published 1908).

Bacquet, K. (2001). Enemies within: Conflict and control in the Baha'i community. *Cultic Studies Journal 8*, 109–140.

Bacquet, K. (2006). When principle and authority collide: Baha'i responses to the exclusion of women from the universal house of justice. *Nova Religio: The Journal of Alternative and Emergent Religions* 9(4), 34–52.

Baha'i International Community. (2010). *The Covenant of Bahá'u'lláh*. Retrieved February 1, 2010, from Baha'i Topics website: http://info.bahai.org/covenant-of-bahaullah.html

Bahá'u'lláh (1976). *Gleanings from the Writings of Bahá'u'lláh*. Shoghi Effendi (Trans.). Wilmette, IL: Bahá'í Publishing Trust. (Original work published 1952).

Bahá'u'lláh (1987). *Prayers and Meditations by Bahá'u'lláh*. Shoghi Effendi (Trans.). Wilmette, IL: Bahá'í Publishing Trust. (Original work published 1938).

Bahá'u'lláh (1988a). *Tablets of Bahá'u'lláh*. Habib Taherzadeh (Trans.). Wilmette, IL: Bahá'í Publishing Trust. (Original work published 1978).

Bahá'u'lláh (1988b). *Tablets of Baha'u'llah, Revealed after the Kitáb-i-Aqdas*. Habib Taherzadeh (Trans.). Wilmette, IL: Bahá'í Publishing Trust.

Bahá'u'lláh (1988c). *The Hidden Words and Selected Holy Writings*. Penang, Malaysia: Ganesh Printing Works Sdn. Bhd. (Original work published 1985).

Bahá'u'lláh (1992). *The Kitáb-i-Aqdas*. Anne Arbor, MI: Edwards Brothers.

Bahá'u'lláh, The Báb, & 'Abdu'l-Bahá (1985). *Baha'i Prayers*. Wilmette, IL: Bahá'í Publishing Trust. (Original work published 1954.)

Blue, D. (2004). *Sensual Orthodoxy*. Saint Paul, MN: Cathedral Hill Press.

Cole, J. R. I. (1998). The Baha'i faith in America as panopticon, 1963–1997. *The Journal for the Scientific Study of Religion* 37(2), 234–248.

Cole, J. R. I. (2002). Fundamentalism in the contemporary U.S. Baha'i community. *Review of Religious Research* 43(3), 195–217.

Cooper, B. (1992). The disabled god. *Theology Today* 49(2), 173–182.

Effendi, S. (1987). *God Passes By*. Wilmette, IL: Bahá'í Publishing Trust. (Original work published 1944).

Extracts from the Writings Concerning Health, Healing, and Nutrition. Retrieved February 1, 2010, from Baha'i Academics Resource Library: http://bahai-library.org/compilations/health.healing.html

Khan, P. (2000). *Talk at New Zealand National Teaching Conference*. Retrieved February 5, 2010, from The Baha'i Studies Web Server: http://bahaistudies.net/khan.html

National Spiritual Assembly of the Bahá'ís of the United Kingdom. (2000). *A Baha'i Perspective on Disability*. Retrieved February 5, 2010, from http://www.bahai.org.uk/dp/disability.htm

Reynolds, T. E. (2008). *Vulnerable Communion*. Grand Rapids, MI: Brazos Press.

Universal House of Justice. (1990). *Ridván 1990*. Retrieved February 1, 2010, from *Baha'i* Academics Resource Library: http://bahai-library.com/published.uhj/ridvan/90.html

Universal House of Justice. (1991). *Ridván 148 B.E./1991 A.D.* Retrieved February 1, 2010, from *Baha'i* Academics Resource Library: http://bahai-library.com/published.uhj/ridvan/91.html

Universal House of Justice. (1992). *Ridván 1992*. Retrieved February 1, 2010, from *Baha'i* Academics Resource Library: http://bahai-library.com/published.uhj/ridvan/92.html

Universal House of Justice. (1993). *Ridván 150*. Retrieved February 1, 2010, from *Baha'i* Academics Resource Library: http://bahai-library.com/published.uhj/ridvan/93.html

Universal House of Justice. (1996). *Ridván 153*. Retrieved February 1, 2010, from *Baha'i* Academics Resource Library: http://bahai-library.com/published.uhj/ridvan/96.html

Universal House of Justice. (1997). *Ridván 154*. Retrieved February 1, 2010, from *Baha'i* Academics Resource Library: http://bahai-library.com/published.uhj/ridvan/97.html

Universal House of Justice. (1998). *Ridván 155–1998 AD*. Retrieved February 1, 2010, from *Baha'i* Academics Resource Library: http://bahai-library.com/published.uhj/ridvan/98.html

Universal House of Justice. (1999). *April 1999–Ridván 156*. Retrieved February 1, 2010, from *Baha'i* Academics Resource Library: http://bahai-library.com/published.uhj/ridvan/99.html

Universal House of Justice. (2002). *April 2002–Ridván 159*. Retrieved February 1, 2010, from *Baha'i* Academics Resource Library: http://bahai-library.com/published.uhj/ridvan/2002.html

Wolfe, G. (2009). Thirty seconds away. *Image* 63, 3–6.

CHAPTER 3

Since Feathers Have Grown on My Body: Madness, Art, and Healing in Celtic Reconstructionist Spirituality

Erynn Rowan Laurie

I have borne many a fight without cowardice
since feathers have grown on my body;
each night and each day
more and more do I endure ill.

. . .

The madman of Glen Bolcain am I,
I shall not hide my gnawing grief;
to-night my vigour has come to an end,
not to me is there no for grief.
                    J. G. O'Keefe (Trans.) (1913: 199, 133)

Geilta in the Celtic Literary Traditions

Celtic myth is rife with "mad" figures: men and women who abandon society after battle, trauma, or being cursed. Suibhne Geilt, Myrddin Wyllt, Mís, LíBán, and others within the tradition fled their homes and social roles after trauma, with symptoms that in modern terms resemble such emotional and psychological disabilities as posttraumatic stress disorder (PTSD), panic, paranoia, schizophrenia, and depression.

These tales and poems are filled with sharp images of suffering, the compassion of friends and family, and the daily struggles of the *geilta* or mad/wild figures. The loneliness and isolation of those who have fled to the wilderness is poignant, but the struggle to become whole again is a strong undercurrent in the literature. Some of these figures succeed, while others die on the edge of society, unable to reintegrate and reclaim those aspects of civilized humanity that have been lost to them.

Although the tradition describes people with what appear to be symptoms of mental illness, most modern scholarship does not touch on this interpretation of the texts, instead choosing to read it as an allegory of some other meaning (Partridge 1980, 25). Shamanism (Nagy 1983: 45) and Christian ascetic sainthood (Bergholm 2009: 148–152) are two common angles of approach. Despite this, it is still possible to make useful readings of the texts that include the idea of mental illness or disability without ignoring more metaphorical or allegoric shades of meaning.

The Irish word *geilt* (pl. *geilta*) is defined as "one who goes mad from terror; a panic-stricken fugitive from battle; a crazy person living in the woods and supposed to be endowed with the power of levitation; a lunatic" (DIL, s. v. geilt). The etymology of the word is problematic, though several possibilities have been offered, including a derivation from the Old Irish root *gel-*, "to graze." A variant of *geilt* is found in Welsh as *gwyllt* or *wyllt*, which has a very similar meaning (Chadwick 1942: 106). The Old Norse language borrows the word quite directly as *gjalti* and attributes it in a derogatory sense to the Irish, conflating this madness with cowardice and loss of masculinity (Sayers 1994: 164–165). The word calls forth images of wildness or the act of grazing, and Suibhne and other *geilta* are described as having a vegetarian diet. This "wildness" is contrasted with civilization, separating the *geilta* from their communities in ways that include dress, diet, and behavior.

The behavior of the *geilta* outside of settled society is defined as "mad" and regarded with both fear and sympathy by those who are not so affected. Attempts are often made to cure the *geilta* and return them to a productive position. Because it is a multifaceted problem, these attempts are not always, or not wholly, successful.

In the Celtic literary tradition, *geltacht* (DIL, s. v. geltacht), defined as "panic, terror, frenzy, insanity," is a specific response to trauma involving violent death or battle, acted out in mythic territory. It separates the *geilta* from their homes and families, leading them to isolate themselves in the wilderness. The hypersensitivity and hyperawareness of the *geilt* makes being around others uncomfortable, generating responses of paranoia and panic that can be eased only by self-imposed isolation. Civilization is experienced as painful, ugly, and horrifying.

Even in the society of others like themselves, human contact is tenuous and easily shattered. Individual *geilt* might be helped or retriggered by contact with other *geilta* (O'Keefe 1913: 61).

CúChulainn was famous in the Ulster Cycle of tales for his "battle frenzy." Unlike the condition of *geltacht*, this was regarded as a positive response to the stresses of battle, imbuing him with heroic strength and the ability to terrorize his enemies (Kinsella 1985: 77). Norse warriors, as well, might enter a state of *berserk*[1] madness that, while not particularly discriminating, was seen as a good thing when pointed at the enemy (Cleasby and Vigfusson 1874, s. v. Berserkr). *Geltacht*, on the other hand, was seen as a panic reaction causing flight rather than engagement with the enemy.

In some texts, *geltacht* was believed to be the result of looking up into the sky during battle and catching sight of the spirits of the battlefield. This sight drove warriors out of their minds. This was particularly seen as a risk to younger warriors, but older, seasoned veterans might also succumb. The sight of these spirits, accompanied by the deafening clamor of battle, could prove a chaotic and devastating combination (Chadwick 1942: 115–116; Sayers 1994: 161–162, 164–165;).

For most veterans, the sight of these spirits and the sound of battle were assumed to encourage their warlike behavior. Song and chant, like the *dord* of the Fianna, were used to enflame the heat of battle that might inure men to its hardships and horrors (DIL, s. v. dord).

In some cases, however, there is an external influence that complicates the situation. The tale of Suibhne offers a preliminary scene where he interacts with a Christian cleric before going to war. Suibhne was presented as a specifically pagan king who attacked Saint Rónán for his attempt to establish a church in Dal nAraide. This resulted in Rónán placing a curse on Suibhne, prophesying his future as a *geilt* and the manner of his death (O'Keefe 1913: 9, 11).

The most famous *geilt* in Irish literature is Suibhne, a fictional king of the Dal nAriad, whose tale is told in the *Buile Suibhne* or "Frenzy of Sweeney." The tale has inspired many literary treatments from the time it appeared. The novel of Flann O'Brien (author Brian O'Nolan), *At Swim Two Birds* (1939), deals with the stories of Finn and Sweeney, two of Ireland's most famous poet-warriors. Seamus Heaney's poetic rendering *Sweeney Astray* (1983) is a popular and well-known version of the tale. Other modern poets have also treated the work,[2] and it is one of the most influential tales in the Irish corpus.

The Welsh Myrddin Wyllt, more commonly known as Merlin, was likewise regarded as a mad figure, living in the wilderness among the animals, reciting poetry and prophecy. Much like Suibhne, Myrddin went mad in the aftermath of battle and fled his community to seek solitude in the wilderness. His tale is initially told by Geoffrey of Monmouth in the *Vita Merlini* (Clarke [Trans./Ed.] 1973). Merlin is a figure well enough known that references should come easily to mind, from T. H. White's *The Once and Future King* (1958) to John Boorman's film *Excalibur* (1981), though most of the popular material elides his madness in favor of eccentricity.

Another Welsh case, presented explicitly as the result of trauma in battle, is that of Cyledyr the Wild. In the tale *Culhwych ac Olwen*, we are told, "He [Gwyn apNudd] killed Nwython, cut out his heart, and forced Cyledyr to eat his father's heart; because of that, Cyledyr went mad" (Ford 1977: 151).

After long sojourns in the wilderness, the *geilta* were perceived as part-bird or part-animal, ambiguously-gendered, taloned, growing feathers or fur in place of clothing.[3] Yet they are also closely and intricately linked with poetry, prophecy, visionary states, and music. Some were healed through their art and isolation while others died in misery after repeated attempts were made to reincorporate them into society. Their wildness was feared, though it did not appear to be considered contagious.

Traditional tales offer examples of both male and female *geilta* (*bangeilta* or "madwomen"), though men are more commonly portrayed. Both male authorship and the association of *geilt* status with the activity of warriors are likely to be factors in this. Where men lose themselves as a result of their own actions or terrifying visions, or of assaults upon them in battle during wartime, women's loss of self traditionally occurs in the context of the death of loved ones and as the result of profound grief. Witnessing the death or finding the body of a loved one who has died violently triggers this descent into "madness."

The most common generative source of the state of *geltacht* is the clamor of battle. Both Suibhne and Myrddin become *geilta* during or immediately after being engaged in combat, and at the battles of Magh Rath and of Allen, seven or nine unnamed men became *geilta* on the same day (Bergholm 2009: 60). Norse literature warns against particular actions during battle that may result in *gjalti*. This is contrasted with the *berserk*'s high-status battle-madness among Norse warriors (Davidson 1988: 79–80).

Suibhne's initiation into *geilt* is described thus:

> Thereafter, when both battle-hosts had met, the vast army on both sides roared in the manner of a herd of stags so that they raised on high three

mighty shouts. Now, when Suibhne heard these great cries together with their sounds and reverberations in the clouds of Heaven and in the vault of the firmament, he looked up, whereupon turbulence (?), and darkness, and fury, and giddiness, and frenzy, and flight, unsteadiness, restlessness, and unquiet filled him, likewise disgust with every place in which he used to be and desire for every place he had not reached. His fingers were palsied, his feet trembled, his heart beat quick, his senses were overcome, his sight was distorted, his weapons fell naked from his hands, so that through Rónán's curse he went, like any bird of the air, in madness and imbecility.

Now, however, when he arrived out of the battle, it was seldom that his feet would touch the ground because of the swiftness of his course, and when he did touch it he would not shake the dew from the top of the grass for the lightness and nimbleness of his step. He halted not from that headlong course until he left neither plain, nor field, nor bare mountain, nor bog, nor thicket, nor marsh, nor hill, nor hollow, nor dense sheltering wood in Ireland that he did not travel that day, until he reached RosBearaigh, in Glenn Earcain, where he went into the yew-tree that was in the glen. (O'Keefe 1913: 15)

Here we see the origins of Suibhne's descent into panic, paranoia, illness, and an animal state after raising his eyes above the field of battle, resulting in his literal flight from society, which he now finds a source of horror and disgust. The Welsh Merlin's grief-stricken flight comes about in the aftermath of battle. Unlike Suibhne, he manages to get through the fray, only to disintegrate as the enormity of the situation overwhelms him:

Merlin called his companions from the battlefield and instructed them to bury the brothers in a richly-decorated chapel.

He mourned for his heroes; his flooding tears had no end. He threw dust upon his hair, tore his clothes and lay prostrate on the ground, rolling to and fro. Peredur and the other princes and commanders offered comfort. He would not take the comfort and rejected their entreaties. So for three long days he wept, refusing food, so great was the grief that consumed him.

Then, when the air was filled with these repeated loud complainings, a strange madness came upon him.

He crept away and fled to the woods, unwilling that any should see his going. Into the forest he went, glad to lie hidden beneath the ash trees. He watched the wild creatures grazing on the pastures of the glades. Sometimes he would follow them, sometimes pass them on his course. He made use of the roots of plants and of grasses, of fruit from the trees and of the blackberries in the thicket. He became a Man of the

Woods, as if dedicated to the woods. So for a whole summer he stayed hidden in the woods, discovered by none, forgetful of himself and his own, lurking like a wild thing. (Clarke 1973: 55, 57)

As with the description of Suibhne's descent into madness, we see Merlin assimilated into wildness as horrifying sound echoes in the heavens, and he flees the company of his fellows, now mad with grief and horror.

The story of Mís offers another *geilt* tale, this one of a woman going mad from grief after the death of her father in battle. The *bangeilt* Mís is regarded as a predator, unlike the male *geilta*; she violates the boundaries of femininity in her animal status.[4] Yet even here, there is regard for her condition and the hope that she can be brought back into the human fold.

He [Dáire Dóidgheal] brought her with him as she was his only daughter, and after the battle she came with a multitude searching through the slaughter for her father's body, and having found the severely wounded body, she began to suck and drink the blood from the wounds so that eventually in a fever of lunacy she rose aloft and flew to Sliabh Mís, and remained there for the aforesaid time, and there grew on her whiskers[5] and hair of such length that they used to scour the ground behind her. Moreover, the nails of her feet and hands curved inwards, so much that no man or beast encountered her but was torn apart on the spot.

Furthermore, her lunatic frenzy caused her to move at such speed that she ran like the wind and so used to outstrip whatever she wished. And she did not hesitate to eat each and every animal and person that she killed, and to drink as much as she wanted of their flesh and blood, so much that the region called the Barony of Clanmaurice became a wilderness with scant population for fear of her, because King Feidhlimidh issued a general edict that she was not to be killed on any account. (Koch and Carey 2003: 283)

All of these events can be seen as terrible traumas. Slaughter, bloodshed, and the wounding and death of loved ones and friends often result in posttraumatic stress and depression, along with other mental disturbances.

In the tale of Suibhne, a curse is understood as the instigating force behind his becoming a *geilt*. It has always been a puzzle why some people manage to remain whole in the face of trauma while others react with panic, hypervigilance, depression, nightmares, flashbacks, and other disabling symptoms of posttraumatic stress disorder. It is possible to see the saint's curse as a metaphor for this mysterious mechanism, the tipping point from sanity into horror and unassailable grief.

Stories of male *geilta* include resolutions where the individual's art is highly regarded. Poetry, prophecy, and the capacity for supernatural vision and ability are associated with these men. Their tales and songs are recorded, their visions sought out, and their spiritual discourse is valued.

Women *geilta* are rarely given a voice beyond the narration of their history. We rarely see them associated with creative arts or spiritual mastery. Most often, if a *bangeilt* is returned to society, she vanishes into the traditional role of wife to the man who has "cured" her. Her potential for art and spiritual accomplishment is silenced by the expectation that she will once again become the property of a man, and her independent will is negated.

Beyond the difference in ways that gender was treated in stories of the *geilta*, we also find tales with aspects of gender-transgression. Some figures apparently change gender during their loss of self in the wilderness (O'Keefe 1913: 17). Suibhne was at least once regarded as female at the beginning of his madness:

> Thereupon they began describing aloud the madman; one man would say that it was a woman, another that it was a man, until Domnall himself recognized him, whereupon he said: "It is Suibhne, king of Dal Araidhe, whom Ronan cursed the day the battle was fought." (O'Keefe 1913: 17–19)

The earliest known tale of the mad wild-man is the Sumerian account of Enkidu in the Epic of Gilgamesh. Enkidu is a forest-dweller, wild and uncontrollable, overgrown with hair and acting as a wild animal. His similarities with Suibhne's wildness and association with animals is unmistakable.[6]

> But as for him, Enkidu, born in the hills—
> With the gazelles he feeds on grass,
> With the wild beasts he drinks at the watering place,
> With the creeping creatures his heart delights in water—(Prichard
>   1958: 44)

In order to bring Enkidu into the fold of civilization, Gilgamesh instructs a woman to go into the wild and bare herself. She is to tempt him and have him lie with her in sexual embrace. When he has lain with her for six days and seven nights, she offers him civilized food and "strong drink." When he has partaken of these, the animals no longer come to Enkidu but flee from him as they would from any ordinary man.

Now a part of civilization, he anoints himself with oil, sheds his bestial hair, puts on clothing, and takes up weapons. In the words of the text, Enkidu "became human" (Prichard 1958: 48).

The Irish story of Mís echoes this transformation by sexual encounter. She, like Enkidu, is extremely hairy. Her finger and toenails are long and curved like claws, and she eats men like a predator.

Hearing of her, the harper Dubh Rois offers to go out and bring her back. He takes his harp with him, along with gold and silver. He sets himself up in a place in the wild, scattering the metal on his cloak, exposing his genitals, and begins to play the harp. Mís, intrigued by the music, comes down to find him. When he meets her, he shows her the metals, which she recognizes. She is curious about his genitalia and asks about his penis and testicles:

> When she gave a side-glance, she caught sight of his fine nakedness, and the sporting pieces. "What are these?" she asked, of his pouch or nest-eggs. "That," he said, "is a tricking staff." "I don't remember that," said she. "My father didn't have the like." "A tricking staff," she said again; "what's the trick?" "Sit beside me," said he, "and I'll do that staff's trick for you." "I will," said she, "and stay with me." "I will," said he, and he lay with her and made love to her and she said: "Ah, ha, ba, be, ba! That's a fine trick, do it again!"

He plays the harp for her again and serves her bread, which she remembers from before her madness. She brings Dubh Rois a deer and, instead of allowing her to eat it raw, he cooks it for her, serving it to her with bread. After further conversation where Mís remembers her prior life, he stands her in the cooking pit where the deer was boiled and bathes her in the broth and remains. There are echoes here of the cooling of CúChulainn's warrior frenzy in three cauldrons of water when he returns from battle (Kinsella 1985: 92).

The pair stays in the forest for two months, until Mís's long hair falls away, and she is returned to sanity and can be safely brought back into society (Koch and Carey 2003: 284–285).

Both these tales illustrate the use of human intimacy to restore health and sanity that was lost or never known in the first place. The use of sexuality as a treatment for *geltacht* is problematic in a modern context.

Issues of informed consent arise, and for many people suffering from posttraumatic stress, sexual assault may have been causative in itself. Yet regaining an ability to enter into and enjoy consensual acts of sexual pleasure may be a measure of progress in the healing of some individuals who are so afflicted.

Geilt tales often involve the equation of the *geilt* with animals. Their wildness is symbolically equated with that of beasts. Yet the tales go further than simply asserting that the *geilt* is *like* an animal. Suibhne grew feathers. In one Breton tale, Merlin is regarded as a bird (Constantine 2005: 96). LíBán, also known as Muirgeilt or "sea-*geilt*," initially appeared to the narrating saint as a salmon with a woman's head (de Vries 2007: 42–43).

Werewolf transformations are common in tales about Irish warriors; foreign warriors and other foreigners are also called *cúglas* (grey-wolf) (DIL, s. v. cúl(f)). The color-word *glas* has deep and subtle connections with liminal and transformative states that emphasize the betweenness of the wolf-warrior (Siewers 2005: 31–66). That *geltacht* was regarded as a function of the failed warrior is significant in its link to this animal transformation.

In the tales of Suibhne and of other *geilta*, the bird-motif occurs again and again. In both Irish and Norse literature, the *geilt* is said to grow feathers after spending time in the wilderness. Flight is implied or expressly described in the tales, with the *geilta* leaping from tree to tree, springing away from the battlefield on the tips of spears, and dwelling among the branches.

Some petroglyphs of warriors in Ireland and Scotland are shown with the heads of birds on human bodies (Ross 1974: 316). This is brought into a normative state in the tale of Conaire Mór, a mythological king who has descended from Otherworldly bird-people. Like the *geilta*, he is part-avian, but as king he is assumed to be a fully functional—indeed, flawless—member of human society. His royal tenure was called "the Bird Reign" or *énlaith* and regarded as one of the golden periods of Irish mythical history (Cross and Slover 1981: 96–98).

Among the *filid* or sacred poets of Irish society, a mark of rank was the *tugen*, a cloak made of bird feathers. It is described as being made of "the necks of swans above and the necks of drakes below" (Joyce 1903: 447). This cloak of white and brilliantly colored feathers signified the *fili*'s association with Otherworld sight and, possibly, with the ability to travel into the Otherworlds. The druid Mog Ruith, wearing a bull hide and feathered headdress, is described as flying over a battlefield raining fire down upon the enemies of his people (Davidson 1988: 51).

Yet while the *filid* earn their feathers by 20 years of painstaking study and practice, the *geilta* grow feathers through their years of suffering and isolation in the wilderness. It seems significant that these feathers grow out of the bodies of the *geilta*, a natural occurrence that accompanies their epiphany of madness. Rather than being able to take on and put off their feathers as a poet in civilized society does, the *geilta* are compelled to feathers, flight, and art. Their feathers, like their madness, cannot be shed at will. They are an inherent part of their being.

Wild, raw food is a common theme in several *geilt* tales. Leafy plants such as watercress and fruits such as wild apples or berries are often mentioned. The *Buile Suibhne* offers this description of the diet of the *geilta*:

> For it is thus Glen Bolcain is: it has four gaps to the wind, likewise a wood very beautiful, very pleasant, and clean-banked wells and cool springs, and sandy, clear-water streams, and green-topped watercress and brooklime bent and long on their surface. Many likewise are its sorrels, its wood-sorrels, its *lus-bian* and its *biorragan*, its berries, and its wild garlic, its *melle*, and its *miodhbhun*, its black sloes and its brown acorns. The madmen moreover used to smite each other for the pick of watercress of that glen and for the choice of its couches. (O'Keefe 1913: 23)

If *geilt* is indeed derived from the Old Irish root *gel-*, "to graze," this origin could signify at least the perception of a vegetarian diet among those so defined. Such a diet would be unusual by the standards of the time, but for an individual living alone in the wilderness, it might be the only practical answer to the problems posed by hunting, trapping, or fishing without tools. That this vegetarian diet is noted so often indicates that it was considered remarkable. These cold, vegetarian foods place the *geilta* more strongly into the field of the nonhuman, grazing or foraging as animals do, rather than hunting, farming, and cooking one's food as the civilized majority would.

Such restricted diets also have a long history of association with ascetic practices and with medicinal or healing regimens.[7] In taking to a vegetarian diet, the *geilta* may have been attempting to regulate their health through herbal simples and purification practices. Beneath all of this, however, is the constant reminder that many of the *geilta* are participating in the community of vulnerable prey animals, eating as they do, sleeping in the trees like birds, and fleeing from the approach of the civilized.

The societal response to someone becoming a *geilt* is usually an attempt to bring the individual back to his or her senses. Most stories include one or more scenes of capture, persuasion, temptation by music, food, or sexual availability. The stories also give the *geilta* the chance to tell their own story in the hope that narration will provide a sort of confessional.[8] The *geilta* may be held against their will (O'Keefe 1913: 59), just as someone today might be involuntarily institutionalized by concerned family members who fear self-harm or danger to others by someone who has become seriously mentally or emotionally unbalanced. The distress of the family and friends of the *geilt* is genuine.

If the *geilt* cannot be brought back willingly, a spouse or friend might go into the wilderness to accompany him or her (Clarke 1973: 131; O'Keefe 1913: 49). There are poignant passages where poetic dialogue is exchanged between the *geilt* and the one who has sought them out, expressing grief, longing, and frustration by both parties.

In the academic discussions of Suibhne and Myrddin, *geiltacht* or madness is rarely addressed as genuine mental illness (Bergholm 2009: 8). It has been viewed as symbolic of a variety of things, from saintly hermitage in "white martyrdom" (Siewers 2005: 33)[9] to shamanic initiation and journeying. While these various readings are valuable in examining the *geilt* figure, the catalogue of the *geilt*'s suffering and mental anguish is downplayed and not regarded as mental or emotional disability. At the same time, many items associated with *geiltacht* match up quite well with actual mental illnesses.

Given that the *geilta* are literary and mythological figures, I will not argue that they are diagnosable individuals suffering from mental illness. I will, however, suggest that many of the symptoms of the *geilta* are very similar to those suffering from PTSD. The examination and cataloguing of some of these points of similarity is useful for understanding how *geltacht* can be approached as a model for understanding trauma and resulting disabilities.

The primary motif of the *geilt* is one of isolation and homelessness. Without exception, the *geilta* flee from society, even though they may maintain some distant contact with it. It is one of the defining aspects of the type (Partridge 1980: 26). This loss of society is intimately connected with perceived loss of humanity. To be outside of the circle of family and culture is to exist as an animal.

The *geilta* are wanderers, unable to stay in one place for long. They must be constantly on the move, fleeing their fears and moving toward the unfamiliar, seeking some respite from their pain. The poems of the *geilta* bemoan this constant motion and lack of any settled place

(O'Keefe 1913: 29–33). Even those places where the *geilta* gather are only temporary shelters. They come and go, blown about like feathers on the wind.

Panic is one of the motive forces of the *geilt*. It is an unreasonable fear of people and the trappings of civilization that cause their motion. They cannot abide the sound of bells, of battle, the songs of humanity. A marked preference is expressed for the belling of stags, the songs of birds, the sound of wind through sheltering boughs. Natural sounds are the sounds of safety, free of the conflicts that drove them away in the first place. Human society brings with it war, destruction, and violence, deliberate cruelties inflicted upon one human being by another. The *geilt* seeks peace and freedom from panic in isolation, where violence is most often far away (O'Keefe 1913: 31, 71).

Along with panic and isolation comes depression. Many of the poems of the *geilta* are laments, expressing deep sorrow at their loss of connections with their previous lives (O'Keefe 1913: 25–29). Yet they cannot relieve the sorrow or heal the damage simply by returning to what has harmed them. Merlin, in particular, comes to his madness through what might be interpreted as depression and survivor guilt after the horrifying slaughter of battle and the burial of so many of his people.[10]

Nothing can be done to restore the lives lost to violence. The rent in the fabric of the *geilt*'s mind is filled with the poetry of loneliness, fueled by an inability to return home. Human love becomes impossible because humanity itself is a deep and abiding source of pain. Even when the *geilta*'s loved ones attempt to join them in their exile, the depression cannot end. Compassion for the suffering the loved one is undergoing on the *geilt*'s behalf leads to further sorrow, aggravating the cycle and deepening it further (O'Keefe 1913: 43). The *geilta* cannot be raised from their depression or joined in their exile until they have experienced a psychological and spiritual transformation that reconnects them with those they love and offers them a renewed sense of identity and belonging.

Whenever the *geilt* is near other people, even other *geilta*, he or she is in a constant state of alert. Suibhne and his compatriot Ealladhan spend a year together in Britain, fearful but attempting to protect one another.

> "O Suibhne," said Ealladhan, "let each of us keep good watch over the other since we have placed trust in each other; that is, he who shall soonest hear the cry of a heron from a blue-watered, green-watered lough or the clear note of a cormorant, or the flight of a woodcock from a branch,

the whistle or sound of a plover on being woke from its sleep, or the sound of withered branches being broken, or shall see the shadow of a bird above the wood, let him who first shall hear warn and tell the other; let there be the distance of two trees between us; and if one of us should hear any of the before-mentioned things, or anything resembling them, let us fly quickly away thereafter." (O'Keefe 1913: 103, 105)

Every out of place sound, every shadow, is potential cause for alarm and for flight. The startle response combines with paranoia and panic to trigger an escape attempt. The rational mind is not engaged in analyzing the actual threat level, rather the *geilta* react instinctively to protect themselves from any potential contact with others.

When Suibhne is roaming Sliabh Mís, he encounters visions of floating, disembodied heads and headless torsos that pursue him vigorously. These heads are of goats and dogs and other indescribable creatures (O'Keefe 1913: 123–125). He flees from them just as he flees from the attentions of the people of Dal nAraide. The disembodied heads are regarded as demonic and may well be some of the same spirits that are said to hover over the battlefield and drive warriors into a state of *geltacht* when they are seen (Chadwick 1942: 115–116).

Suibhne's flight from the beastly heads once again takes up the theme of feathers and leaping, birdlike, from tree to tree in an attempt to escape his torments. The heads jabber and shriek, recalling the war-cries of the battlefield and the screams of the dying. He is re-exposed to the experiences that drove him from the field in the first place. In their recurrence, they reinforce and maintain the state of *geltacht* within which he dwells. These are the echoes of his traumas made manifest.

These moments of horror backed by the appearance of apparitions have the same emotional resonance as flashbacks and nightmares (Matsakis 1996: 22–23), appearing suddenly with varying degrees of perceived reality. The feeling of pursuit by terrifying monsters or memories is an extremely common nightmare (Galvin and Hartmann 1990: 238), and this panicked feeling may also manifest during waking hours in flashbacks that range from feelings of discomfort to a sense of absolute immersion in the traumatic past as it is relived over and over again (Matsakis 1996: 22).

The tale of Suibhne ends tragically with the death of the protagonist (O'Keefe 1913, p. 155). During the course of Suibhne's madness his people went into the wilderness three times to capture him and bring him home (O'Keefe 1913: 37). During one of these returns to civilization the madness leaves him, and he resumes his duties and his position (O'Keefe 1913: 61). Even this healing, however, was temporary.

While living with his people, Suibhne is confronted by the Mill Hag, who taunts him about his period of *geltacht* and urges him to demonstrate his leaping and flight. At first, Suibhne refuses, wishing to leave that part of his life behind. With each refusal, the woman's demands grow more insistent, until Suibhne makes a leap from floor to bedpost. She insults him and duplicates the feat, pushing Suibhne until he is unable to maintain his sanity and flies out the window, leaping from treetop to peak, pursued by the woman, whose leaps are as prodigious as his own.

Suibhne's final leap takes him over the cliffs of Dun Sobairce, where the woman falters and is dashed on the rocks below (O'Keefe 1913: 83). It is this incident that consigns Suibhne permanently to the wilderness. He never returns to civilization, and the closest he comes to other people is lurking at the boundaries of a hermitage, talking with the cleric there and taking a pittance of milk left for him daily in a dunghill by a sympathetic woman (O'Keefe 1913: 143). It is this final association with humanity that leads to his death, murdered by the woman's husband, who believes that Suibhne has seduced her (O'Keefe 1913: 143, 145).

In the case of Myrddin, there is a partial but controlled return to civilization. His madness is regulated but after a time, he wearies of civilized life. Rather than returning to the raw wilderness, he builds an observatory with many doors and windows so that he can practice his arts and make his prophecies but still remain sheltered. He is joined in this semi-exile by his sister and an aide (Clarke 1973: 81, 131–133).[11]

Myrddin is no longer seen as mad, though he maintains some characteristics of the *geilt*. His place in society is respected and his wisdom sought out by those wishing to know the future. His life at the periphery is much more managed and manageable than Suibhne's, and his situation is his own choice. Although he is isolated and communes with the wild beasts, he is not bereft of human company or of the benefits of society.

In the tales of Mís and LíBán, there is a complete cure and, in the case of Mís, a return to society (Koch and Carey 2003: 285). Her period of *geltacht* resulted in no poetry, though her name is attached to Sliabh Mís, a mountain where much of her tale was said to have occurred (Stokes 1892: 484). LíBán was also brought back into the fold of civilization—cured, in a sense—but this resulted in her death and her ascent into heaven, for she had already spent centuries in the shape of a woman-headed salmon and her cure resulted in her return to an extremely aged human form (de Vries 2007: 42). Both women experienced some amount of erasure as a part of their reintegration; it was their madness, their difference, which had given them their notoriety in the first place. Once the cause of that notoriety was removed, Mís was no longer of interest and vanished from the field without leaving behind a body of poetry, prophecy, or art. LíBán disappeared physically, though her legacy remains in the celebration of St. Muirgelt (de Vries 2007: 50), whose feast day is January 27th.

It is art that marks the *geilta* as useful in their cultures, even when they are unable to join with the majority in ordinary ways. Poetry is its primary manifestation in the tales, and the prophetic aspect of their knowledge is normally presented in this form. Like most prophetic utterance, it may be obscure until the prophecy comes to pass, yet the form itself is often regarded as a thing of beauty.

The poetic laments of the *geilta* are among the most beautiful passages in the Celtic literatures. The articulations of loneliness, suffering, and longing echo even today, able to move people removed from the *geilta* by barriers of culture, language, and time.

The experiences of the *geilta* in their pain, their isolation, and their art are part of the universal human condition. Their ability to reach through the barriers between the everyday world of society and the spiritual world of wilderness and the presence of the deities offer a possible route to a nonordinary form of integration. They hold a mirror to our lives today, particularly when we are suffering and feeling alone and unable to reach out to join family and friends around us through the experiences of our traumas.

Geilta as Healing Models in the Celtic Reconstructionist Pagan Community

The spiritual community I inhabit is that of Celtic Reconstructionist (CR) Paganism. It is a modern polytheist, animist spirituality inspired by and based upon the texts, myths, folklore, and spiritual principles of the pre-Christian Celtic peoples of Europe (CR FAQ). These sources are not seen as infallible but rather as exemplary texts offering commentary on human behaviors, spiritual principles, and models, both positive and negative, for ritual or daily life.

The movement is amorphous and tends to be localized, with small groups or individuals interpreting and developing the traditions for themselves in ways that connect us to what we know of early Celtic cultures and the deities and spirits we encounter through our spiritual work and our understandings of the tales and poems. In addition to spiritual connection, there is an emphasis on attempts to reconstruct relevant aspects of pre-Christian spirituality in ways that are supportive and valuable to people living in a global technological culture that is under extreme environmental, economic, and population stresses.

The mythologies, folklore, and folk practices of the Celtic nations are our wisdom-texts, our parables, and the basis of our practices. Within this complex, the role of poet, musician, artist, and walker-between-worlds is highly respected. The positive ideals of the warrior—honor, strength, generosity, justice, defense of the weak—are held in esteem, though much of the movement is also involved with peace and social justice issues. The fact that CR contains a specific place of spiritual experience and authority for the "wounded healer," for a so-called sacred madness, is of profound import and offers a hopeful model for those suffering from mental illness.

The *geilt* is a figure who stands in liminal space between the poet and the warrior, damaged but ultimately valuable as someone potentially capable of interacting with the sacred in ways that can be beneficial to the community and that might not be available to those living more normalized lives. *Geilta* may be perceived as "wounded healer" figures who have learned through their suffering and their difficulties and who may be able to share the knowledge gained to help others. The practice of the arts of the *geilta* can be read as similar to modern ecotherapy (Greenway 2009: 132–139), art and talking therapies, journaling, poetry, dream analysis, spiritual retreats, and group therapy can all be seen as having predecessors in the techniques of the *geilta* in their search for wholeness.

Personal Notes Regarding *Geilt* and Healing from PTSD

I will not attempt here to define disability. I am not an academic nor am I a medical expert. I have, however, been diagnosed with PTSD, chronic clinical depression, fibromyalgia, and other psychiatric and physical conditions. For the intents and purposes of the US government, I am considered a disabled person. My daily life is significantly affected, and I live on a disability pension.

Daily life can be a struggle. Nightmares, flashbacks, depression, side effects of medication, and chronic physical pain all take their toll, yet I continue making efforts to improve my physical and emotional life and to work toward healing to the best of my ability. When I'm able, I have an active social and spiritual life and a vast network of friends all over the world.

I keep exceedingly irregular hours, and days-long bouts of insomnia are not uncommon. The people who regularly associate with me are aware that I have a much greater chance than their other friends of canceling appointments with them. They are aware of my physical limitations and generally make allowances for them.

Socially, I present myself as a "professional madwoman." In claiming this status, I claim the *geilt* identity, deliberately and knowingly challenging the normative assumption of modern Western society that everyone not visibly impaired is whole and able-bodied. Invisible chronic illnesses such as PTSD are often disregarded, and to call attention to the fact that my own "disabilities" are invisible brings them back into open discourse. I have neither the time nor the energy to deal with people who cannot accept me on my own terms. This has been, for me, part of the lesson of the *geilta*. In claiming the role of *geilt*, I carve out for myself an extremely useful and empowering semantic and ontological space within my spiritual community and the larger world.

In my healing work, I have taken Suibhne and other *geilta* as inspirational models and "heroic" figures, not because they were healed, but because they were able to function and bring beauty to the world in some way even though they were broken. Despite their isolation or, perhaps, because of it, they were able to take inspiration from their situation and contribute to society through their art. As a disabled veteran, a poet, and a writer, this is a deeply resonant and appealing model. It suggests very powerfully that I do not have to be "normal" to be creative, generative, inspired, or useful.

Within my spiritual community, the figure of Suibhne is recognized and understood, even if the word *geilt* is not always part of the vocabulary. Myrddin Wyllt is also a well-known figure within the mythology. This role of outsider-poet[12] is accepted as a valued mode of being within our community, as a variant on the seer-poet-magician who acts as an advisor to those seeking knowledge of the Otherworlds.

In following the model of Suibhne, I have engaged in wilderness retreats (Laurie 2007: 193–196). These have been taken in the company of one or two other people because of the potential danger to one woman backpacking or wilderness camping alone. Being solitary in the wilderness could be triggering in and of itself for some people, since forests provide cover for any number of real or imagined dangers. My companions are chosen for their understanding of my spiritual goals. Most of my encounters with wildlife have been with herbivores or birds, though in the Pacific Northwest rainforest there is always a possibility of running into a cougar or a bear, another reason for going in company rather than alone.

Silence is often a component of these retreats, with an eye to confronting the numinous in the wilderness and to then express these experiences in poetry or through journaling. Meditation takes the form of physical activity such as hiking, gathering firewood, or purifying immersion in a body of water such as the sea or a river.

Another common activity is sitting vigil overnight, tending a fire as a meditative focus. The necessity of feeding the fire helps maintain a mindful wakefulness throughout the process. The soft sounds of fire, wind, and water aid in detaching from the everyday rhythms of urban life. Part of the purpose is to enter a mental and emotional space where contact with deity and spirit becomes easier and where the stresses of day-to-day life are reduced and, potentially, tamed. There is an openness that can be achieved under such conditions that is much more difficult under the unrelenting sound of a 60-cycle hum or the whine and buzz of fluorescent bulbs in a "silent" building.

These methods encourage direct experience of other-than-human powers including animals, plants, and land and water features, as exemplified in the *geilt*'s identification and communion with the natural world. During these times, it may be easier for some individuals to confront the emotional realities of living with the effects of trauma, placing them in a larger context that may help bring healing perspective. The modern field of ecopsychology advocates such practices (Harris 2009: 84–91) as methods of connection with something greater than ourselves to restore a sense of balance with the world in which we live; being too immersed in human society, as the *geilt* understands, can be harmful to the soul. To be open and aware in nature can chip away at some of the shielding and distancing mechanisms we use to insulate ourselves.

Eremetic isolation is also a part of my daily life, as it was for the *geilta*. I live alone and avoid using the phone. Most of my interaction when I am feeling unwell is done online, offering both comfortable distance and vital connection at the same time. Quiet is necessary for a feeling of control over my environment and because of the hours I keep. This is much more possible for me than it would have been for a *geilt* in the medieval world. Their isolation was near-complete, encounters with other human individuals being rare and emotionally fraught.

Yet isolation is not a prop for some semblance of sanity; it is a spiritual act, my day bounded by ritual and contemplation to help order my world and remind me of my connection to the sacred. Deliberate isolation is an alembic in which growth and transformation may occur.

This isolation is my primeval forest. This is my Glenn Bolcan. It is a place for the incubation of writing and poetry, for pursuing meditation and self-examination away from the disturbance of the outside world. It is the base from which my peregrinations are made and to which I return when my travels are finished.

The possibility of connection and communication without the need to expose myself to physical contact with others creates a safe boundary that the *geilta* of the tales might only experience in meeting someone at the edge of a hermitage or the verges of the forest. The Internet creates a liminal space that is neither wilderness nor civilization but partakes of aspects of both. It makes safe isolation possible without requiring the difficult physical work of maintaining a cabin in the woods. I can live in monastic silence when it is needed, yet I am still able to touch the human community if I find myself too ill, exhausted, or fragmented to leave the house.

In the course of working through my PTSD, poetry serves a deeply therapeutic role. Expressing sorrows and traumas creates a way to make sense of these incidents. To name something gives it shape, and shape shows ways to grasp and engage with trauma. It can bring a feeling of control over how one reacts to memories and accompanying physical sensations. To give these forbidden things voice helps moderate their effects and sheds light on them.

Poetry, moreover, is regarded as a form of magic in Celtic culture and within CR spirituality. The shapes and sounds of words are resonant with power, weaving spells and demanding results of the universe. When Suibhne speaks of his torments, he speaks in verse, surrounding his pain and classifying it. This expression is expected and his dialogues with would-be helpers, the cursing cleric, and his fellow *geilta* are all couched in formal quatrains. Turning posttraumatic terror into art helps bleed away its power to harm and allows those who suffer to lance the wound so that it may heal.

My mother sometimes jokes that I was dropped off on her doorstep by the alien armada. While understandably humorous because I am very different from the rest of my family in temperament, there is a small grain of truth in this Othering. My disabilities are only one thing that sets me apart from my family and mainstream society. My religion is different, unrelated to the majority's monotheism. My sexuality is different, for I am not heterosexual, homosexual, or monogamous. Like Suibhne and LíBán, I am neither fish nor fowl, yet I bear the images of both salmon and raven on my skin, permanently inscribed to acknowledge my spiritual relationship to both.

Gender fluidity and nonheteronormative sexuality are common in alternative spiritual communities, and CR is no exception. These fluidities are seen as part and parcel of what it can mean for the *geilt* to touch the Otherworlds. The images on my body are a mirror of shapes taken outside mundane realms. They are expressive of who I become in the Otherworlds and of the modes in which I interact with what dwells there. These coded symbols are recognizable as sacred art within CR and the wider Pagan communities.

The moment of embracing a *geilt* identity is transformative. Deep ambiguity is accepted as a part of this process. The *geilt* accepts a liminal state of being that reaches into the healing capacity of wilderness by becoming part of that wilderness. *Geltacht* is an acceptance of our animal bodies, our living, breathing selves beyond all social markers. It is a redefinition of madness or disability as a state that embraces and encompasses creativity and art as a part of its potential and sacralizes it within a specific spiritual context.

To follow the path of the *geilt* to forest or seaside or wild, open meadow is to take in the potential for peace outside of human society. It offers an expansive inner space for exploration and experimentation, wearing other forms and experiencing other ways of perception. This may appear crazy to people who have no experience of the loss of boundaries that can come with PTSD.

Following the example of the *geilta* who congregate in the glens to speak together and share experiences, I engage in group work at the Veterans hospital, as well as make use of individual therapy. My counselors are aware of my alternative spirituality, the importance within that framework of communications to me from Otherworlds, and my practice of ritual and magic through poetry, art, and writing. These professional contacts help keep me from veering too far from reality, acting as a system of checks and balances that alert me if I am beginning to take a path that may cause harm to myself or others. They acknowledge that my approach is unusual but agree that it has been helpful to me.

Journaling is also a part of this process, allowing me to look back upon and reflect on my work and my progress, much as Christian clerics recorded the words and lives of the *geilta*. To write about my experiences, both in my daily life and regarding the traumas in my past, helps me sort through my emotions and gain a greater understanding of my reactions and my direction. Because I do a great deal of this journaling online, it also allows me to share my life openly with others, who often have useful commentary and suggestions when I find myself in a difficult place. For me, this is the dialogue of Suibhne and Ealladhan, and the astronomical observatory of Myrddin.

In all of this, taking the examples of myth and literature, it must be emphasized that I am not reifying an identification of "madness" with either artistic ability or genius. For many people, to follow this path might result only in further psychological harm, particularly if they undertake this work without the support of a spiritual community. Art may help in healing and in giving voice to torment and transformation, but an inborn spark of talent and a keen desire for this expression must already be present for that art to be realized. Isolation and wilderness practices pursued without forethought and due caution can place the practitioner in situations that may be fatal.

It should also be noted that poetry and writing done for therapeutic purposes may be helpful without being at all "beautiful" or "artistic" in any conventional sense. It may take years before art develops out of the raw materials; wounds must be opened and cleansed before they heal properly, ideas must be cultivated and tended before they come to culmination. In some sense, genuine art might be regarded as a serendipitous side effect of the process of healing.

In an ideal world, the *geilt* strives for healing through shape-shifting soul-flight, expressed in art, and gifted to the community when they meet at the edge of the world. The community of CR practitioners and the examples of its traditional sources and perspectives offers fruitful soil for the work.

Notes

1. The *berserk* warrior is associated with shape, shifting into forms such as bears or wolves, and with battle-fury such as that of CúChullain.
2. John Ennis, *Near St. Mullins*, Dedalus Press (Dublin 2002), Michael Routery in Jamie Robles (Ed.), *f(actions)*, New College of California (San Francisco 2005), "Astray," p. 35.
3. Ranke de Vries in Joseph Falaky Nagy (Ed.), *Myth in Celtic Literatures*, *CSANA Yearbook 6*, Four Courts Press (Dublin 2007), "The Names of LíBán," pp. 42–43, O'Keeffe (1913), p. 17, John T. Koch and John Carey, *The Celtic Heroic Age*, 4th ed., Celtic Studies Publications (Aberystwyth 2003), p. 283.
4. The resemblance of Mís with her long, unkempt hair to the maenads of Greek tradition, wild and rending humans and animals alike in their frenzy, is notable.

5. Whiskers here refers to pubic hair.
6. Both Enkidu and Suibhne bear a great resemblance to the Biblical figure of Nebuchadnezzar (Dan. 4: 31–33), who grew animal fur and fed on grass, fleeing the company of men. While the Irish scribes would not have known of Enkidu, Nebuchadnezzar would have been a very familiar figure to the scholars of the time.
7. Bergholm (2009), p. 149 for βοσκοί, "grazers," Caroline Walker Bynum, *Holy Feast and Holy Fast: The Religious Significance of Food to Medieval Women*, University of California Press (Berkeley 1988), pp. 33–39.
8. The tales of Suibhne, Merlin, Mís, and LíBán all have these characteristics.
9. White martyrdom is described as exile or pilgrimage, red martyrdom as death, and *glas* martyrdom as separation from physical desires in fasting and asceticism.
10. See Davidson (1988).
11. Clarke (1973), bower p. 81, lines 550–559, companions pp. 131–133, lines 1465–1473.
12. The outsider-poet role is also expressed by other figures in Irish mythology; Finn Mac Cumhaill, the leader of the Fíanna and the subject of an entire cycle of stories, is an example of the outsider-poet who does not suffer from *geilt*. Joseph Falaky Nagy, *The Wisdom of the Outlaw: The Boyhood Deeds of Finn in Gaelic Narrative Tradition*, University of California Press (Berkeley 1985).

References

Berserkr. (1874). In R. Cleasby & G. Vigfusson (Eds.), *An Icelandic-English Dictionary* (p. 61). London: Oxford University Press.

Bergholm, A. (2009). *The Saintly Madman: A Study of the Scholarly Reception History of Buile Shuibhne*. Unpublished doctoral dissertation, University of Helsinki.

Boorman, J. (Director). (1981). *Excalibur* [motion picture]. United States: Orion Pictures.

Chadwick, N. K. (1942). Geilt. *Scottish Gaelic Studies 5(2)*, 106–153.

Constantine, M. (2005). Neither flesh nor fowl: Merlin as bird-man in Breton folk tradition. In C. Lloyd-Morgan (Ed.), *Arthurian Literature XXI: Celtic Arthurian Material* (pp. 95–114). Cambridge: D. S. Brewer.

The CR FAQ. Retrieved Februray 8, 2010, from http://www.paganachd.com/faq/

Cross, T. P., & Slover, C. H. (Eds.). (1981). *Ancient Irish Tales*, Totowa, NJ: Barnes and Noble.

Davidson, H. R. E. (1988). *Myths and Symbols in Pagan Europe: Early Scandinavian and Celtic Religions*. Syracuse, NY: Syracuse University Press.

deVries, R. (2007). The names of LíBán. In J. F. Nagy (Ed.), *Myth in Celtic Literatures, CSANA Yearbook 6*. Dublin, Ireland: Four Courts Press.

Ford, P. K. (Ed./Trans.) (1977). *The Mabinogi and other Welsh Medieval Tales.* Berkeley, CA: University of California Press.

Galvin, F., & Hartmann, E. (1990). Nightmares: Terrors of the night. In Stanley Kripner (Ed.), *Dreamtime and Dreamwork: Decoding the Language of the Night.* Los Angeles, CA: Tarcher.

Geoffrey of Monmouth. Basil Clarke (Ed./Trans.) (1973). *The Life of Merlin: Vita Merlini.* Cardiff, Wales: University of Wales.

Greenway, R. (2009). The wilderness experience as therapy: We've been here before. In Linda Buzzell & Craig Chalquist (Eds.), *Ecotherapy: Healing with Nature in Mind* (pp. 132–139). San Francisco, CA: Sierra Club Books

Harris, S. (2009). Beyond the "Big Lie": How one therapist began to wake up. In L. Buzzell & C. Chalquist (Eds.), *Ecotherapy: Healing with nature in mind* (pp. 84-91). San Francisco: Sierra Club Books.

Heaney, S. (1983). *Sweeney Astray.* New York, NY: Farrar Straus Giroux.

Joyce, P. W. (1903). *A Social History of Ancient Ireland*, Vol. 1. London, UK: Longmans, Green, and Co.

Kinsella, T. (Trans.). (1985), *Thetain.* Philadelphia, PA: University of Pennsylvania Press.

Koch, J. T., & Carey, J. (2003). *The Celtic Heroic Age*, 4th ed. Aberystwyth, UK: Celtic Studies Publications.

Laurie, E. R. (2007). *Ogam: Weaving Word Wisdom.* Stafford, England: Megalithica.

Matsakis, A. (1996). *I Can't Get Over It: A Handbook for Trauma Survivors.* Oakland, CA: New Harbinger Publications.

Nagy, J. F. (1982). The wisdom of the geilt. *Éigse 19(1),* 44–60.

O'Brien, F. (Brian Nolan). (1939). *At Swim-Two-Birds.* London, UK: Longman, Green, and Co.

O'Keeffe, J. G. (Ed./Trans.). (1913). *Buile Suibhne: The Frenzy of Sweeney*, Vol. XII (pp. 119, 133). Dublin: Irish Texts Society.

Partridge, A. (1980). Wild men and wailing women. *Éigse 18(1),* 25–37.

Prichard, J. B. (1958). *The Ancient Near East: An Anthology of Texts and Pictures.* Princeton, NJ: Princeton University Press.

Ross, A. (1974). *Pagan Celtic Britain.* London, UK: Cardinal.

Sayers, W. (1994). Deployment of an Irish loan: ON "verða at gjalti" 'to go mad with terror.' *The Journal of English and Germanic Philology 93(2),* 157–182.

Siewers, A. K. (2005). The bluest-greyest-greenest eye: Colours of martyrdom and colours of the winds as iconographic landscape. *Cambrian Medieval Studies 50,* 31–66.

Stokes, W. (Trans.). (1892). The Bodleian Dinnshenchas. *Folklore 3,* 484.

White, T. H. (1958). *The Once and Future King.* London, UK: Fontana/Collins.

SECTION 2

Religion, Accessibility, and Disability

The authors in this section combine narrative description with questions and issues pertinent to cultural and religious inclusion. As articulated in the Introduction to this collection, accessibility has long been at the center of the disability rights movement. People have called into question the common attitude that accommodation for people with disabilities is a matter of social benevolence, asserting instead that members of the disabled community have a civil right to access in societal institutions and public resources. Accessibility then means the availability of the same choices that are accorded to able-bodied people. It means opening the meaning of "normal" to the ordinary lives of people with disabilities. But access goes beyond physical modification and institutional accommodation to include issues associated with social integration, dispositional orientation, and full participation in voluntary affiliations such as religious groups. Each chapter in this section investigates the intersection of disability, accessibility, and religion in unique and divergent narratives, highlighting the multiple issues associated with the ongoing quest for full social inclusion.

Jo Pearson opens Section 2 by presenting an analysis of Wiccan perceptions of disability and priest/esshood, with specific focus on how both physical and mental disabilities affect access to an exclusive rite of initiation process and postinitiation participation in Wiccan ritual. After a brief introduction to Wicca and a synopsis of Wiccan ritual, Pearson demonstrates how each coven will decide for itself issues of access to initiation and why some Wiccans feel more able to support and train initiates with certain disabilities than do others. A marked difference emerges in attitude toward those disabled persons seeking initiation, and those already initiated and trained as priests and priestesses who later develop a disability. Having already gained experience they are deemed able to bypass their disability, especially if it is physical. When a disability is located in the mind, the situation can be more problematic in some Wiccan contexts. This chapter addresses how physical and mental disabilities affect access to participation in religious rituals.

In Chapter 5, Jeff McNair and Abigail Schindler combine narrative description with social critique by demonstrating that while physical integration of people with intellectual and developmental disabilities (I/DD) into many communities in the United States is common, true social integration often goes unrealized. Research indicates that while a significant portion of the population participates weekly in religious services, individuals with I/DD are less likely to participate socially in religious communities. The authors argue that some type of religious group is a normative structure in human experience, and as such it offers numerous benefits for individuals with I/DD and their families. In addition, the authors suggest the need for interreligious collaborative efforts to increase social integration across religious traditions. By way of example, McNair and Schindler consider issues regarding the restrictive nature of rules governing independent living arrangements and their effect on the religious liberty of group home residents.

In Chapter 6, Darla Schumm and Michael Stoltzfus incorporate core themes in Daoism to access alternative ways for thinking and talking about disability and chronic conditions. After a brief and incomplete synopsis of important values and texts, central elements of Daoism are mined for their potential to offer both critical and distinctive modes of responding to chronic disabilities that move beyond the standard models used in Western social-scientific discourse. Daoism helps to illustrate how many forms of human embodiment and capacity are elements of a single, ever-changing way and invites the integration of disability into the understanding of human life without necessitating categorization, definition, or cure. The authors demonstrate that seeking a way of dynamic balance in the midst of uncertainty and ambiguity is both a core teaching in Daoism and an everyday experience of individuals living with chronic disability or illness.

In Chapter 7, Lavonna L. Lovern integrates social analysis with narrative description as she highlights the myriad historical, cultural, spiritual, and bureaucratic challenges Native American and Alaskan Native people face in their efforts to access quality health care. Native

Americans, because of various legal and international issues, were excluded from the initial Americans with Disability initiatives, and this lack of inclusion created a situation that kept individuals from receiving the needed medical and rehabilitation services. Lovern helps readers understand the assimilation debate and elements of Native American traditional beliefs operating as currents that flow beneath the surface of the discussion of Native American health care issues. The web of bureaucracy faced by Native American and Alaskan Native people attempting to access health and disability care is described through the process of anonymous first person narratives. The efforts of those who work to mitigate the bureaucratic maze to help disabled individuals are celebrated.

CHAPTER 4

Disabled Rites?
Ritual and Disability in Wicca

Jo Pearson

Introduction

This chapter is based on early fieldwork—on my own experience of being in ritual with disabled people; discussion on a closed e-mail list and other personal mailings; and on demographics—the increasing age of the Wiccan population and concomitant percentile of disabled Wiccans—what one priest called the "new tradition of 'limp, grimp and groan.'" I shall begin by giving a necessarily brief introduction to Wicca, and providing a synopsis of Wiccan ritual. I shall then go on to examine disability in a preinitiatory context, highlighting issues and concerns that my research has brought to light, including Wiccan perceptions of disability and priest/esshood. Lastly, I shall explore reactions of Wiccans to what I term, tongue in cheek, "postinitiation-onset" disability, using three specific examples: an unseen disability (a priest who has diabetes), a mental disability (a priestess who experienced debilitating depression linked to her menopause), and a physical disability (a priestess with advanced arthritis).

Wicca

Wicca is "the only religion England has given the world" (Hutton 1999: vii),[1] and it is with the British traditions of Gardnerian and Alexandrian Wicca that I am concerned in this chapter. This "English religion" emerged in the New Forest in the 1940s, among a group of respectable citizens associated in one way or another with a retired civil servant named Gerald Gardner. Gardner and his associates formulated Wicca based largely on the magical secret societies and occult lodges of the late nineteenth/early twentieth centuries, Freemasonry, and the mystery religions of the ancient classical world. From the latter, Wicca draws its identity as a modern day mystery religion, in which men and women are initiated as priests and priestesses.

This is the entry point into Wicca, and usually the first experience of the ritual practice that is central to Wicca as an orthopraxic religion for Wicca operates within a rich ritual framework that includes rites of passage (including a series of three initiations), seasonal rites (the sabbats of the Wheel of the Year), and training/lunar rites (esbats). In addition, many work ritual in specific magical systems, such as (practical, or occult) kabbalah. According to Wiccans, the true meaning of their religion can be expressed and experienced *only* through direct participation in its rituals. Ritual is regarded as a legitimate means of "knowing," an embodied, incarnate means of knowing. It is not empty, or simply a reinforcing interpretation of something else, nor is it "simply an alternative way to express certain things . . . [for, as Rappaport states,] certain things can be expressed *only* in ritual" (Rappaport 1979: 174, emphasis added). Ritual thus has a central place in Wicca, and while its importance is not denied by disabled initiates, disability does offer challenges both to the *ways* in which ritual is practiced and to underlying philosophies of mind and body evident in Wiccan understandings of what happens in and through ritual praxis.

Wiccan rites tend to take place at night, either in private homes or at outdoor working sites—there are no easily identifiable Lodge buildings or temples. It might be stating the obvious, then, to note that Wiccan covens tend to be small, 13 being the traditional number of stereotype, but the average coven in fact consisting of between four and ten people—depending on the size of one's living room, bedroom, attic, or cellar! This very brief synopsis may already have alerted you to potential problems with regard to the inclusion of disabled people within Wicca, and these will be addressed before going on to explore the issues within the rites themselves.

At the Edge of the Circle: Issues before Initiation

Wicca's self-identity as a small mystery religion of priestesses and priests, entry to which is by a rite of initiation, is, of course, exclusivist, even elitist. The practice of adult initiation rites containing oaths of secrecy creates strong, resilient boundaries—there are most definitely insiders and outsiders. Wiccan covens do not take all-comers, and there is no right to initiation, any more than there is any right to ordination. However, while a disabled candidate for ordination training in, say, the Church of England has recourse to the law if he or she feels discriminated against, and the Church has a duty to enable that person's training and future work if he or she is selected,[2] there is no such recourse in Wicca. Because Wicca is not an institutionalized religion and its members gather in each other's private homes, it is not subject to the 2006 Equality Act.[3]

This is not to suggest that Wiccans on the whole discriminate against disabled people (though some do), but rather to acknowledge that there is no one body that can be held to account. In fact, each coven will decide for itself, and the decision will be based on certain practical and logistical considerations before anything else. Thus, a potential initiate with physical impairments affecting his or her mobility may not be able to access a temple located upstairs, or an outdoor working site. The coven must then decide whether it is willing or able to make adjustments, such as using the lounge rather than a bedroom, or working indoors rather than out. However, it is generally the case that potential initiates are expected to fit the coven, not vice versa. This may be fine if it is a new coven and the disabled person is the first initiate, but may be far more difficult if the coven is established, with long-standing members and preferred ways of working. As one priest opined:

> I judge people on whether I get along with them, not on their physical problems...in *some* cases, you cannot expect a coven to change their complete way of working in order to accommodate someone with a handicap. [T]he new initiate must fit the coven, not the other way around. However, quite often the people will put their "handicap" forward as THE reason, as a convenient scapegoat for refusal [of initiation].

In addition to logistical considerations and people's feelings that they perhaps have the "right" to be initiated, there may be medical concerns. Wicca is not a paid priesthood, and the majority of initiates have to work. Some are medically trained, in one or more areas: my contacts include general practitioners, nurses, radiographers, mental health professionals, psychologists, psychiatrists, and British Sign Language interpreters/translators. But whether medically trained or not, some Wiccans will feel more able to support and train initiates with certain disabilities more than others, and so one might expect a spectrum of response. For instance, some might be very happy to work a rite with a person with hearing difficulties, but feel completely incapable of training him or her as one's own initiate if he or she does not know advanced sign language. Or, because of the nature and purpose of Wiccan ritual as transformative psychospiritual practice, concern might be expressed as to the effect such rites may have on someone with a mental disability. As "Steve" reported:

> I have personally witnessed how Wicca/ritual practice/the initiatory jour-
> ney has provided a platform for transformation and growth . . . (although
> as I write this I am aware of the dangers, for some, of this journey and
> the added responsibility for coven elders in terms of, for example, ritual
> practice precipitating additional mental health issues).

So if we turn now to what happens *within* Wiccan ritual, we can begin to examine the potential problems that might arise.

A Brief Guide to Wiccan Ritual

The generic framework of Wiccan ritual has been formulated from ritual practices inherited from ceremonial magic via The Hermetic Order of the Golden Dawn, and involves the casting of a circle to create sacred space, its consecration and purification, and the calling of the four quarters (north, east, south, and west) to guard and protect the circle. Formalized words and gesture are used to communicate the stages of removal from the everyday into the ritual working space,[4] from the purification and consecration of the space and people, to the casting of the circle. This is then often immediately followed by the Witches' Rune,[5] a dance and chant in which formalization gives way to movement controlled only by the rhythm of the chant and the holding of hands in a circle. From the slow circumambulations that constitute the building up of the circle, the Wiccans join together in a faster, smaller circular movement, in which they feel the power produced by their dancing bodies creating what the Wiccans call the "cone of power" in the center of the circle. This dance operates as a bridging mechanism between the formalized framework of the ritual construction of sacred space and entering into a liminal space. The hypnotic rhythms of dancing and chanting help Wiccans "to enter into a deeper state of consciousness . . . [where] we are both separate and joined, individual yet one" (Crowley 1996: 86).

For those with physical disabilities, the potential problems are pretty obvious: there are references here to gesture, walking, dancing, kneeling, and standing for long periods. Yet these problems relate to physical movement in the preliminary stages of ritual; the next stage brings up another issue, that of embodying the divine.

The energy raised by the dance is focused in the invocation of the divine, which forms the central part of the rite. The spiritual force of a Goddess and/or God is believed to be drawn into the body of a Priestess and Priest, in a process known as "Drawing down the Moon/Sun" or, more commonly in the United Kingdom, as "invocation." The Priest or Priestess who is to be invoked stands before the altar and empties his or her mind, becoming still, becoming an empty vessel that the Divine can enter. The invoker kneels before the Priest or Priestess and uses the words of an invocation to imagine an image of the deity, visualizing the image forming behind the body of the Priest/Priestess and then merging into his or her etheric body/aura. The energy of the Divine is perceived as held within the body of the Priestess/Priest who, for the duration of this time, is considered to *be* the Goddess or God invoked.

In the center of the ritual, then, Wiccans *experience* the divine, a process that Jane Ellen Harrison observes in her *Epilogomena to the Study of Greek Religion*. Harrison (1962: xliv–xlvi) writes that the dancer who plays a god in a sacred rite "cannot be said to worship his god, he lives him, experiences him."[6] This experiencing of the divine *through the body* is particularly marked by the practice of ritual nudity, which draws attention to the physicality of the process of invocation through which the divine is incarnated or embodied.[7] Through the practice of ritual nudity, it can be argued that Wicca challenges the cultural forces that inform the way in which we think about our bodies, taking the body outside the context of the lived experience of everyday life. At the same time, the body is presented as a site—or potential site—of divine presence; physical action enables divine encounter. The body becomes ambiguous, reflecting both the divine and the human, life and death, youth and age, reproduction and degeneration, along the lines of Bakhtin's Renaissance body or Mellor and Shilling's Baroque modern bodies. Thus, a priestess who has never given birth—either through choice or through infertility—might be invoked as a mother goddess, or a young priestess as a crone goddess (or vice versa), or a priest in the prime of life might be invoked as Lord of Death at Samhain.

In esoteric terms, the deity force is believed to merge into the etheric body that surrounds the physical body; it does not *necessarily* take over the flesh, though the process does often have an effect on the physical because of its close connection to the etheric. In what sense, then, is the physical body normative, stable, or fixed? And if the etheric or subtle body is the locus of transformative experience, the site of divine presence, to what extent is it necessary that the physical body be "without defect"? If the magical energy required for the process of invocation is released from the body and concentrated by the mind, the two loci of disability in medical and legal terms, does this mean that disabled people cannot operate as Wiccan priests and priestesses? These are some of the questions that must be asked in considering disability and ritual in the Wiccan context, especially because Wicca *already* challenges Western cultural meanings assigned to the body and the mind in ways that, on the surface, ought to make it easier for disabled people to function fully as priests and priestesses within its rites. The body is most definitely celebrated, joyously; yet it is clearly a focus of pain and entrapment for many, especially those with a physical impairment, and may issue a challenge to notions of embodiment as "good," and the body as a host for the divine.

Disability and Priesthood

The cofounder of the Alexandrian tradition of Wicca, Maxine Sanders, tells of her first encounter with a disabled person wanting initiation. Paul was paralyzed from the waist down and used a "sporty wheelchair" that, she reports, he was able to haul up and down steps if there was no one to help him. However, his request for initiation, she says,

> hit me like a sledgehammer. One of the unwritten rules of the coven I had been initiated into dealt with precisely this: initiating the disabled was not allowed. It had not occurred to me to question this as no disabled person had ever approached us. That first coven had strict rules regarding who was allowed to take on the mantle of the priesthood... [t]he physically handicapped or crippled and anyone who was not whole in body was... disallowed.[8] (Sanders 2008: 190–191)

Here, we witness the lack of challenge to unwritten rules that stems from the privileged position of the temporarily able-bodied. It was only after a period of time in which Paul's intent shone out as true, Maxine "questioned the law of the Craft, and found *it* wanting," and so she disobeyed the law and initiated him. Psychological problems followed, and Paul was eventually admitted to hospital for treatment of clinical depression. A year after his initiation, Paul himself suggested that this law should not be broken again, since "The next man may not be so strong" (Sanders 2008: 191).

Although Sanders claims that "Times, opinions, laws change!" (Sanders 2008: 191), the idea that being "whole in body and mind" is a necessary prerequisite for priesthood continues to retain some currency. In discussion with a Wiccan priest on initiating disabled people, he said precisely that, using the ancient mystery religions as his reason for maintaining this view.[9] According to the Classicist Mary Beard, qualifications required for Roman priestly roles [such as *pontifices* or augur] were "freebirth, Roman citizenship, and *an absence of bodily defects*" (Beard 1990: 22, my emphasis)—but that was in the third century BCE. The intervening millennia seem irrelevant to some, though they would not dream of indulging in some other dubious practices of the mystery cults, such as blood sacrifice. Selective affinity with a romanticized and conflated construct of ancient priesthood can therefore fuel contemporary ideals of what constitutes priesthood in Wicca;[10] that discrimination is rare may well be solely because very few physically disabled people seek initiation.

And yet, if priest/esshood is understood as being in some way "active in relation to the gods" (Beard and North 1990: 9) and as such the process of invocation is central to that priest/esshood, and if we are encountering Wiccans claiming that disabled people, by virtue of their disability, cannot embody the divine, then the "disabled divine" is also being dismissed.[11] The ancient pagan pantheons and myths mined by Wiccans for their rites include lame gods and wounded healers. The most obvious is, of course, Hephaestus. Born weak and crippled,[12] he was thrown from Olympus by his mother, Hera, but was saved and became god of artisans and of the blacksmiths' fire; importantly, he was given as his bride Aphrodite, goddess of beauty, reflecting that ambiguity that brings together the apparently irreconcilable—in this case the grotesque and the beautiful.[13] Other examples include Chiron, the great teacher and master of healing who could not heal himself, and Odin, the All-Father of Norse mythology, who gave up the sight in one eye in order to become all-knowing and all-seeing.[14]

And of course, there are also "crazy gods." Dionysus, for example, was struck with madness by Hera and sent to wander the earth. He is well known as the inspirer of ritual madness, freeing us from our normal selves by means of wine, ecstasy, or—importantly—through madness. Pan inspires sudden fear in lonely places ("Pan-ic") and brings madness to those who see him face to face. It is interesting that both these gods associated with madness supplied much of the symbolism for the Christian version of Satan: divine madness becomes demonized. They are also gods strongly linked with nature, wildness, and unexpected, powerful encounters,[15] and both are popular deities in the Wiccan ritual context. The encounter with madness in some form is, in a sense, an accepted part of Wicca, and deities associated with madness are more integral to Wicca than those associated with physical impairments. As Stanislav Grof (2002) has observed in *Spiritual Emergency*, "the gods are crazy and so are we, especially when we are forced to encounter them and the craziness is part of the encounter. It is dangerous, creative, and liminal. And very, very rich in potential." In fact, Wicca does not dismiss divine madness but rather seeks to engage with it in some controlled way, and the disabled body can and does embody the divine in the same way as the temporarily able body. Although there does appear to be a certain amount of prejudice toward the *idea*[16] of initiating someone with a physical disability, the greater concern tends to be for those with an existing mental disability. This is because Wicca actively seeks and engages with spiritual emergence, if not spiritual emergency,[17] and it is therefore felt to be inappropriate—even dangerous—for those with an existing mental health problem to be subjected to such crises of transformation, when "the process of growth and change [can] become [ ] chaotic and overwhelming... [and people] may even fear for their own sanity" (Grof and Grof 2002, back cover).[18] If we now turn to the three case studies I mentioned at the beginning of this chapter, we can see how three experiences of disability are responded to within Wicca.

Case Studies

Matthew[19], a Wiccan priest, happens to have diabetes, for which he is dependent on insulin to control. He was rather surprised to find diabetes listed as a disability under the Disability Discrimination Act of 2004 (DDA), as he has never considered himself to be disabled and "reacts extremely badly to anyone trying to categorize me as disabled... it's a 'hidden impairment' and I do my best to keep it that way." He does, however, need to check blood glucose levels before any rituals, consider how it might change during the course of the ritual, and make any necessary adjustments to ensure that he maintains blood glucose levels during the ritual to prevent slipping into a hypoglycemic coma, though he points out that this is something he would do before anything for which physical and mental competence is essential. But ritual has a specific danger. As he points out,

> A problem with hypoglycemia is that as brain function deteriorates, there can be a sense that one is on the brink of understanding some

great mystery, that one is having an intense mystical experience. This can be more dangerous than usual under ritual conditions if you are in an altered state of consciousness and hoping such an experience may ensue! That's happened to me once. My partner noticed and took appropriate action. Unfortunately, it also meant the end of that ritual.

He feels that his constant need to be a "control freak" means that he is *deeply aware* of his body· "I know all the way down to my bones that I am mortal. That's a good thing. I don't take life for granted," and "Blood glucose levels can give you a crude insight into the amount of energy you have used because for the body, glucose is effectively fuel". In this way, he feels his condition is of benefit to him as a Wiccan.

He says, "The physicality of the craft is one of its many strengths. The way ritual can actively engage body, mind, emotions and spirit through all five senses, so that we can engage with the sacred as whole people." Here, "knowledge is gained from a *thinking body* in which sensuous understanding involve[s] *all* of the body's senses, and from the intricate links which exist[ ] between the fleshy, physical body and the mind" (Mellor and Shilling 1997: 23). For him, it is important that "the disabled witch doesn't feel they're being treated as a passenger"—ritual needs to be tailored to everyone's strengths, not reduce to the "lowest common denominator":

> In the closeness of a Wiccan circle, having a group of people who know, love and respect you also watching with a degree of concern in case you malfunction would for me be more painful than reassuring. A circle of equals is just that. It is not just that you trust them, they must be able to trust you.

In fact, only a couple of people very close to him are even aware that he has diabetes and know how to respond if he does show signs of hyperglycemia—though he states that his response to their concerns is somewhat fierce, "even though it's saved my life a couple of times." He has not, at any point, considered his "disability" to be something that disables his activities as a Wiccan priest. Rather, Matthew has used his "disability" to acquire knowledge *through* the body, knowledge that he uses to enhance his ritual experience as well as his normal, everyday life.

For others, however, disability has had a negative effect on ritual experience. There are, for instance, priestesses who, having reached a point where they felt their disability was preventing them from embodying the Goddess, have made the decision to close down their coven and stop working Wiccan ritual. For Samantha, the disability was ongoing, long-term depression. She had suffered from progressive osteoarthritis since birth, which became bad enough to prevent her from dancing, kneeling, and standing for long periods. But, she said:

> It never occurred to me to stop working as a High Priestess. Our coven members were very helpful, understanding and we managed to adapt to have a chair in the circle... I felt quite frustrated because I wasn't able to participate as much as I wanted to, but still everyone was ok with that.

After her hip replacement, she could fully participate again. The real problem came some four years ago, linked to the hormonal changes of the menopause. She says:

> I started to feel depressed and couldn't focus on anything, felt incapable, my self-esteem was very low and I felt suicidal at times and I couldn't connect with the Gods. I really wasn't up to fulfilling the role of HPS. So at that time I felt I needed to close the coven.

In her case, where a physical impairment could be worked around and managed, a temporary mental disability dis-abled her spiritual life to the extent that she made this decision. At no point did anyone tell her what that decision should be.

My second example is Tabitha, a 48-year-old woman, for whom the pain of arthritis had become crippling, to the extent that she felt she was no longer able to perform all the activities required of her as a Wiccan High Priestess (HP). Because her training had been hard-line to the point of being abusive, she felt she would be breaking her third-degree initiation oaths if she continued to run her coven as Gardnerian in that particular lineage.[20] She wrote,

> The general opinion was that if one was not fit to run around, sit on the floor etc., then one was not fit to be participating in or running a Gardnerian coven... I've always felt I had to push myself to take part in B&$ every circle, dancing etc., even when it took me a week in bed to get over it and a huge amount of painkillers before and after circle... I felt very sad that the Gardnerian way of working is not flexible enough to allow for disability. I felt very sad that I had to take the steps I did because I couldn't manage to run the coven "properly"... Maybe other lines of the Craft are not so inflexible, but unfortunately I was trained in one that was... having to do this has been very, very difficult indeed,

and I have felt, rightly or wrongly, rather "abandoned" because of something I have to live with.

In this case, clearly her decision was hugely influenced by the prejudicial and discriminatory attitudes of the coven in which she had been trained, in particular the pronouncements of her own initiating HP. Happily, as a result of the discussion and support she got from others on the list, Tabitha is now very aware that her "hard-line" training is considered by others to be abusive, and is not the norm—a point that is reflected anyway in the fact that Tabitha herself has not continued such practices with her own initiates even though she retained those expectations that had been imposed upon her. She finally decided to continue running her coven, making adaptations as she needs—wearing a robe and/or cloak instead of working skyclad and so on. She says:

> I now have a large, sheepskin-lined rocking chair at the side of the altar, and we are working on developing magical techniques such as "gealdor" (sung spells), rune work etc. It has to be a tradition where it is OK to be "disabled" and that is "workable" for the rest of my life.

Neither Samantha nor Tabitha stopped identifying as a priestess, but equally neither, at least temporarily, felt able to continue practicing Wicca in a coven setting or in a hard-line Gardnerian lineage. In the first case, no one told Samantha what she "should" do; in the second, Tabitha acted on oaths she had made to her HP and thus, in a sense, was told what she should do. Although in Samantha's case, part of the physical impairment had been lifelong, the disabilities that affected both women's Wiccan activities were not present prior to initiation—both had, in fact, been long-standing Wiccan priestesses with a great deal of experience before they experienced "dis-ablement." Their problems arose, then, as a result of what the medical literature would no doubt call "postinitiation-onset disability," which appears to engender a different response from Wiccans to those presenting for initiation with a disability.

Conclusion: Once a Priest/ess, Always a Priest/ess?

In the same way that one would not disown a child, partner, sibling, and so on who, as the result of an accident or illness, develops a disability, so Wiccans would be highly unlikely to reject a priest or priestess who found himself or herself in such a position. Instead, compromises would be reached and "reasonable adjustments" made in negotiation with the disabled person. As the husband of a Wiccan priestess who, as the result of a motorbike accident, had one of her legs amputated, wrote,

> Sabrina is a human being just like the rest of us, and she doesn't want to be treated differently than the rest of us or be made to feel different. So really all we do is try to make things as easy as possible for her without making a big fuss.[21]

Contrary to the ideas about priesthood and wholeness expressed earlier, then, there is no suggestion from anyone—not even those who hold to this idea—that any of these or countless other examples suddenly became unfit to be priestesses or priests when they experience disability, and must therefore leave Wicca. There is thus a marked difference in attitude toward those seeking initiation who are disabled—both by their impairment and sometimes by Wiccan ritual—and those already initiated and trained as priests and priestesses who later develop a disability. Having already gained experience they are, it seems, deemed able to bypass their disability, although it appears that physical disabilities are more easily accommodated both by the person with the impairment and by their fellow priests and priestesses.[22]

When a disability is located in the mind, it appears that the situation can be more problematic. Undoubtedly, the relationship between spirituality and mental health is complex, seemingly more than that between physical health and ritual: even Paul, with severe physical impairments, became debilitating only once a mental disability presented, while depression, as Samantha's case revealed, may "block" someone from feeling the divine, so that he or she no longer feels able to operate as priests or priestesses. It appears that the psychospiritual transformation actively facilitated by Wiccan ritual is regarded as dangerous and thus unsuitable for those with a preexisting mental health condition. Thus, while psychological change is both sought and expected, and is facilitated by ritual practice, Wiccan ritual is believed to have the potential to intensify the experience of inner psychological processes, and anything that opens an individual up even further to intense spiritual energy is felt to encompass risk as well as potential. It seems, then, that while the body can be allowed to inhabit an ambiguous, unstable space without firm or fixed boundaries, the mind cannot be allowed to inhabit a similarly liminal space. Rather, fixed boundaries are established in order that there can be an equally fixed boundary between pathological mental disorders and spiritual experience—in an attempt to avoid, rather than embrace, transforming spiritual *emergence* into spiritual *emergency.*

Notes

1. And despite the antics and publications of various high-profile Wiccans since the 1950s, Wicca does not proselytise—it does not seek converts, and has no desire to become a numerically significant, mainstream religion (which rather confuses those sociologists of religion for whom size is everything!).

2. So long as they can meet the requirements of selection—communication etc. Ability to form relationships, for example, might be difficult for a person with Asperger's syndrome. We might also note here the Catholic tradition of "ex defectu," which covers both "bodily defects" and "defect of reason." Bodily defects "constitute an impediment to Sacred orders, either because they render a person unfit for the ministry or because his deformity would make him an object of horror and derision." They include "mutilated persons, those having an artificial limb or who are unable to use their hand or thumb or index finger; the blind and those whose vision is too dim to allow them to read the Missal,,, Total deafness, dumbness, and stammering to such an extent as to make it impossible to pronounce complete words are likewise impediments. Paralytics, the lame who cannot properly perform the ceremonies, those who cannot drink wine without vomiting, lepers, those afflicted with the falling sickness, and in general all whose deformity is very notable are irregular." Defect of reason includes the insane, energumens, and simpletons. Reception of Holy Orders calls for integrity of body, mind, will, and faith, lack of which is an irregularity that either impedes ordination or invalidates Orders already entered. Retrieved January 29, 2008, from http://www.newadvent.org/cathen/08170a.htm.

3. This Act came into force on October 1, 2007.

4. "[S]timulating an awareness of the hidden side of reality" (Starhawk 1989: 27) that, S. Gablik laments, we have lost—"we no longer have the ability to shift mind-sets and thus to perceive other realities, to move between the worlds...One way to access these worlds is through ritual where something more goes on than meets the eye—something sacred" (Gablik, 1992: 22 in Carpenter 1996: 65).

5. Written by Doreen Valiente. See Crowley (1996: 87) and Farrar ([1971] 1991: 13).

6. The Protestant theologian Friedrich Schleiermacher (1768–1834) defined the experience of the Divine, or the infinite, as the essence of religion. This experience, says Peter Berger (1979: 130) in his commentary on Schleiermacher, is what religion is all about—*not* theoretical speculation, *nor* moral preachings...The underlying experience of all religion, its

essence, is one of encountering the infinite within the finite phenomena of human life.

7. This is in stark contrast to the Protestant re-formation of the body in which it is "the 'spirit,' separate from the impurities of the sensuous body" that seeks contact with the divine (see Mellor and Shilling 1997: 30).

8. [cf] Origen, whose self-mutilation (castration) prevented his ordination. Also Deut. (23: 1): "No one whose testicles are crushed or whose penis is cut off shall be admitted to the assembly of the LORD."

9. Of course, this is also true of Catholic priesthood—see Note 1.

10. And in Catholicism!

11. We are also, surely, entering similar territory to that which argued against women's ordination as priests: that they are "disabled" by their gender in a manner that prevents them from standing *in locus Christi*.

12. Hephaestus was reported in myth as *cholōs*, "lame," crippled, halting (*ēpedanos*) and misshapen, either from birth or as a result of his fall (see *Iliad* xviii.397; *Odyssey* viii.308, etc.). In vase-paintings, he is sometimes shown with his feet back-to-front, *Hephaistosamphigyēeis*.

13. Although this was an arranged marriage that did not please Aphrodite, and from which there was no issue. However, given the still taboo subject of "disabled sex," it is also pertinent to note that Hephaestus did have several children, by both mortals and immortals.

14. He surrendered the eye to drink from the Mimir's Well of Knowledge, and hung pinned to Yggdrasil with a spear for nine days, so that he could gain the knowledge of the runes.

15. And of course, Dionysus is coupled with Apollo as the irrational/rational dichotomy in Nietzsche's *The Birth of Tragedy* (1872).

16. I say "idea of" since disabled people asking for initiation seems to be a rare occurrence.

17. Lukoff (1998: 11) clarifies the difference between the two thus: "In spiritual *emergence*, . . . there is a gradual unfoldment of spiritual potential with minimal disruption in psychological/social/occupational functioning, whereas in spiritual *emergency* there is significant abrupt disruption in psychological/social/occupational functioning."

18. Similarly, a person going through an experience that is psychologically traumatic—including divorce, important exams, grief—or lacking in psychological maturity—the average age of Wiccans at the time of initiation is 35—would have to wait for initiation.

19. All names have been changed.

20. Unfortunately my ill health does not allow me to fulfil all the criteria I am oathed to fulfil by the HP who trained me and I do not wish to be forsworn. I am aware that I would not be fulfilling the role I was trained to fulfil if I missed out the very important parts of the ritual such as B & $, even if only for myself as well as other traditional duties incumbent upon a third-degree HP.

21. Another priestess with a hearing impairment shares the attitude of simply getting on with it rather than making a fuss. Well aware that, on the disability spectrum, she is "nowhere near as bad as other people," she has become increasingly reliant on untrained lip-reading. Of course, in the darkness of a candlelit room or the open spaces of a large outdoor rite, this is near impossible. Her answer? "I get someone to poke me in the ribs when it's my turn to say or do something!"

22. As one priestess suggested,

> [I]f we tie the practice of the Craft to the functionality of the body, then at some point in most of our lives we will have to stop practicing the Craft... since the true practice of the Craft is within the heart that rejoices in our service and love of the God and Goddess, then the flesh is just a vessel of it, no matter how it functions.

References

Beard, M. (1990). Priesthood in the Roman Republic. In M. Beard & J. North (Eds.), *Pagan Priests: Religion and Power in the Ancient World* (pp. 17–48). London, England: Duckworth.

Berger, P. L. (1979). *The Heretical Imperative: Contemporary Possibilities of Religious Affirmation*, New York, NY: Anchor Press (Doubleday).

Carpenter, D. D. (1996). Emergent nature spirituality: An examination of the major spiritual contours of the contemporary pagan worldview. In J. R. Lewis (Ed.), *Magical Religion and Modern Witchcraft* (pp. 35–72). New York, NY: SUNY.

Crowley, V. (1996). *Wicca: The Old Religion in the New Millennium*. London, England: Thorsons.

Gablik, S. (1992). The artist as enchanter. *Common Boundary 10*(2), 20–27.

Grof, S., & Grof, C. (Eds.). (2002). *Spiritual Emergency: When Personal Transformation Becomes a Crisis*. Harmondsworth, England: Penguin.

Hutton, R. (1999). *The Triumph of the Moon: A History of Pagan Witchcraft*. Oxford, England: Oxford University Press.

Irregularity. Retrieved January 29, 2008, from http://www.newadvent.org/cathen/08170a.htm

Lukoff, D. (1998). From spiritual emergency to spiritual problem: The transpersonal roots of the new DSM-IV category. *Journal of Humanistic Psychology 38*(2), 21–50. Retrieved October 22, 2008, from www.spiritualcompetency.com/jhpseart.html

Mellor, P. A., & Shilling, C. (1997). *Reforming the Body: Religion, Community and Modernity*. London, England: Sage.

Nietzsche, F. ([1872], 1993). *The Birth of Tragedy: Out of the Spirit of Music*. Harmondsworth, England: Penguin.

Rappaport, R. (1979). *Ecology, Meaning and Religion*. Berkeley, CA: North Atlantic Books.

Sanders, M. (2008). *Firechild: The Life and Magic of Maxine Sanders, 'Witch Queen'*. Oxford: Mandrake Press.

Starhawk. ([1979], 1989). *The Spiral Dance: A Rebirth of the Ancient Religion of the Great Goddess*. San Francisco, CA: HarperCollins.

CHAPTER 5

A Secular Case for Religious Inclusion of Individuals with Intellectual and Developmental Disabilities

Jeff McNair and Abigail Schindler

Consider Jack,[1] a man with developmental disabilities who is well known in a local church. He regularly participates in social opportunities there, including overnight men's retreats. Church leaders often refer to him as an example of enthusiasm for and dedication to the church. Originally, Jack was referred to the faith community through a state agency caseworker, a devout Jew who determined that the client was interested in attending a Christian church.[2] After doing research, this caseworker found a potential church, and transported him there until both she and Jack felt confident that it was a good match. Shortly thereafter, the church took over responsibility for his transportation, and he has been a devoted member for more than ten years.

Now, consider Damien, a man with developmental disabilities who was regularly involved with a church for more than five years, including work with children's ministry and leadership within a program serving adults with disabilities. When Damien's caseworker died suddenly, she was replaced by another caseworker who felt that it was outside of her role to support him in his religious involvement. She encouraged him to move in with his girlfriend and within about six months of the new caseworker's association with him, Damien began living with a girlfriend, relied on a state agency for assistance with his Social Security Insurance (SSI) (as opposed to unpaid individuals in his personal network), and ultimately moved 20 miles away from the extensive network that he had in the community. When people in his church network protested, his caseworker joked, "I am leading him to a life of sin." At times, agency workers may manipulate individuals with intellectual and developmental disabilities (I/DD) to reflect their imposed biases.

These brief scenarios illustrate two approaches to supporting adults with disabilities in the community. One appears to be informed about the benefits of participation in a religious community. The other is antagonistic and uninformed about these potential benefits. Both highlight the importance of support workers respecting the values of the individual they are supporting, instead of imposing their own values. They also illustrate the need for support workers to understand the benefits of religious inclusion for people with intellectual disabilities. This chapter proposes a rationale for caseworkers to assist clients in fulfilling their desire to participate in the religious community of their own choosing.

Normative Experiences

A "normative structure in social experience" (Rappaport 1993: 246) is a structure experienced by most individuals in a society. Such structures include religious organizations, political parties, and even families, in contrast to social service agencies where clients come to receive services from professional helpers (McKnight 1987). While all people will have experiences with state agency structures across their lifetimes, these kinds of interactions are normative only when used rarely, for short time periods, and with the expectation that one will be able to recover to the point that such structures will no longer be required. For instance, within American culture it is expected that people will get off welfare, out of the unemployment lines, out of the hospital, and cease to use social security benefits when not "really" in need of them. Agencies themselves will periodically evaluate consumers to determine whether there is a continuing need for services. The desire to move away from state agency support accompanies the normative experience of living independently, where one relies on natural, social structures for support.

Over time, social supports have gradually been replaced by governmental social services (McKnight 1985). At the same time, the proliferation of governmental social services is the result of various communities advocating for the development of such services (Ryan and Thomas 1980). Too often, community services have been supplanted by governmental services to the point that there is a greater reliance on the government for the support of one's neighbor, causing many to relinquish this responsibility. In order to more fully utilize natural supports, human service professionals must nurture the normative structures the general public is already using, but which state structures tend to overlook. Efforts might aim to transform these formal supports to the greatest extent possible and supplement them with informal, natural supports.

When supporting individuals to make community connections and foster network development, religious groups are obvious sources of natural support that often go ignored (Hoeksema 1995). Normative structures become normative because they meet the needs of the people using them. In a survey of parents of individuals with disabilities, 81 percent reported that using religious beliefs or religious activities helps them feel better, 65 percent rated religion as at least moderately helpful, and 29 percent rated religion as being the most important thing that keeps them going (Rogers et al. 2002). Despite the fact that many parents believe their religion is a pervasive cultural theme in their and their child's life, "this fact is not reflected in the literature" (Weisner, Beizer, and Stolze 1991: 649).

Community Integration

The state will often attempt to facilitate community through enforced physical integration (e.g., the Americans with Disabilities Act, inclusion in schools, programs to facilitate less restrictive settings at work, and independent living). However, the assumption that physical integration into the community will lead to social integration is not well supported (Cummins and Lau 2003), and there are no guarantees that the former will lead to the latter. True community "needs to be constantly nourished and revitalized" in order to prevent it from becoming "soulless institutions... places where rules and organisation are more important than communion and friendships" (Vanier 2008: 185). The typical experience of an individual with intellectual disabilities with his or her community is one that is regulated and controlled by professionals. These professionals are themselves regulated to the point that it is difficult for the individual with I/DD to break through his paternalistically protected life in order to experience anything approximating natural community.

Those with I/DD often have small and restricted social networks that include only those they reside with, paid support workers, and family members (Bigby 2008; Forrester-Jones et al. 2006; Lippold and Burns

2009; Robertson et al. 2001; Verdonschot et al. 2009). Wolfensberger describes this substitution of unpaid relationships with "boughten" ones as a wound experienced by devalued people (Wolfensberger 2000: 109). A systematic review of the literature revealed that though people with I/DD in integrated settings fare better than those in segregated or institutional settings, social participation levels for individuals with I/DD remain low across settings. People with I/DD were found to have an average of only 3.1 individuals in their social network, with one usually being a paid staff member. In addition, they were less likely than their nondisabled peers to participate in community groups and other leisure activities (Verdonschot et al. 2009). These findings expose the limitations of service providers in supporting and facilitating relationships for individuals with I/DD.

A potential source of natural relationships for people living in group homes is a church, parish, synagogue, mosque, Buddhist meditation group, or some other religious institution/network. These communities are often overlooked though they have the potential to enrich the lives of people with I/DD and increase the number of nonpaid relationships they experience (Hoeksema 1995: 292). Much like all communities, though, simply attending a place of worship or religious function may not be enough, since "being in is not the same as belonging to" (Turnbull and Turnbull 2007: xii). People with disabilities may face architectural, attitudinal, communicational, programmatic, and liturgical barriers to participation in religious communities, but those communities must be proactive about providing for their full inclusion (Carter 2007).

Benefits of Religious Participation

The literature provided here strongly supports "secular benefits" to persons involved with religious groups. Professionals who are aware of the benefits of religious participation to individuals with disabilities should pass on this understanding to the support vendors with whom they work. Some direct benefits of religious participation to individuals with disabilities and their families include the interpretation of disability, network participation, and natural supports. Supporting an individual with I/DD in the religious group of his or her own choosing does not necessarily call for the establishment of any particular religion, and can in fact meet the criteria of achieving a secular purpose.[3] Let us briefly consider some of the secular benefits of religious participation.

Interpretation of Disability

The manner in which a disability is interpreted by the family has profound effects on the family member with disability. As Heifetz and Franklin argue, "families are embedded in a complex of social systems that help to define and interpret the experiences associated with disability" (Heifetz and Franklin 1982: 128). A modern understanding of disability is that the deprivations people with disabilities experience are not simply due to impairments and functional limitations but due to their environment (Barnes 1995; Shakespeare 2006). Therefore, the way individuals within a social network understand intellectual disability influences the self-perception of persons with I/DD. As Fitzgerald claims, external influences "play a disproportionately large role in shaping self-perception" for people with disabilities (Fitzgerald 1997: 407).

Such interpretations of self are critical, and the basis upon which the perceptions are built are equally critical. Culturally normative assumptions of disability may or may not be constructive or even realistic. Even healthy understandings of who one is may contain wishful falsehoods or platitudes, which although well intended may be demeaning or destructive when carried to their logical conclusion. Family interpretations of disability are "powerful and are probably learned and shared to some extent by the child with developmental delays" (Weisner, Beizer, and Stolze 1991: 660). Although religious schemas are subject to the same negative platitudes of other systems, "... religious belief systems are generally regarded as having a positive impact on family adjustment because they provide a valuable interpretive framework" (Haworth, Hill, and Masters Glidden 1996: 271). Even this interpretive framework will sometimes cause dissonance in socially normative situations because of the sheltered nature of such interactions, or because it challenges the preconceived notions of actors within the systems. Fitzgerald observed that

> This process of confronting our inability to control everything, to surrendering to a force beyond ourselves, to being open to vulnerability and the trusting of others' responses to our vulnerability, is part of a deep spiritual understanding which most of us are confronted with at some times in our lives; a surrendering which most of us also seek avidly to avoid because it fails to fit with the conception of self we have become accustomed to in our Western liberal tradition. (Fitzgerald 1997: 411)

However, the systematic treatment of the topic of disability by religious groups has significant potential for framing disability in the lives of the religious.

Network Participation

Fewell (1986) lists various supports received from religious institutions by individuals with disabilities and their families. These include instrumental supports (Unger and Powell 1980), which are the material supports individuals receive from support networks, emotional or social supports, educational supports, and structural supports associated with the family life cycle. Individuals with disabilities experience the same benefits of religious participation as those without disabilities, including the experience of group belongingness, expression of religious beliefs, and use of religious beliefs to guide their moral behavior (Hoeksema 1995). Many individuals with I/DD both express an interest in and find fulfillment from religion (Kregel et al., 1986; Rose 1997), and church attendance is one of the most favored activities of young persons with disabilities (Scuccimarra and Speece 1990). Although recent data are unavailable, it has been estimated that approximately 60 percent of individuals with mild disabilities and 50 percent of individuals with developmental disabilities report attending church (McNair and Smith 2000; Riordan and Vasa 1991; Scuccimarra and Speece 1990). In addition, 61 percent of parents of children with disabilities reported themselves as regular church attenders (McNair and Rusch 1991). Berger and Neuhaus (1977) describe "mediating structures" as bridges between people, linking people who might not otherwise gain the mutual benefit of their interactions. These individuals are often critical in the development of social networks. As normative community structures, religious communities hold the potential for being important mediating structures in these individuals' lives.

Natural Supports

Research also indicates that individuals with disabilities and their families receive a wealth of supports from religious groups and religious participation. Dunst, Trivette, and Cross (1986) observed that informal supports have a greater influence on family well-being than do formal supports. Others point to religious groups as informal supports, stating, "to increase the effectiveness of interventions...providers need to be cognizant of families' religious beliefs and build on informal resources provided by churches" (Heller et al. 1994: 297).

A wide variety of supports are regularly provided to individuals with disabilities by religious communities (McNair and Swartz 1997). These include food, money, social interaction opportunities, and emotional support. Haworth, Hill, and Masters Glidden state that "... religious services, Sunday school, and other activities offered by the church ... provided [mothers] with a network of social supports in which they found friendship and comfort" (Haworth, Hill, and Masters Glidden 1996: 277). Fewell (1986) observed that mothers of children with Down's syndrome who had high religious support also received more support from family and friends, and were more satisfied with the support they received than were less religious mothers. She further states,

> For far too long, professionals who work with families of handicapped children, including professionals associated with religious organizations, have failed to understand and realize the importance of these sources of religious support. Although neglected and rarely taken seriously by professionals, it has not been overlooked by parents, and from these sources they often derive much of the strength they need to nurture their child with special needs. (Fewell 1986: 314–315)

This religiosity of families with disabilities was also the pivotal factor in research completed by another group.

Weisner, Beizer, and Stolze (1991) studied the religiousness of parents as the independent variable in comparisons of perceptions of disability, and supports received by families of individuals with disabilities. The researchers placed families into four groups using four criteria in assessing each family's "religiosity." Criteria were (1) church/temple involvement and attendance, (2) sense of spirituality, (3) support from church/temple, and (4) influence of religion. Families were then characterized as nonreligious, somewhat religious, religious, or highly religious. Questionnaires were provided, and responses grouped according to religiosity. Religious families reported receiving more material help from friends and neighbors, more positive feedback from professionals, and more participation in social activities with friends. The authors state, "highly religious parents were also more likely to seek support for their family in the form of child care aid or group activities than were nonreligious parents" (Weisner, Beizer, and Stolze 1991: 658).

McNair (1997, 2000) has described the "local church" as a network of supporting adults with disabilities in the community. As a rule, religious communities are durable and stable networks. Although they are born and die every day, they typically have a lifespan measured in years, perhaps even decades. Faith communities may also be extensive in terms of the types of people one finds like oneself (laterality), the types of persons one finds different from oneself (variability), the types of persons one finds "above or below" oneself (in terms of education, employment, etc., also known as verticality), and the sheer number of members in the network. This offers the opportunity for integration across a wide variety of individuals with whom one might not typically interact.

Role of Persons with Disabilities in Religious Communities

The inclusion of individuals with disabilities in religious communities also results in various benefits to the religious community itself. These include accessing the gifts for service these members bring. Religious communities also grow spiritually through relating with persons with disabilities and their families. One can make the case that persons with intellectual or developmental disabilities are indispensable to the spiritual development of religious groups as a whole (McNair 2008; Reynolds 2008). In the Christian church, for example, 1 Corinthians (12: 14–27) compares individuals within the church to parts of Christ's body, prioritizing the "weaker" parts, which are said to be "indispensable." However, this does not imply a utilitarian notion of people with disabilities to religious groups, since a person is not disabled so that a person without a disability can gain something from his or her presence (Byzek 2000). Instead, this passage necessitates correcting the wrong of exclusion. We must not exclude anyone on the basis of our perceptions of who they are as in reality, all people, even those who "seem to be weaker" to us, are in fact indispensable to a body of religious participants if they are to be a complete body of participation. It is also not some form of religious affirmative action, but a recognition of the fact that people having every form of difference must be included if a whole body is to be a whole body.

Conclusion

As normative social structures, faith communities offer numerous benefits for individuals with I/DD and their families, including individual and familial framing of disability, social network participation, and a broad array of natural supports. The religious community itself also benefits from the gifts, resources, and diversity offered by people with I/DD. Efforts to include persons with I/DD in religious communities of their own choosing should occur across religious groups and ought to be included in the basic transition services provided by local school districts and adult service agencies. Through interfaith collaborative efforts, true community integration can be achieved for a group who often experience deprivation in social networks and community inclusion.

These secular benefits provided by faith communities serve as a call to service professionals, who have a duty to provide the best supports possible for individuals with I/DD. Supporting full societal inclusion of people with developmental disabilities necessarily includes supporting their participation in religious activities (Vogel, Polloway, and Smith 2006), though service providers may struggle to include this dimension of individuals' lives into their support plan. However, the full commitment to accessing the benefits of religious communities for people with disabilities does not fall on service providers. The religious communities themselves have a responsibility to proactively reach out to and support individuals with I/DD (Carter 2007). Access to religious communities will be inadequate if the religious community and the culture employed by that community are not welcoming (Reinders 2008). Since communities themselves may be considered a "manifestation of our need to belong," they directly benefit from embracing people with I/DD and acknowledging the mutual vulnerability of human existence (Reynolds 2008: 129).

Finally, although this chapter focused on secular benefits, there are obviously significant religious benefits to religious participation including the opportunity to develop one's spiritual self and the chance to be among like-minded people. Although these types of benefits might not be sought by the secular person, they are life enhancing and life defining for people who participate in a religious community.

Notes

1. Names have been changed to protect the identity of those involved.
2. For the purposes of this chapter, the terms "church" and "faith community" are considered synonymous.
3. For an investigation of issues involved in church/state separation, see Cnann's (2002) *The Invisible Caring Hand*, or Monsma's (1996) *When Sacred and Secular Mix*.

References

Barnes, C. (1995). Disability, cultural representation and language. *Critical Public Health 6*(2), 9–20.

Berger, P., & Neuhaus, R. (1977). *To Empower People: The Role of Mediating Structures in Public Policy*. Washington, DC: American Enterprise Institute for Public Policy Research.

Bigby, C. (2008). Known well by no-one: Trends in the informal social networks of middle-aged and older people with intellectual disability five years after moving to the community. *Journal of Intellectual & Developmental Disability 33*(2), 148–158.

Byzek, J. (2000, November/December). Jesus and the paralytic, the blind, and the lame: A sermon. *Ragged Edge Magazine*. Retrieved September 4, 2009, from http://www.raggededgemagazine.com/1100/1100cft1.htm

Carter, E. W. (2007). *Including People with Disabilities in Faith Communities: A Guide for Service Providers, Families, and Congregations*. Baltimore: Paul H. Brookes.

Cnann, R. (2002). *The Invisible Caring Hand: American Congregations and the Provision of Welfare*. New York, NY: New York University Press.

Cummins, R. A., & Lau, A. L. D. (2003). Community integration or community exposure? A review and discussion in relation to people with an intellectual disability. *Journal of Applied Research in Intellectual Disabilities 16*, 145–157.

Dunst, C. J., Trivette, C. M., & Cross, A. H. (1986). Mediating influences of social support: Personal, family, and child outcomes. *American Journal of Mental Deficiency 90*, 403–417.

Fewell, R. R. (1986). Supports from religious organizations and personal beliefs. In R. Fewell & P. Vadasy (Eds.), *Families of Handicapped Children*. Austin, Texas: Pro-ed.

Fitzgerald, J. (1997). Reclaiming the whole: Self, spirit and society. *Disability and Rehabilitation 19*(10), 407–413.

Forrester-Jones, R., Carpenter, J., Coolen-Schrijner, P., Cambridge, P., Tate, A., & Beecham, J. (2006). The social networks of people with intellectual disability living in the community 12 years after resettlement from long-stay hospitals. *Journal of Applied Research in Intellectual Disabilities 19*, 285–295.

Haworth, A. M., Hill, A. E., & Masters Glidden, L. (1996). Measuring religiousness of parents of children with developmental disabilities. *Mental Retardation 34*(5), 271–279.

Heifetz, L. J., & Franklin, D. C. (1982). Nature and sources of the clergy's involvement with mentally retarded persons and their families. *American Journal of Mental Deficiency 87*(1), 56–63.

Heller, T., Markwardt, R., Rowitz, L., & Farber, B. (1994). Adaptation of Hispanic families to a member with mental retardation. *American Journal of Mental Retardation 99*(3), 289–300.

Hoeksema, T. B. (1995). Supporting the free exercise of religion in the group home context. *Mental Retardation 33*(5), 289–294.

Kregel, J., Wehman, P., Seyfarth, J., & Marshal, K. (1986). Community integration of young adults with mental retardation: Transition from school to adulthood. *Education and Training of the Mentally Retarded 21*(1), 35–42.

Lippold, T., & Burns, J. (2009). Social support and intellectual disabilities: A comparison between social networks of adults with intellectual disability and those with physical disability. *Journal of Intellectual Disability Research 53*(5), 463–474.

McDermott, R., & Varenne, H. (1995). Culture as disability. *Anthropology & Education Quarterly* 6(3), 324–348.

McKnight, J. (1985, Summer). A reconsideration of the crisis of the welfare state. *Social Policy*, 27–30.

McKnight, J. (1987, Winter). Regenerating community. *Social Policy*, 54–58.

McNair, J. (1997). *A Discussion of Networks Supporting Adults with Disabilities in the Community*. Retrieved from http://www.jeffmcnair.com/CSRD/networks. htm

McNair, J. (2000). The local church as a network supporting adults with disabilities in the community: One perspective. *Journal of Religion, Disability & Health* 4(1), 33–56.

McNair, J. (2008). The indispensable nature of persons with intellectual disabilities to the church. *Journal of Religion, Disability & Health* 12(4), 321–329.

McNair, J., & Rusch, F. R. (1991). Parent involvement in transition programs. *Mental Retardation* 29(2), 93–101.

McNair, J., & Smith, H. (2000). Church attendance of adults with mental retardation. *Education and Training in Mental Retardation and Developmental Disabilities* 35(2), 222–225.

McNair, J., & Swartz, S. L. (1997). Local church support to individuals with developmental disabilities. *Education and Training in Mental Retardation and Developmental Disabilities* 32(4), 304–312.

Monsma, S. (1996). *When Sacred and Secular Mix: Religious Nonprofit Organizations and Public Money*. Lanham, MD: Rowman& Littlefield.

Rappaport, J. (1993). Narrative studies, personal stories and identity transformation in the mutual help context. *Journal of Applied Behavioral Science* 29, 239–256.

Reinders, H. (2008). *Receiving the Gift of Friendship: Profound Disability, Theological Anthropology, and Ethics*. Grand Rapids, MI: Eerdmans.

Reynolds, T. E. (2008). *Vulnerable Communion: A Theology of Disability and Hospitality*. Grand Rapids, MI: Brazos Press.

Riordan, J., & Vasa, S. F. (1991, June). Accommodations for and participation of persons with disabilities in religious practice. *Education and Training of the Mentally Retarded* 51–155.

Robertson, J., Emerson, E., Gregory, N., Hatton, C., Kessissoglou, S., Hallam, A., & Linehan, C. (2001). Social networks of people with mental retardation in residential settings. *Mental Retardation* 39, 201–214.

Rogers, S. A., Poey, E. L., Reger, G. M., Tepper, L., & Coleman, E. M. (2002). Religious coping among those with persistent mental illness. *The International Journal for the Psychology of Religion* 12(3), 161–185.

Rose, A. (1997). "Who causes the blind to see": Disability and quality of religious life. *Disability and Society* 12(3), 395–405.

Ryan, J., & Thomas, F. (1980). *The Politics of Mental Handicap*. New York, NY: Penguin Books.

Scuccimarra, D. J., & Speece, D. L. (1990). Employment outcomes and social integration of students with mild handicaps: The quality of life two years after high school. *Journal of Learning Disabilities* 23, 213–219.

Shakespeare, T. (2006). The social model of disability. In L. Davis (Ed.), *The Disability Studies Reader* (pp. 197–204). New York, NY: Routlege.

Turnbull, R., & Turnbull, A. (2007). Foreword. In E. W. Carter (Ed.), *Including People with Disabilities in Faith Communities: A Guide for Service Providers, Families, and Congregations* (pp. xiii–xvii). Baltimore: Paul H. Brookes.

Unger, D., & Powell, D. (1980). Supporting families under stress: The role of social networks. *Family Relations 24*, 134–142.

Vanier, J. (2008). *Man and Woman God Made Them*. New York, NY: Paulist Press.

Verdonschot, M. M. L., De Witte, L. P., Reichrath, E., Buntinx, W. H. E., & Curfs, L. M. G. (2009). Community participation of people with an intellectual disability: A review of empirical findings. *Journal of Intellectual Disability Research 53*(4), 303–319.

Vogel, G., Polloway, E. A., & Smith, J. D. (2006). Inclusion of people with mental retardation and other developmental disabilities in communities of faith. *Mental Retardation 44*, 100–111.

Weisner, T., Belzer, L. & Stolze, L. (1991). Religion and families of children with developmental delays. *American Journal on Mental Retardation 96*(6), 647–662.

Wolfensberger, W. (2000). A brief overview of social role valorization. *Mental Retardation 38*(2), 105–123.

CHAPTER 6

Beyond Models: Some Tentative Daoist Contributions to Disability Studies[1]

Darla Schumm and Michael Stoltzfus

Seeking a way of dynamic balance in the midst of uncertainty and ambiguity is both a core Daoist teaching and a central experience of individuals living with chronic disability or illness. In an effort to minimize ambiguity and explain disability, Western social-scientific models tend to isolate and label individual bodies with descriptive categories such as healthy or sick, normal or abnormal, abled or disabled. Medical, religious, and social models are some examples of the types of explanations offered to help people define disability, and if possible, minimize or eradicate it from the human experience. In this chapter some of the standard models used to categorize those with disabilities are highlighted. Elements of a Daoist perspective on the importance of destabilizing conventional categories in order to enable a creative and harmonious response to an ever-changing reality are offered.

Daoism is a multifaceted, complex combination of religious and non-religious traditions indigenous to ancient China. The authors are not experts in Daoism, and this chapter makes no effort to simplistically summarize a complicated and diverse spiritual tradition in a few pages. There are many approaches to Daoist views of wellness and difference; however, there are some important similarities that can be used to help us think about disability. In this chapter we humbly and incompletely articulate some tentative contributions that Daoism might make to the expanding field of disability studies.

One of the challenges for persons with disabilities is resisting the imposition of the various models and definitions onto their bodies, lives, experiences, and perceived capacities. Those who live with disabilities and chronic conditions know all too well that human bodies defy categorization and explanation. It seems to be human nature to want to explain the unexplainable. Thus, the desire to neatly compartmentalize and explain away the body's lack of cooperation with "normal" functioning is understandable, but, on a cellular level, is futile. Questions and statements such as "Why did this happen to you/me?" "Can't it be fixed?" "What are God/the universe trying to teach you/me?" "You/I are disabled because...," or "you/I would be healed if you/I just..." are often more frustrating and infuriating than the actual physical challenges of illness or disability. The purpose of this essay is to explore disability, or life experience, as one form of many human variations. The life experiences of the "disabled," no more than the "abled," do not adhere neatly to a particular model of what it means to be human, abled, or disabled.

How then, given human propensity for explanation and categorization, might the topics of disability and chronic conditions be explored, avoiding the limitations and restrictions of models and definitions? The purpose in this essay is to map an alternative way (to use Daoist terminology) for thinking and talking about disability and chronic conditions. The metaphor of a map is used intentionally because unlike many models and definitions, a map often reveals various routes or ways that can lead to one's ultimate destination. Some of the routes are straightforward and direct, others are slower but more scenic, while still others are windy, hilly, and more challenging, but each can direct a traveler to a destination. The route taken may be dependent on point of origin, on resources and/or abilities, or on goals and objectives for the journey. No one way or route is necessarily superior to another, just different with different challenges and rewards. A few helpful notions from the broad, complex fabric of Daoism are the map or guide in this essay for thinking about disability. Some central elements of a Daoist worldview can offer alternative ways of thinking about and responding to chronic disabilities that move beyond the accustomed models. Other authors (Miles 2002) have argued for a different, more socially holistic model of disability based on Daoist perspectives. Daoism, however, does not simply offer an alternative model, but helps to destabilize taken-for-granted categories that enable more creative, innovative, and harmonious thinking about disability and its pervasive role in human experience.

Elements of Daoism

While Daoism is vast and diverse, there exists broad scholarly agreement that two classical Chinese texts, the *Daodejing* (Book of the Dao and its Virtue) and the *Zhuangzi* (Book of the Master Zhuang), are central in the establishment and development of Daoist traditions. The *Daodejing* is a short text in about 5,000 characters, divided into 81 brief chapters written in steady verse, dating to the third century CE. Although the *Daodejing* has often been hailed as representing the core of the Daoist worldview, it is a multifaceted work that can be read in at least two different ways: as a document of early Chinese culture or as a scripture of universal significance (LarFargue 1992).

The basic concept in the text is *dao* or "way." It can be understood either metaphysically as the underlying source and power of the universe or practically as the way in which the world functions. The text does not make its understanding easy. Rather the first chapter begins by saying that *Dao* cannot be named or known with ordinary human senses. Although ideally at the root of an ordered cosmos, the *dao* over the course of human history and the unfolding of culture has come to be buried under the complexity of social structures and conventional patterns of thought. To recover the original harmony of all and thus a state of peaceful balance, people should practice simplicity, nonaction, that is, cultivate freedom from all invasive and personally motivated tendencies, and embrace all beings while developing peace within and benevolence without (LarFargue 1992).

Similar ideals are also present in the *Zhuangzi*, compiled in the mid-third century BCE and associated with the thinker Zhuang Zhou (c. 370–290 BCE). The text consists of 33 chapters and is written in prose (Watson 1968, 1996). Its many stories, fables, and fictional dialogues made it the first text of classical Chinese fiction, and its worldview and language have inspired literary works as well as religious visions over the centuries (Mair 1983). The book defines the *dao* not only as the core power of the universe but also as the inherent quality all people and beings have that determine the way they think and act. All beings can find an ideal state of "free and easy wondering," realize their inner core of spontaneity to the fullest, and attain "perfect happiness" by being who they are and accepting where they stand in life (Graham 1982).

Daoism bears witness to a history of perpetual transformation. Western religions tend to place their trust in an invisible stability that somehow transcends the fleeting experience of time, whereas Daoism recognizes and celebrates the profound and mysterious creativity within the very fabric of time and space itself. In the most general terms, Daoism seeks dynamic harmony in the midst of constant change. The *dao*, or way, is affiliated with rhythms of cosmic energy that ebb and flow beyond the limits of human understanding but nonetheless maintain a discernable pulse or pattern. The intellectual historian Benjamin Schwartz describes it as "organic order"—"organic" in the sense that it is part of the world and not a transcendent God, "order" because it can be felt in the sense of organized patterns (Schwartz 1998). *Dao*, as the one power underlying all, is beyond human cognition at its center but manifests in natural rhythms on its periphery (Kohn 2001).

The name for this rhythm in Daoism, and in all of Chinese culture, is *yin* and *yang*. The words themselves refer to the shady side of a hill and the sunny side of a hill, respectively. The shady and sunny sides of the hill are always provisional. The cycle begins again in a continuous process of arising and decaying. From this basic pattern two important points emerge. The first is that everything in the cosmos is constantly transforming itself. The second is that opposites in the world are complementary. Daoism rejects a conflict dualism rooted in absolute distinctions between good and evil, heaven and hell, health and illness, ability and disability. Nothing is purely matter or spirit, good or evil, day or night, *yin* or *yang*. All things are flowing in the midst of everything else. Summer and winter, male and female, stability and change are all an expression of the underlying *yin* and *yang* in eternal interplay. When one fully internalizes this realization, it becomes clear that the goal toward which human beings should strive is complementary harmony rather than the absolute victory of one conflicting perspective over another, since there are no unchanging absolutes. The *yin/yang* symbol represents and affirms the holding together of contrasts in a balanced synthesis, the integrating of divergence into a synthetic whole (Smith 1998: 77–90).

In Daoism, the preeminent space wherein balance and harmony operate is the human body in its interaction with the natural environment. The body forms an integral part of a body-mind-cosmos continuum that cannot be separated and is seen as one (Kohn 2007). The underlying potency at the center of this continuum is the *dao*. Human health and vitality have to do with the whole of one's body; the mental, the emotional, the physical, the spiritual, and the environmental are viewed synthetically, in constant interaction; and one is not given priority over the other. The body is understood as a system of vital energy that is the foundation for both physical and spiritual well-being. What many in the West call "matter" and "spirit" or "body" and "soul" are, in Daoist understanding, both organic functions of the energy systems of the human body (Yuasa 1987).

The starting point for the Daoist view of the body is *qi* (pronounced chee). *Qi* is the concrete aspect of the dao, the material energy of the universe, the basic element of nature (Kohn 2007). *Qi* is often translated as vital energy or breath, and it is quite literally the stuff of life. If a Daoist were to come across the story of how the god of the Bible breathed life into Adam, she would say that the divine creator was transferring *qi* energy into him. In Daoism, however, *qi* is not bestowed by some almighty creator, but is simply the natural operation of the universe, the dynamic pattern of *yin* and *yang*, expansion and contraction, the rhythm of the *dao*. The *dao* has no special relationship with humanity and does not bless or punish humanity. The *dao* abides in all things that exist, from rocks to bananas, imbuing each with a unique manifestation of its energy or *qi*. When *qi* is flowing in and out, then we have life; when *qi* stops moving, then we have death. Flexibility, movement, adaptation, and transformation are thus critical to maintaining a harmonious and healthy life.

One way of explaining the *dao* energy flow is to imagine *qi* as a string. Thus, a stimulus in one area produces a correlative resonance in all other areas just as plucking a guitar string sets off harmonic vibrations through the wood and all the other strings. Musical harmony exists in the midst of chaotic vibrations and flux. All interactions, all energy, all existence is always evolving into a natural state of chaotic harmony and balance.

Daoism, as incompletely described above, seeks a way of balance in the midst of continuous process. Flexibility is an important Daoist virtue because of the recognition that dynamic balance is not reducible to static concepts, models, or definitions. "Dao that may be daoed is not enduring Dao;/Name that may be named is not enduring Name" (DDJ, 1).[2] All human attempts to explain the Dao are misleading, and all efforts to categorize human health and vitality into neat medical distinctions and arbitrary social or religious definitions are incomplete. This basic Daoist understanding has important implications for disability studies as outlined in the following sections.

Some Typical Models of Disability

One reason that disability studies are so rich and interesting is because "disability," like the *dao*, defies definition. There are porous boundaries between disability and apparent health. More significant, disability cuts across all races, classes, genders, ethnicities, nationalities, and generations because it can potentially happen to anyone at any time because of an accident or a degenerative disease of the limbs, ears, eyes, or nervous system (Wendell 1996: 11–33). In 2000, it was estimated that some 64 million or 20 percent of Americans had one or more physical or intellectual disabilities or chronic illnesses and that number is increasing as the population ages (Davis 2002; Harrington n.d.). This makes people with disabilities the largest and most diverse minority group in the United States. There is simply no coherent way to accurately define or categorize this large amorphous group.

In spite of this vast diversity, efforts to define those with disabilities abound. Four models that are used to categorize people with disabilities are highlighted. First, the most basic and simplistic disability paradigm reflects an impairment or deficit model. In this worldview of disability it is the physical or intellectual impairment, the blindness, deafness, paralysis, or chronic illness, that differentiates disabled people from others who are thought to have more able or whole bodies. There tends to be a dualistic distinction that creates a pseudo sense of separation and isolation, rather than the integration of diverse human embodiments into a complementary whole (Tremain 2002).

Second, medical models of disability also emphasize deficits or impairments but stress a restitution narrative focusing on diagnosis, treatment, and cure. It is defined by a progressive sequence involving distinct phases: illness, treatment, and recovery (Garland-Thomson 2005; Longmore and Umansky 2001; Reynolds 2008). This narrative does not work well for people with chronic disabling conditions because it tends to isolate people and sets up unrealistic expectations of recovery. An overemphasis on "discovering a cure" reinforces the conflict dualism of the deficit model. A person is not whole, not really able, unless one is "cured." This model does not address ongoing issues of healing and renewal in everyday life (Goering 2002). Health and harmony are not necessarily associated with the absence of disability. Indeed, such thinking implies that people with chronic disabilities might never experience healthy and holistic lives at all.

In contrast to the restitution narrative favored by medical discourse, Arthur Frank (1995) advocates for a quest narrative that views illness and disability as part of a person's life journey and as an opportunity for ongoing moral, physical, and spiritual cultivation. A central question in the quest narrative is: What does physical, mental, and spiritual healing mean when cure is unlikely? A chronic condition requires perpetual healing actively constructed by the person moment to moment, day to day (Charmaz 1991). This type of dynamic harmony and balance, viewed as a provisional and ongoing process, fits in well with the brief summary of Daoism presented above.

Third, religious models of disability tend to associate chronic impairment or deficit with individual spiritual deficiency. There is a persistent insinuation that chronically disabling conditions somehow involve merited suffering (result of sin or lesson to learn), and well-meaning people from multiple religious traditions often struggle to offer religious explanations and religious solutions to the "problem" (Koosed and Schumm 2005; Reynolds 2008; Schumm and Stoltzfus 2007; Simundson 2001). Religious models tend to mimic the restitution narrative associated with medical models of disability, where religious explanations and solutions replace medical explanations and solutions. If the restitution narrative is granted a religious legitimacy, then people may feel that they are spiritually defective because of the physical or intellectual difficulty that they experience. Restitution narratives, whether medical or religious, do not fit well with people who struggle with chronic conditions and seek not a resolution but a way of balance in the midst of a transforming process.

In contrast to the three models mentioned above, the social model of disability tends to gloss over impairment as just another "natural" form of embodiment and focuses on disability as an oppressive social and historical construct. Many in the disabled population argue that social attitudes, prejudice, paternalism, an inaccessible environment, economic hardships, and excessive individualism often pose greater difficulties than the actual condition although this is certainly not always the case (Davis 2002; Garland-Thomson 2005; Linton 1998; Longmore and Umansky 2001; Wendell 1996). Demeaning ideas associated with disability are everywhere. For example, consider such everyday expressions such as "a crippled or paralyzed economy," "blind obedience/rage," "that's so lame," or "his suggestion fell on deaf ears" (Wendell 1996: 77–88). In addition, freak shows, medical experimentation, and high rates of sexual assault upon persons with intellectual disabilities are all part of the sociocultural fabric of disability in the United States (Shapiro 1994).

The social model helps to challenge trivializing representations of disability and exposes concrete historical oppression. However, Alexa Schriempf (2001) and others (Morris 1991) critique the social model for deemphasizing impairment: "The social model, in focusing on the social construction of disability, has amputated disabled (especially women's) bodies from their impairments and their biological and social needs" (Schriempf 2001: 60). Even when taking into account that disability evades easy definition, the fact remains that in many medical, legal, and personal situations, deafness, blindness, or paralysis fits the context as a partial descriptive account. A dualistic contrast between nature and culture or body and mind may not be the best way to discuss the multiplicity of disability, the integrating of distinction into a synthetic whole.

Disability and Daoism: Beyond Categories

Just like women, people of color, and sexual minorities, many with disabilities have come to equate breaking free of social and medical categories as a form of liberation and a way to challenge historically contingent ideas of normality. Daoism offers several routes or paths for discovering liberation and breaking free from oppressive and limiting social and medical categories. Daoism suggests that arbitrary models or definitions are always incomplete and represent a society dominated by "cunning intellect" or "artificial interference" (DDJ, 3, 57, 58, 65). A narrow calculating approach to social organization is compared with a person who "is self-pretentious . . . self-important," and hence constitutes "leftovers and cancerous growths" (DDJ, 24). Dispositions marked by control and excessive interference may be peeled away by means of "daily diminution" (DDJ, 48). The *yin/yang* symbol represents multiplicity and unity in the midst of a continuous process where harmony is constantly regenerated, there is no intention to "claim mastery" (DDJ, 2, 10), and nothing is purely matter or spirit, abled or disabled. Daoism invites a culture to integrate disability naturally, even harmoniously, into its understanding of humanity without having to control it, cure it, or categorize it. Daoism might help illustrate many forms of human expression and embodiment as aspects of a single, dynamic way.

To counter "cunning intellect" and "artificial interference," Sandra Wawrytko (2005) suggests several Daoist realignments: "It's not what you think that matters but what you unthink. It's not what you do that matters but what you undo" (90). "Unthinking" and "undoing" narrow models and dysfunctional dualisms are illustrated as "an infant who has yet to smile" (DDJ, 20). Wawrytko emphasizes the importance of Daoist flexibility and adaptability by highlighting the cognitive ability of infants to learn more quickly than adults because their brains are less molded by taken-for-granted categories and less cluttered by conventional patterns of thought. "The Daoist sage has been able to wring

the saturated sponge dry again..., has swept it clean of the accumu-
lated dust and debris of imposed conditioning. Hence, the Sage is able
to respond to reality co-creatively" (94). "Unthinking" and "undoing"
the dysfunctions of cultural conditioning help to stimulate innovative
spontaneity often symbolized in Daoism by the fluid images of water
flowing around, beneath, and above obstacles. "Dao in the world is
like a river flowing home to the sea" (DDJ, 32). Water is flexible and
unthreatened by adaptation and change (Seong-Won 2005). Daoism
invites our minds, bodies, and communities to become flexible and
adaptable like flowing waters or smiling infants.

The integration of disability as a natural and normal element of
social awareness enables us to "unthink" old models and destabilizes
inflexible categories. Increasingly, disability theorists tend to argue
against essentializing disability and for recognizing disability as fluid
and heterogeneous. Rosemarie Garland-Thomson (1994) articulates this
well when she writes "Disability can be painful, comfortable, familiar,
alienating, bonding, isolating, challenging, infuriating, or ordinary"
(586). This variability and contingency raises the familiar Daoist issue
of whether one is ever able to speak with any assurance about a social or
medical category. The multiplicities of disability are increasingly moving disability theorists and activists to organize for a world that is more
accessible to all, rather than for generalized assertions about isolated
individuals or some generalized disabled group identity (Davis 2002;
Tremain 2002).

Daoism, Irony, and Disability

Another route that Daoism offers for unthinking disability is that of irony.
It is better to be small, humble, weak, and imperfect than to stand out from
all the rest for those who "stand on tip toe" are not well balanced (DDJ,
24). Daoism uses irony as a tool for negotiating the paradox of human
endeavor—for finding a way to cherish living in the midst of ambiguity
and difficulty regardless of imposed cultural values and labels.

Two stories from the *Zhuang Zi* exemplify Daoist irony. The first
story involves a carpenter dreaming about a giant crooked oak tree that
he earlier deemed useless for making doors, coffins, and vessels.

After Carpenter Shih had returned home, the oak tree appeared to
him in a dream and said, "What are you comparing me with? Are you
comparing me with those useful trees? The cherry apple, the pear, the
orange, the citron, the rest of those fructiferous trees and shrubs—as

soon as their fruit is ripe, they are torn apart and subject to abuse. Their big limbs are broken off, their little limbs are yanked around. Their utility makes life miserable for them, and so they don't get to finish out the years Heaven gave them, but are cut off in mid-journey. They bring it on themselves—the pulling and tearing of the common mob. And it's the same way with all other things. (Watson 1996: 60)

It is the conventional uselessness of the oak tree that enables it to grow old and that protects it from being subject to the utility of the "common mob." Irony is expressed in the story by demonstrating the "use of the useless" (63), that nonconformity to conventional standards of judgment can empower freedom and flourishing. The story also demonstrates how human patterns of thought affect the natural world.

A second story highlights the connection between crippled bodies and conventional expectations.

There's Crippled Shu—chin stuck down in the navel, shoulders up above his head, pigtail pointing at the sky, his five organs on the top, his two thighs pressing his ribs. By sewing and washing, he gets enough to fill his mouth; by handling a winnow and sifting out the good grain, he makes enough to feed ten people. When the authorities call out the troops, he stands in the crowd waving good-by; when they get up a big work party, they pass him over because he's a chronic invalid. And when they are doling out grain to the ailing, he gets three big measures and ten bundles of firewood. With a crippled body, he's still able to look after himself and finish out the years Heaven gave him. How much better, then, if he had crippled virtue. (Watson 1996: 62)

This story expresses irony by highlighting human ability in the midst of chronic disability and by demonstrating the potential usefulness of nonconforming bodies in raising questions about conventional values and taken-for-granted patterns of thinking and acting.

Disability artists and activists also use irony to unsettle the implied superiority of ablism, to call attention to inflexible categories, and to highlight ability in the midst of ambiguity and contingency. For example, Ruthann Robinson (1999), a legal theorist, expresses irony in the poem "Literary Ambition":

to write a poem
spare, clear, and lyrically
honest
unabashedly autobiographical
*   *   *

to write a poem
that begins: Twenty
No, better, Thirty
Years ago, they pronounced me incurable
* * *

to write a poem
without closure (286)

Robinson invites the reader to imagine and explore what it means to live with a medical diagnosis of "incurable," with knowing that there is no final "closure." Robinson expresses irony by articulating her precarious context poetically, living and creating in a culture that often equates disability with inability. Irony is one way to cultivate harmony in the midst of situations that resist resolution while at the same time destabilizing the restitution narratives favored by medical discourse.

Perhaps one of the most challenging aspects of disability is to convince nondisabled people that even when it involves pain and hardship, disability is not always a tragedy or burden but in fact provides much of value. For example, as physical and/or mental outsiders, disabled people offer a valuable critique of a world that nondisabled people take for granted. Susan Wendell writes, "When people cannot ground their self-worth in their conformity to cultural bodily ideals or social expectations of performance, the exact nature of those ideals and expectations and their pervasive unquestioning acceptance becomes much clearer" (69).

In her eloquent memoir *My Body Politic: A Memoir*, Simi Linton (2006) boldly articulates how she grew to appreciate the value of her disability, while at the same time learning to negotiate the new physical, mental, and societal challenges it inevitably presented her. Linton writes:

> For it wasn't until some time after I sustained the injury to my spine that immobilized my legs, after I learned to use a wheelchair, and after I had reckoned with myself and the world for a while in this new state—it wasn't until then that I gained the vantage point of the atypical, the out-of-step, the underfooted (3).

Linton's story generates irony through the new ability that living in a disabled body brings in terms of "unlearning" and "undoing" typical patterns of thinking. Her words also highlight the fluidity and contingency of all human identity claims and the effort to find balance while recognizing the mobility of all vantage points. Irony offers a bridge to help navigate the turbulent terrain of striving for a transformed world in which things are not arranged in neat systems and categories; a world where challenging conventional ways of prioritizing people and things is quite useful and valuable. Daoism has long used irony as a tool for negotiating the paradox, dependency, and fragility of human endeavor. Those living with and writing about disability also use irony as a means to destabilize the implied superiority of abilism, to recognize opportunity in the midst of difficulty, and to free people from the illusion of self-sufficiency.

Daoism, Interdependence, and Disability

Daoism tends to view humans existing as a unified body, mind, and spirit that are part of a universal and interdependent scheme. Ancient Chinese thinkers developed correlative thinking as a way of mapping the patterns of the *dao* to help explain the connections between three important elements of our interdependent existence: the body, the communal/environmental, and the cosmos (Kohn 2004; Miller 2003: 53–73). It is critical that the personal body, the communal/environmental body, and the heavenly bodies are functioning harmoniously, with resonance and synchronicity. The Daoist correlative mind enables the individual to perceive and process multiple levels of changing reality in order to cultivate dynamic balance in the midst of multiple interdependent conditioning. One of these multiple layers involves the interaction of energy or *qi*.

The basic physiological principle at work in traditional Chinese medicine is the continuous exchange of vital energy or *qi* according to the process of *yin* and *yang*, expanding and contracting, activating and storing. As the lungs inhale and exhale and the heart contracts and pumps, so also *qi* pulsates through the body. Liva Kohn (2007) writes, "There is only one *qi*, just as there is only one *dao*. But it, too, appears on different levels of subtlety and in different modes" (105). Daoist cosmology correlates the energy flow in human bodies with the basic modalities of the cosmos, the phases of the moon, the orbits of the stars, the changing of the seasons, the beating of the heart. In this more cosmic view of *qi*, the energy that gives life to our bodies is nothing less than the basic energy of the universe (Kohn 2004). The interrelationship between person, environment, and universe makes them mutually conditioned and interdependent.

An important way that disability studies enhance the exploration of interdependent relational dynamics is by recognizing its field as interdisciplinary and multidimensional. Disability studies invite scholars to think about disability not as an isolated, individual medical pathology but instead to synthesize and correlate the dynamic connections between multiple fields of analysis including historical, religious, social, medical, legal, psychological, economic, and other perspectives. Disability scholarship also embraces interdependence by its critical appraisal of the dominant individualist narrative so prevalent in US history (Linton 1998). For example, capitalistic economic systems often are predicated on able-bodied values of self-mastery, independence, control, and strength. Douglas Baynton (2001) demonstrates how in the history of the United States, opponents to suffragists, immigration, and abolitionists all used disability to discredit undesirable group's claims to citizenship, while women, African Americans, and immigrants bristled at being associated with disability. Increasingly, disabled people "declare that they prize not self-sufficiency but self-determination, not independence but interdependence, not functional separateness but personal connection, not physical autonomy but human community" (Longmore, quoted in Fries 1997: 9). Although it is easy to come up with situations in which someone with a disability might need support or assistance, interdependence and human community suggests more complex relational and social dynamics.

Rebecca Green (2006), a public health nurse who lives with Crohn's disease, suggests that the physical vulnerability associated with chronic illness helps to free people from the illusion of self-sufficiency and leads to an increased availability to accept comfort and care from others. By recognizing their own vulnerability and need to receive comfort from others, the chronically ill and disabled also become aware of the importance of responding to others with care and flexibility. The giving and receiving of care is a complementary process, not a one-way street. Living with a disability or relating to someone with a disability clarifies how interrelated our lives really are, how much we physically, socially, and spiritually need each other. Human beings are never free from vulnerability and a need for mutual support. The quest for individual cure, so emphasized in the medical model, makes little sense in the context of interdependence.

In her article "The Blind Man's Harley: White Canes and Gender Identity in America," Katherine Kudlick (2005) discusses her experience at what she dubs "blind boot camp," and provides an example of the tension between the seemingly competing desires for interdependence and independence within herself and within the blind community. While not the primary focus of her article, Kudlick notes a debate in the blind community surrounding the choice of mobility aids. There are those who argue that white cane use is far superior to guide dogs because the cane promotes total independence and autonomy, while using a guide dog still requires dependence on another being. There is an implicit acceptance of the value of rugged individualism on the part of those who argue for the superiority of cane use, which also dismisses the potential advantages and benefits of learning how to be interdependent with not only other people but also other beings in the world.

Darla Schumm reflects on both the paradox and the irony that many people who live with disabilities experience in trying to establish balance between excessive dependence and excessive independence. Darla is legally blind and the coauthor of this essay:

> For years I stubbornly resisted using any mobility aids. I have some limited sight and was able to travel relatively safely on my own without a cane or dog. I saw this ability as a mark of my self-sufficiency and independence. It was not until I was preparing to get married that I realized that my stubborn independence was becoming an obstacle to the things I really craved: self-determination, interdependence, personal connection, and human community (as described by Lawnmore above). Amidst sobs, my fiancé begged me to consider using a mobility aid because he feared for my safety when I traveled alone and negotiated busy intersections and crowded streets without any assistance. I eventually got a guide dog and what I have realized is that my "dependence" on my guide, Papaya, not only allows me to provide comfort and care to my husband by giving him peace of mind, but allows me to be even more independent (and it goes without saying, safe) in my mobility. The great irony is that while there are those who would negatively or condescendingly describe my use of a guide dog as just another form of dependence, it is my interdependence with Papaya which keeps me safe and affords me a newfound level of independence. Additionally, Papaya has taught me much about the rewards of reciprocal care. She takes care of me on a daily basis by keeping me safe, and I in turn take care of her on a daily basis by providing her shelter, food, affection, and love.

The scenario highlighted above suggests that the experience of disability can open new relational perspectives that question cultural narratives grounded in excessive notions of individualism and independence. Paradoxically, a culture that prizes individual achievement tends to idealize individuals who overcome a disabling condition and achieve a high level of self-sufficiency and independence. Consequently, "supercrip" becomes an internalized role for some with disabilities:

> By acting as if we have no needs, we may perpetuate a "super-crip" image—disabled people can do anything we want if we only try hard enough. We may exhaust ourselves trying and come to believe that we are better than other disabled people who have not accomplished as much. (Woronow 1985: 174)

Darla Schumm addresses the "supercrip" dynamic by reflecting on her own experience and internal struggle with the label:

> I have always struggled with the idea of the "supercrip." To look at me, you would not necessarily know that I had any disability. Since I did not use mobility aids until I was in my mid thirties, for most of my life I had no external markers which identified me as disabled. Growing up my parents, teachers, and other important adults in my life always told me I could do whatever I wanted to do and they all encouraged me to take risks and set my goals high; consequently, I have accomplished quite a bit academically and professionally. It was not until after I had received my Ph.D.—which was one of my life long goals and one of my greatest challenges as a person with a disability—that I began (and it contin- ues to be an ongoing process) to deconstruct how I had internalized a "supercrip" identity. The "supercrip" label is certainly pinned on many of us with disabilities by others, but it is the internalization of this label that I find most troubling. I have tried to "pass" as nondisabled, felt superior to other blind people who have not achieved as much "success" as I have by societal standards, and lived with a fair amount of anxiety and exhaustion doing these things. As I began to become more comfort- able with my disability and with myself as a person with a disability, my judging of both others and myself decreased. Reading, researching, writing, and talking more openly about disability has enabled me to more fully incorporate my disability as just one of many interesting (and some not so interesting) aspects of who I am. I am learning to break free of models and labels and see disability as simply one form of human variation, no better or worse, no more or less embarrassing, or no more or less worthy of praise and admiration than any other form of human variation. By attempting to shed my internalization as a "supercrip," I have discovered new and deeper understandings of my own sense of self, as well as of what it means to be a part of human communities—with my disabled and nondisabled friends alike.

Darla's comments highlight the paradoxical tensions that many with dis- abilities experience as they try to navigate the delicate balance between independence and interdependence. Those with hidden disabilities may face particular difficulties in our fast-paced, individualist society, especially if they are living with a less well-known chronic condition such as fibromyalgia or lupus. In many cases, people are torn between trying to keep up without accommodation, passing as nondisabled, or "coming out" and having to struggle for support without pity, recognition, and paternalism. Exploring these tensions helps in the development of a harmonious approach that challenges exaggerated self-reliance while recognizing that independence and interdependence are complementary, not flatly oppositional.

Conclusion

Daoism seeks dynamic balance in the midst of constant change. All efforts to categorize human health and vitality into organized medical distinctions and constructed social models are fluid and incomplete. A Daoist worldview helps to destabilize typical categories used for defining chronic disability enabling us to think more creatively and holistically about the complicating role of disability in human experience. Daoism illustrates that many forms of human embodiment are aspects of a single, dynamic way and invites the integration of disability into the understanding of human life without necessitating categorization, definition, isolation, or cure.

Disability theorists, activists, and artists are increasingly trying to organize for a more interdependent human community, rather than for generalized assertions about a particular group identity. In his essay "The End of Identity Politics and the Beginning of Dismodernism," Lennard Davis (2002) argues for a "clouding of the issue of disability identity" and calls for a "new ethics of the body" that he names a "dismodernist ethics" (27). Davis's dismodernist ethics seeks to destabilize heretofore standard models of identity politics and constructions of the body by envisioning new ways of constructing community. Davis writes:

> In a dismodernist mode, the ideal is not a hypostatization of the normal (that is, dominant) subject, but aims to create a new category based on the partial, incomplete subject whose realization is not autonomy and independence but dependency and interdependence. (Davis 2002: 29)

Davis's position fits nicely with the long-held Daoist suggestion that harmony is not affiliated with a fixed point or an absolute perspective but rather involves a fluid and dynamic balance, perpetually regenerated by the ongoing integration of a body-community-cosmos continuum. Those who live with chronic illness or disability often comprehend intuitively that harmony exists in the midst of multiple layers of perpetual process as people move within an interdependent flow of events that resist isolated control, rigid categorization, or medical resolution.

A final example from Darla's life as a parent illustrates the importance of Daoist flexibility and adaptability by highlighting a recent exchange with her young son. Darla observes:

> My two-and-a-half-year-old son Henry demonstrates the innovative spontaneity of a child's response to my disability. Henry has grown up with a Mommy who is virtually blind. At a very young age, Henry understood that Mommy navigated the world differently than the other people in his life. On a recent afternoon we were preparing to leave the house and go on an outing. As we headed for the door, Henry looked up at me and asked: "Mommy, Are you going to drive?" I said "no," at which point Henry very matter-of-factly stated, "You can't see, you would crash into other cars." What was most striking to me with this exchange was not that my two year old understood at some level that I can't see, but that his observation was lacking any type of judgment or categorization about what it means to be blind. For Henry my blindness is as natural and normal as the fact that when it is cold outside he must wear a coat. I am not lacking anything in Henry's mind; I simply can't see and therefore do things differently than the people he knows who can see. In his own way, Henry has learned that I am blind; what he has not yet learned are the societal prejudices, attitudes, or stereotypes about what it means to be blind or disabled. Through the wisdom of a child, Henry embodies one of the contributions that Daoism can make to disability studies: The less cluttered our minds are by the imposed conditioning of conventional standards of judgment regarding disability, the more flexible we are in responding to both the beauty and the challenge of living with chronic disability.

Daoism maps a way to destabilize old models and definitions while at the same time making fluid claims for balance and harmony in the midst of the unresolved ambiguity associated with chronic disability. The aim of this essay has not been to offer an alternative model based on Daoism, but rather to provide some cracks in the very structure of how we tend to think about disability. Daoism helps us to understand that nonconformity to conventional attitudes and judgments can empower freedom and flourishing. Indeed, Daoist interdependence, irony, transformation, and synthesis help to map a world where harmony and balance are found in the midst of the chaos, rewards, insights, challenges, and beauty of all bodies—disabled and nondisabled alike.

Notes

1. This chapter was previously published in 2011 in *Disability Studies Quarterly* *31*(1) and is reprinted here with permission.
2. All quotations from the Dao De Jing have been translated by Charles Wei-hsun Fu and Sandra A. Wawrytko, indicated by DDJ and the appropriate chapter number.

References

Baynton, D. (2001). Disability and the justification of inequality in American history. In P. Longmore & L. Umansky (Eds.), *The New Disability History: American Perspectives* (pp. 33–57). New York, NY: New York University Press.

Charmaz, K. (1991). *Good Days, Bad Days: The Self in Chronic Illness and in Time.* New Brunswick, NJ: Rutgers University Press.

Davis, L. (2002). *Bending over Backwards: Disability, Dismodernism & Other Difficult Positions.* New York, NY: New York University Press.

Frank, A. (1995). *The Wounded Story Teller: Body, Illness, and Ethics.* Chicago: University of Chicago Press.

Fries, K. (1997). *Staring Back: The Disability Experience from the Inside Out.* New York, NY: Plume Books.

Garland-Thomson, R. (1994). Redrawing the boundaries of feminist disability studies. *Feminist Studies 20*, 586.

Garland-Thomson, R. (2005). Feminist disability studies. *Signs: Journal of Women in Culture and Society 30*(2), 1558–1587.

Goering. S. (2002). Beyond the medical model? Disability, formal justice, and the exception for the profoundly impaired. *Kennedy Institute of Ethics Journal 12*(4), 373–388.

Graham, A. (1982). *Chuang-tzu: Textual Notes to a Partial Translation.* London: University of London.

Green, R. (2006). Unpublished Interviews: 8-30-06 and 9-4-06.

Harrington, C. (n.d.). Disability Statistics Center. Retrieved from http://dsc.ucsf.edu/main.php

Kohn, L. (2001). *Daoism and Chinese Culture.* Cambridge, MA: Three Pines Press.

Kohn, L. (2004). *Cosmos and Community: The Ethical Dimension of Daoism.* Cambridge, MA: Three Pines Press.

Kohn, L. (2007). Daoin: Chinese healing exercises. *Asian Medicine 3*, 103–129.

Koosed, J. L., & Schumm, D. Y. (2005). Out of the darkness: Examining the rhetoric of blindness in the gospel of John. *Disability Studies Quarterly 25*(1). Retrieved from http://www.dsq-sds.org/index.

Kudlick, C. (2005). The blind man's harley: White canes and gender identity in America. *Signs: Journal of Women in Culture and Society 30*(2), 1590–1606.

LarFargue, M. (1992). *The Tao of the Tao-Te-Ching.* Albany: State University of New York Press.

Linton, S. (1998). *Claiming Disability: Knowledge and Identity.* New York, NY: New York University Press.

Linton. S. (2006). *My Body Politic: A Memoir.* Annarbor: The University of Michigan Press.

Longmore, P., & Umansky, L. (Eds.). (2001). *The New Disability History: American Perspectives.* New York, NY: New York University Press.

Mair, V. (1983). *Experimental Essays on Chuang-tzu.* Honolulu: University of Hawaii Press.

Miles, M. (2002). Disability on a different model: Glimpses of an Asian heritage. *Journal of Religion, Disability & Health 6*(3), 89–108.

Miller, J. (2003). *Daoism: A Short Induction.* Oxford: Oneworld.

Morris, J. (1991). *Pride Against Prejudice: Transforming Attitudes to Disability.* London, UK: The Women's Press, Ltd.

Reynolds, T. (2008). *Vulnerable Communion: A Theology of Disability and Hospitality.* Grand Rapids, MI: Brazos Press.

Robinson, R. (1999). Literary ambition. In Susan Raffo (Ed.), *Restricted Access: Lesbians on Disability.* Seattle: Seal Press.

Schriempf, A. (2001). (Re)fusing the amputated body: An interactionist bridge between feminism and disability. *Hypatia 16*, 56–72.

Schumm, D., & Stoltzfus, M. (2007). Chronic illness and disability: Narratives of suffering and healing in Buddhism and Christianity. *Journal of Religion, Disability & Health11*(3), 5–21.

Schwartz, B. (1998). The worldview of the Tao-te-ching. In Livia Kohn & Michael LaFargue (Eds.), *Lao-tzu and the Tao-to-ching* (pp. 189–210). Albany, NY: State University of New York Press.

Seong-Won, P. (2005). Economy of water: A spiritual basis for an alternative economy. *Ecumenical Review 57*(2), 171–178.

Shapiro, J. (1994). *No Pity: People with Disabilities Forging a New Civil Rights Movement.* New York, NY: Times Books.

Simundson, D. J. (2001). *Faith Under Fire: How the Bible Speaks to Us in Times of Suffering.* Lima, Ohio: Academic Renewal Press.

Smith, W. (1998). *Patterns of Faith Around the World.* Oxford: Oneworld Publications.

Tremain, S. (2002). On the subject of impairment. In M. Corker & T. Shakespeare (Eds.), *Disability/Postmodernity: Embodying Disability Theory.* London, UK: Continuum.

Watson, B. (1968). *The Complete Works of Chuang-tzu.* New York, NY: Columbia University Press.

Watson, B. (1996). *Chuang Tzu: Basic Writings.* New York, NY: Columbia University Press.

Wawrytko, S. (2005). The viability (dao) and virtuosity (de) of Daoism ecology: Reversion (fu) as renewal. *Journal of Chinese philosophy 32*(1), 89–203.

Wendell, S. (1996). *The Rejected Body: Feminist Philosophical Reflections on Disability*. New York, NY: Routledge.

Woronow, N. (1985). A see-by-logic life. In Susan Brown, Debra Connors, & Nancy Stern (Eds.), *With the Power of Each Breath: A Disabled Women's Anthology*. Pittsburgh: Cleis Press.

Yuasa, Y. (1987). *The Body: Toward an Eastern Mind-Body Theory*. New York, NY: State University of New York Press.

CHAPTER 7

Health and Disability Care in Native American and Alaska Native Communities

Lavonna L. Lovern

In exchange for over 450 million acres of Native lands, American Indians received a commitment from the federal government to provide for the health, safety, and welfare of Indian people into the future.... Native people experience higher disease rates and lower life expectancy than any other racial or ethnic group in the country. Indians experience exponentially higher rates of diabetes, mental disorders, cardiovascular disease, pneumonia, influenza and injuries. The infant mortality rate is 150 percent greater for Indians than that of White infants. Indians have the highest prevalence of Type-2 diabetes in the world, and are 2.6 times more likely to be diagnosed with diabetes. Indians have a life expectancy five years less than the rest of the U.S. population. (National Congress of American Indians, 2010b)

One of the most unique and relatively continuous aspects of American history involves the interaction between the differing Native American nations and the United States of America. The interplay between the differing nations breaks down into a complex of unresolved treaty issues and legal disputes beyond the scope of our current legal system. While many of the issues and disputes are similar in content to those the United States faces regularly on an international basis, the fact that the Native American nations exist within U.S. borders changes the way the gambits are negotiated. Jurisdiction for tribal issues is unclear within the federal government. On the one hand, Native Americans are members of nations, separate and sovereign, from the United States. On the other hand, Native American people are also citizens of the United States. There is the additional issue of tribes that are only state recognized or remain at this point "unrecognized." The question of Native American nations-American nation relationship remains vague, which creates the loopholes that allow for disparities in economics, health, and education in the Native American populations when compared with the general U.S. population statistics. This chapter is neither intended to hash out the relationship between the various nations nor to chronicle the issues of broken and unratified treaties. Instead, the purpose of this chapter is to examine the results of these historic and current events as they impact Native American health issues.

It is also not the objective of this chapter to lay blame at anyone's door or to reopen old animosities, but rather to come to understand that failed international negotiations have substantial impact on Native American people within the United States. The impact of these failed negotiations continues to cause hardships to American citizens, of both Native and non-Native decent. There is discussion among many Americans aimed at the completion of the assimilation process and the elimination of the sovereignty of the Native nations. This movement often brings with it the notion that either "Native Americans have lost and should give up the concept of separation and fully assimilate" or "it all happened a long time ago and needs to be placed in history with the notion that it is time to get over it and fully assimilate." It seems that regardless of the expressed motivation, the end result is for Native Americans to give up their separate identity and complete the assimilation process. For a great many Native Americans, assimilation seems no more reasonable than asking Canada to give up sovereignty and boundary distinctions to assimilate with the United States.

For many Native Americans, full assimilation means allowing the historical attempts at genocide to become complete. Identification as sovereign people allows for the continuation of cultures, languages, and spiritualities. It is not an option, in the eyes of many Native Americans, to allow the destruction of their way of life or the elimination of their existence because without the cultures, languages, and spiritualities Native Americans will cease to exist. While many Native American nations have already fallen to extinction, the remaining people continue to fight for existence. It is not necessary that all Americans agree with this position, but it is important to understand that there are those among the differing nations who hold strongly to their positions and will not be swayed by any amount of argumentation. It is also important to note that the potential extinction of Indigenous populations is being noted worldwide. The United Nations has recently released the "State of the World's Indigenous People," which chronicles the growing threat of extinction of these populations because of loss of land, poverty, and health crises (United Nations 2010). The continued destruction of Indigenous populations remains tied to colonization and postcolonization issues. The fate of these occupied populations is not an issue just for the United States but has blossomed into a worldwide debate.

For the purposes of this chapter, the debate over the appropriateness of assimilation and the passion involved in resistance will be understood as currents that flow beneath the surface of the discussion of Native American health care issues. While such issues are not always the specific focus of the discussion, they cannot be ignored as they are often the hidden current that guides the flow of the discussion. The fact that the words are often not expressed as overt assertions does not eliminate the power of these positions. Furthermore, the historic and current trends in the negotiations between the differing Native American nations and the American nation resemble advanced game theory. If negotiations are approached in this manner, the result is the loss of connection to actual humans and the process becomes no more than a game. The net result of negotiations-as-game-theory is to focus on the end game; to win, at the loss of "acceptable casualties" or "cannon fodder." It is the intention of this chapter to survey the landscape of Native American health care issues with an understanding that populations and demographics are made up of individuals who deserve respect, dignity, and honor rather than merely becoming cannon fodder in a game of statistics.

Any discussion of Native American health care issues requires context, which is often so convoluted as to cause the most diligent of readers to give up in despair. There is no attempt in this chapter to compile all the relevant information. Instead, the intent is to produce an adequate background for the final portion of the chapter, which includes a discussion of those who are intimately involved in Native American health care. The final section will be devoted not only to identifying the people but also to giving voice to some of the people. Establishing a foundation for that final portion will require several background sections. The first section will be devoted to a brief survey of historical elements related to the discussion of Native American health care issues. The second section will focus on general health care issues in Native American populations and related statistics. The third section will focus on the American Disability Act (ADA) and the role of the ADA/Americans with Disabilities Act with Amendments (ADAA) in the Native American nations. The fourth section will be devoted to issues involving Indian Health Services (IHS) and the operation of these services within Native American populations. The fifth section offers a brief look at barriers involving trust. These issues cannot be ignored in a discussion of health care, as they are often some of the most difficult barriers to eliminate. The final section of this chapter will focus on issues experienced and expressed by those who work in health care and rehabilitation services within Native American communities. It must be noted at this point that a complete and in-depth discussion of these topics is beyond the scope of a single chapter. There are more than 500 federal and state recognized Native American communities and many more that are, as of yet, not recognized. Variations among these communities involve further differences including urban and rural communities, reservation and nonreservation communities, education levels, socioeconomic levels as well as assimilation and traditional concerns. The generalizations discussed in this chapter are to be understood as just that. Within any given community it is understood that perspectives differ between clans, families, and individuals. With this in mind, the information in this chapter should be taken as a small representation of the extensive discussion that needs to be undertaken on Native American health care.

A Brief History

Deloria and Lytle organize Native American history into six periods:

> Discovery, Conquest, and Treaty-Making (1532–1828);
> Removal and Relocation (1828–1887);
> Allotment and Assimilation (1887–1928);
> Reorganization and Self-Government (1928–1945);
> Termination (1945–1961); and Self-Determination (1961–Present).
> (Deloria and Lytle 1983: 1–24)

Each of these periods is marked by specific negotiations and legal actions that mark the relationship between the myriad of Native American nations and the American nation. The general complications of these discussions are multiplied because the American nation did not negotiate equally with each Native American nation. The treaties and legal agreements that were made differed, so that one Native American nation may have vastly different entitlements involving the American nation than those guaranteed to another Native American nation. Add to this the issue that some of the agreed-upon treaties were not ratified by the American Congress and the legal quagmire begins to resemble the La Brea tar pits. The more one struggles with the legal issues, the more one is sucked down into the sticky mess until the tar consumes the individual and no further forward motion is possible. Indeed, watching current negotiations on health care and disability issues in Native American communities is a bit like watching attempts to cross the tar pits. Those working in health care and rehabilitation services are caught in various stages of tar consumption and the observers, often the very individuals in need, are left to simply shake their heads as they watch those caught begin to sink and watch others, unaware of the danger, charge forward.

Using Deloria and Lytle's periods of history, as cited above, we will join those who charge into the tar pit of Native American health care history. In order to avoid sinking too quickly, the first few eras of history will be discussed only briefly. The period of discovery, conquest, and treaty was marked by a cacophony of battles, alliances, and land grabs that culminated in the era of removal and relocation. This second era was a period of annihilation through the use of boarding schools and reservations. Many Native Americans mark this era as the beginning of active government-sanctioned genocide, especially in regard to the actions of Andrew Jackson both before and during his presidency. The General Allotment Act of 1887, sponsored by Senator Henry Dawes, opened the era of allotment and assimilation with a focus on "civilizing the Indian" through continued and extensive boarding school education and agriculture. There are three specific events at the end of this era that are of particular note for health care.

The first event of note involved the Supreme Court findings in *Donnelly v. United States* (1913). This case marked the beginning of the movement in which Native American communities began to litigate in order to define and protect treaty status. Under consideration in this litigation were issues involving whether executive order reservation land was to be considered Indian Country. *United States v. Sandoval* (1913), for example, defined the status of the Pueblo Indians of New Mexico. Both *Donnelly* and *Sandoval* reinforced the federal government's responsibility for the welfare in trust of Native Americans (Deloria and Lytle 1983: 71–74). These cases set the stage for the establishment of the Snyder Act of 1921. The Snyder Act "gave the secretary of the interior general authority to expand federal monies for Indian 'benefit, care, and assistance'" (Deloria and Lytle 1983: 242). Specifically, the Snyder Act states that money is to be used "for relief of distress and conservation of health." While vague in terms of monetary amounts and definitions, the Snyder Act establishes the "trust responsibility" for Native American health services. The final action to be noted in this era involved the granting of citizenship. The Act of November 6, 1919, and the Act of July 19, 1919, "gave citizenship to all Indians who had been members of the armed forces during the (World War I) conflict" with all other Indians born within the United States receiving citizenship on June 2, 1924 (Deloria and Lytle 1983: 221). Deloria and Lytle go on to note that while the gaining of full U.S. citizenship granted certain rights, it also served to muddy the waters in terms of "Indian identity" and Native American status in the United States.

The reorganization and self-government era opened with Lewis Meriam and his associates producing *The Problem of Indian Administration*, or *Meriam Report*, in 1928. This report established the inadequacies of the U.S. trust regarding Native Americans involving economics, health, and education. The report stated that the living conditions were substandard and the death rates, both adult and infant, were high. The living conditions were further described as promoting disease and lacking in proper sanitation. Housing and education were described as significantly below standard and not living up to either treaty or legally agreed-upon Indian Country trust levels. In the closing pages of the report, Meriam and his associates make several "recommendations for immediate action" including the employment of "medical specialists to aid the director of medical work," "the creation of new positions in the field of health," and "establishing public health clinics" (Meriam et al. 1928: 52–53).

Previously, Supreme Court cases, such as *Cherokee Nation v. Georgia* (1831), specifically addressed the relationship between tribes, states, and the federal government. These cases have been used to establish the guardian-ward status between Native American nations and the American nation that established the trust relationship (Indian Health Services 2010a).

The Indian Reorganization Act of 1934 offered a means by which a reorganization of the manner by which Indian Affairs were handled could be enacted. The act officially ended allotment of Indian land and attempted to place Indian bureaucracy within tribal governments instead of in Washington. One problem with the act was that the organization of tribal government and their constitutions had to be approved by the U.S. government. This, in turn, led to a second problem in that only a few tribes voted to accept the act and not all of those completed the reorganization after the vote (Deloria and

Lytle 1983: 14–15). The ambiguity involved in the Reorganization Act continues to be an issue for the dissemination of health care and the implementation of the Americans with Disabilities Act, as will be noted later.

The termination period was ushered in by the events surrounding World War II and the depression. With federal budget cuts being demanded, Congress set its sights on Indian programs. The idea was to terminate federal support for Indian programs according to a list provided by Acting Indian Commissioner William Zimmerman. Zimmerman produced a report that listed tribes as (a) able to self-support; (b) needing some federal support; and (c) dependant. While Zimmerman noted that additional steps would be needed before any of the tribes could be fully self-supporting, the report was followed in 1952 by a notice sent by Indian Commissioner Dillon Myer, who had previously presided over the effort to establish interment for Japanese-Americans, "to all Bureau of Indian Affairs employees alerting them that the government was preparing to withdraw from its Indian programs" (Deloria and Lytle 1983: 17). The introduction of House Concurrent Resolution 108 began formal termination policy in 1954. Termination policies eliminated federal support to the Klamath of Oregon and the Menominee of Wisconsin along with numerous minor and antecedent tribes and put the remaining tribes on notice for potential future termination of programs (HCR 108, 1954). Two weeks later, Public Law 280 (1953) gave civil and criminal jurisdiction to the states of California, Minnesota, Nebraska, Oregon, and Wisconsin and the territory of Alaska eliminating tribal jurisdiction. In 1954, a separate act was passed (68 Stat. 674) that "transferred the hospital and health facilities, property, personnel, and budget funds of the Indian Health Services of the Bureau of Indian Affairs to the U.S. Public Health Service" (Deloria and Lytle 1983: 19). The response to termination on the part of the Native American Nations included both litigation and social resistance. Termination policies were viewed as a violation of individual treaties as well as of law that covered all of Indian Country. Deloria and Lytle discuss the more recent impact of that policy:

Today when anti-Indian sentiment rages among federal and state officials, they clothe their resentments in the citizenship argument (Citizenship Act of 1924), contending that any semblance of tribal relationships and federal protection is in fact a second-class citizenship that should be abolished as a means of assisting Indians. Several of the termination bills recited this litany, indicating that the only purpose of the legislation was to grant "full" citizenship to Indians—a goal that seemed laudable and liberal. (Deloria and Lytle 1983: 221)

The self-determination era of Native American history used the 1964 Civil Rights Act as the foundation for the 1968 Indian Civil Rights Act. The general unrest of the civil rights era was reflected in the Native American populations as seen in the Alcatraz, Wounded Knee, The Trail of Broken Treaties, Oglala, and the Native American protests of the bicentennial. While many view this self-determination period as a revitalization of Native American culture, others see it as a continuation of the termination policy era. Health care and disability law were greatly impacted by the passage of the Rehabilitation Act of 1973. Sections 503 and 504 were especially relevant to this discussion in that they prohibit discrimination, based upon disability, at the hands of employers or federal contractors or providers. Also, in 1973, the Indian Healthcare Improvement Act was passed with the intention of following up on the *Meriam Report* and increasing the standards and effectiveness of Native American health care services. The Americans with Disabilities Act was passed in 1990. In 1991, President George Bush stated:

[T]he concepts of forced termination and excessive dependency on the Federal Government must now be relegated, once and for all, to the history books. Today we move forward toward a permanent relationship of understanding and trust, a relationship in which the tribes of the Nation sit in positions of dependent sovereignty along with the other governments that compose the family that is America. (Bush 1991)

Bush's statement added fuel to the already heated discussion involving the guardian-ward versus the nation-to-nation status between Native American communities and the U.S. government. At issue was whether or not Native Americans were wards of the state placed in specific communities to be guarded by the U.S. government. The position of the Native American Nations was to reassert the nation-to-nation status involved in international treaty negotiation, which, in turn, initializes systems of international law.

On September 30, 2000, Congress allowed the Indian Health Care Improvement Act (IHCIA) of 1976 to expire, throwing the paradigm by which Native American health issues were addressed back to the Snyder Act of 1921. Many Native Americans viewed this congressional action as an attempt to reinforce the guardian-ward relationship and eliminate attempts to invoke international law in nation-to-nation negotiations requiring the upholding of agreed-upon treaties. In 2006, the G. W. Bush Administration actively blocked attempts to reestablish the IHCIA. The Department of Justice claimed that the "question for the Federal government's responsibility to provide health services under the federal trust relationship" was unclear (Northwest Portland Area Indian Health Board 2006: 1). The reasons given for the lack of clarity resulted primarily from the paucity of definition in the Snyder Act as to the exact responsibilities of the U.S. government in matters of Native American health services. Stating that the U.S. government was responsible for Native American health issues was not the same as stating to what extent the government was, in fact, responsible. On September 25, 2008, President Bush signed amendments to the 1990 ADA. These amendments focused on several issues including children with disabilities and the broadening of the definition to one of "substantially limited" rather than one of "significant" or "severe" restriction (Americans with Disabilities Act 2008). The implications of the ADA for Indian Country were debatable as will be discussed specifically in the following section of this chapter.

With the change of presidential administrations, the language of ward-guardian was replaced with language involving nation-to-nation negotiations. Along with this new framework, the stipulations involving Native American health care services also changed. In a press release on May 5, 2009, the IHS reported a proposed budget of $4.03 billion for FY 2010, a 13 percent increase over the 2009 budget. The increase is reported to cover rising costs of care, increased population, and the upgrading of facilities and equipment. The same press release stated that President Obama proposed an increase of $117 million in contract health services funds. These funds are established to assist in the delivery of health care to 1.9 million American Indians and Alaska Natives (Indian Health Services 2009a). On May 15, 2009, IHS came out with an additional press release regarding the distribution of $500 million under the American Recovery and Reinvestment Act of 2009 to cover already allocated monies. This money is to be distributed to cover building and revitalization projects currently underway. The money will also be used to complete 169 sanitation projects and fund 302 maintenance projects (Indian Health Services 2009b). In addition, the House of Representatives introduced a bill to assist Native American Veterans and their families. "The bill is meant to amend an oversight in the Native American Housing Assistance and Self-Determination Act that has caused disabled veterans, their families and survivors to be denied help because they are receiving veterans and survivors benefits"

(Capriccioso 2009). The most recent act by the current administration involved the signing of the Patient Protection and Affordable Care Act (2010). The press release from the White House verifies that within this act is the establishment of the Indian Health Care Improvement Act of 1976 as permanently reauthorized. The administration further reaffirms that "[O]ur responsibility to provide health services to American Indians and Alaska Natives derives from the nation-to-nation relationship between the federal and tribal governments" (The White House 2010). The reestablishment of both the IHCIA and the nation-to-nation language appears to be a follow up to President Obama's meeting with tribal leaders in which he announced a 90-day mandate for his cabinet secretaries to find a way to improve relations between the Native American Nations and the American Nation including an additional $3 billion worth of stimulus dollars that is to be given to Indian programs (Washington Post 2010).

While not an exhaustive discussion of historically important events, the preceding discussion brings the reader about hip-deep into the tar of nation-to-nation policy making involving Native American health care and disability issues. The next step will sink the reader chest-deep into the general health issues before plunging him or her into the depths of Native American health care and disability issues, at which point, breathing reeds (or scuba if you prefer) may be required.

General Health Statistics

The purpose of this section is to acquaint the reader with various significant data. We are limited by format in that we can provide information only of the very general sort. However, the information to be presented is gleaned from the massive amount of data available in order to offer an overview of the extent to which health care services are employed. For the sake of brevity, little discussion or analysis is offered, as the data seem very clear, and there is little to be gained by reiteration.

IHS reports that

-Approximately 57 percent of American Indians and Alaska Natives living in the United States rely on the IHS to provide Access to health care services in forty-five hospitals over 600 other facilities operated by the IHS, Tribes, and Alaska Native corporations, or purchased from private vendors.

-The American Indian and Alaska Native people have long experienced lower health status when compared with other Americans. Lower life expectancy and the disproportionate disease burden exist perhaps because of inadequate education, disproportionate poverty, discrimination in the delivery of health services, and cultural differences. These are broad quality of life issues rooted in economic adversity and poor social conditions.

-American Indians and Alaska Natives born today have a life expectancy that is 4.6 years less than the U.S. all races population (72.3 years to 76.9 years, respectively; 1999–2001 rates).

-American Indians and Alaska Natives die at higher rates than other American from tuberculosis (500 percent higher), alcoholism (519 percent higher), diabetes (195 percent higher), unintentional injuries (149 percent higher), homicide (92 percent higher) and suicide (72 percent higher). (Rates adjusted for misreporting of Indian race on state death certificates; 2003–2005 rates.). (Indian Health Services 2010b)

Furthermore, the following demographic information is indicated by research:

-The 2005–2007 Current Population Survey revealed that the American Indian and Alaska Native (AI/AN) population has larger families, less health insurance (the number of AI/ANs without health insurance is over double that for U.S. all races), and a poverty level nearly twice that of the rest of the population.

-When compared to the U.S. All Races, the AI/AN population lags behind in several areas. The 2000 Census data reveal that Indians have lower educational levels and higher unemployment rates. The AI/AN population is a young population. The approximate median age of the Indian population is twenty-five years compared with thirty-five years for the U.S. All Races. The Indian population served by the IHS is living longer than it did thirty or even twenty years ago. Statistics on age at death show that during 1972–1974, life expectancy at birth for the Indian population was about 63.6 years. Life expectancy has now increased to 72.3 years (1999–2001). Diseases of the heart, malignant neoplasm, unintentional injuries, diabetes mellitus, and cerebrovascular disease are the five leading causes of Indian deaths (2002–2005). (Indian Health Services 2010e)

On the issue of sanitation and potable water, both so essential to health, we learn that

-Safe and adequate water supply and/or waste disposal facilities are lacking in approximately 15 percent of American Indian and Alaska Native homes, compared to 1 percent of homes for the U.S. general population.

-While 1 percent of the U.S. general population lacks access to safe water, 12 percent of Indian homes lack access to safe water.

-There is a backlog of over 3,300 needed sanitation facilities construction projects. The cost to provide all American Indians and Alaska Natives with safe drinking water and adequate sewerage systems in their homes is estimated to be almost $2.9 billion. With inflation, new environmental requirements, and population growth, the current sanitation appropriations are not reducing the backlog. In addition to providing safe sanitation facilities to existing homes, the IHS also provides sanitation facilities to new homes. (Indian Health Services 2010g)

In addition, IHS gives the following data:

-Annually, injuries account for 41 percent of the years of productive life lost for American Indians and Alaska Natives.

-More than $350 million is expended annually for the treatment of injuries.

-Implementation of effective injury prevention programs can improve the quality of life for Indian people and redirect the use of limited health care funds for treatment of other health conditions.

-Unintentional injury deaths to American Indian and Alaska Native people have decreased by 58 percent between 1973 and 2003; however, since 2000, injury deaths have begun to increase. (Indian Health Services 2010c)

Furthermore,

-Injuries are the leading cause of death for American Indian and Alaska Natives from ages one to forty-four years, and the third leading cause of death overall.

-Unintentional injury mortality rates for Indian people are approximately three times higher than the combined all-U.S. races rates. (Indian Health Services 2010d)

The National Congress of American Indians (NCAI) Policy Research Center offers the following *Demographic Profile of Indian Country* for January 10, 2007, as confirmation of the above data and offers additional information.

-Indian life expectancy is 2.4 years less than all other races in the 1999–2001 rates. Indian life expectancy has increased by 4 years from the 1996–1998 rates.

-Native people die at higher rates than other Americans from: tuberculosis, 600 percent higher; motor vehicle crashes, 229 percent higher; unintentional injuries, 152 percent higher; alcoholism, 510 percent higher; diabetes, 189 percent higher; suicide, 62 percent higher.

-Indian youth have the highest rate of suicide among all ethnic groups in the U.S. and is the second-leading cause of death for Native youth aged fifteen to twenty-four. (National Survey on Drug Use and Health 2003)

-The rate of violent crime against American Indians is twice the national average (101 per 1,000 as compared to forty-one per 1,000 annually). (Bureau of Indian Affairs 2006)

-One out of ten American Indians (twelve and older) become victims of violent crime annually. (Bureau of Justice Statistics 2004)

-Poverty rates for AI/AN are 25.4 percent compared with U.S. total populations of 13.3 percent. (National Congress of American Indians 2010a)

The Centers for Disease Control and Prevention (CDC) report that

-Injuries and violence account for 75 percent of all deaths among Native Americans ages one to nineteen. (Wallace 2000)

-Native Americans nineteen years and younger are at greater risk of preventable injury-related deaths than others in the same age group in the United States. Compared with blacks and whites, this group has the highest injury-related death rates for motor vehicle crashes, pedestrian events, and suicides. Rates for these causes are two to three times greater than rates for whites the same age. (Wallace, Patel, and Dellinger 2000)

The CDC also issued a report from 2002 on *Traumatic Brain Injury Among American Indians/Alaska Natives—United States, 1992–1996.* This report states that Traumatic Brain Injuries (TBIs) are the second leading cause of death among Native Americans and Alaska Natives. Furthermore, the majority of these injuries are classified as preventable. During this time period:

IHS, tribal, or contract-care hospitals recorded 4,491 TBI-related hospitalizations among AI/ANs, resulting in 21,107 hospital days (average length of stay: 4.7 days, range 1–292 days). The average TBI-related hospitalization rate was 81.7 per 100,000 population... Of these 4,491 cases, 221 (5 percent) were fatal. Male TBI rates were 2.5 times greater than female rates. The AI/AN TBI rate was similar to the combined incidence rates of TBI hospitalization reports by Colorado, Missouri,

Oklahoma, and Utah (81.7 versus 84.8 per 100,000 population). (Centers for Disease Control and Prevention 2002)

The report goes on to note that the AI/AN reporting rate for TBI is assumed to be a low estimate because many within the Native American population do not use IHS and that records are often coded using the "unspecified" designation (Centers for Disease Control and Prevention 2002). While the incidents of death mentioned in this report are not to be dismissed, for the purposes of this discussion it is the rate of survival that requires attention. Although no statistics were given, it is not unreasonable to assume that a number of the survivors of TBI will require chronic or permanent medical and/or rehabilitation efforts. Such efforts may require in-home treatment as well as institutional placement for care.

Cornell et al. report that according to Toubbeh (1990), "[T]he estimated rate of disabling conditions among American Indians is higher than any other group in the United States, with a rate that is six times higher than the general population..." (Cornell et al. 1999: 1). Cornell further reports that according to Toubbeh (1987, 1990), "...American Indian elders develop secondary health problems from primary disabilities at a rate which is 30 percent greater than other Americans similar in age" (Cornell 1999: 1). Moreover, "[T]he American Indian working-age group was 1.5 times more likely to report work-related disabilities than the general population (Clay, Seekins, and Cowie 1994; O'Connell 1987)" (Cornell 1999: 1). Cornell also reports that according to O'Connell (1987) "...young American Indian male adults have a seven times greater chance of becoming disabled before the age of 26 than any other race of people in the United States" (Cornell 1999: 1). A final section in Cornell (1999) states the following:

An estimated 40,000 American Indians under the age of eighteen were classified as having a disability in 1991 according to the National Indian Justice Center. American Indian adolescents have serious health problems: developmental disabilities such as mental retardation and learning disabilities; depression; suicide; anxiety; low self-esteem; and alienation (Hodge, 1990; Locust, 1990; National Indian Justice Center, 1991; O'Connell, 1987). American Indian infants are born with disabling conditions at three times the rate of all other babies in the United States (Toubbeh, 1990). Bacterial meningitis, otitis media, and congenital anomilies occur among American Indian populations at an overall rate of twice the national average, but varies from tribe to tribe (Hodge & Weinman, 1987). Many American Indians with disabilities are either unserved or underserved. The final report from the National Indian Justice Center's roundtable discussion on "Disabilities and their Effects on American Indians and Alaskan Native Communities" (1991) found that access to services is limited by personnel shortages, inadequate funding, legislative barriers and problems identifying persons eligible for services. (Cornell 1999: 1)

One final set of statistics needs to be added involving violence. While the relevance may not be immediately clear, it must be understood that violence often leads to the need for both physical and mental health care services. The Bureau of Justice Statistics (2004) reports the following:

-American Indians experience a per capita rate of violence twice that of the U.S. resident population.

-On average American Indians experience an estimated one violent crime for every ten residents ages twelve years and older.

-The violent crime rate in every age group below thirty-five was significantly higher for American Indians than for all persons.

-Among American Indians ages twenty-five to thirty-four the rate of violent crime victimization was more than two and a half times the rate for all persons the same age. (Bureau of Justice Statistics 2004: iv)

-The rate of violent victimization among American Indian Women was more than double that among all women.

-Offenders who were strangers to the victim committed most of the robberies (71 percent) against American Indian.

-American Indians were more likely to be victims of assault and rape/ sexual assault committed by a stranger or acquaintance rather than an intimate partner or family member. (Bureau of Justice Statistics 2004: v)

-The rate of violent crime victimization among American Indian females (86 per 1,000) was two and a half times the rate for all females. The victimization rate for American Indian females was much higher than that found among black females (46 per 1,000 ages twelve or older), about two and a half times higher than that among white females (thirtyfour), and five times that of Asian (seventeen) females. (Bureau of Justice Statistics 2004: 7)

-White or black offenders committed 88 percent of the violent victimizations (against Native Americans). (Bureau of Justice Statistics 2004: 8)

The above statistics are confirmed, and further detail is added, on additional sites established by the U.S. Census, CDC, IHS, U.N. Indigenous Report and disability organizations. The following two sections of this chapter are dedicated to discussions of the ADA/ADAA and IHS, respectively, and lead the reader into "full tar immersion" as these discussions require a level of bureaucracy proficiency known to only the most daring of tar swimmers.

ADA/ADAA Issues

The ADA was originally enacted in 1990. In 2008, as was previously mentioned, amendments were added, creating the ADAA. The original act was formed in public law, but was later reformatted into U.S. Code. In this later form,

> [T]he United States Code is divided into titles and chapters that classify laws according to their subject matter. Titles I, II, III, and V of the original law are codified in Title 42, chapter 126, of the United States Code beginning at section 12101. Title IV of the original law is codified in Title 47, chapter 5, of the United States Code. (www.ada.gov/pubs/ada.htm)

The establishment of the ADAA was intended to further the rights of disabled Americans that had begun in 1993 and to continue the Rehabilitation Act of 1973 504 with amendments (29 CFR § 1614.203), which was itself designed to join disability rights to the Civil Rights Act of 1964 (PL 82-352, 78 Stat. 241) (Historical Context of the Americans with Disabilities Act 2008).

The ADAA is designed to ensure the rights of disabled individuals by establishing laws and requirements for areas that include, but are not limited to, access to jobs, transportation, housing, and air travel. The complexity of the document is itself not limited to the language, as was demonstrated in the previous paragraph, but requires that violations or complaints be submitted within a restricted time to the appropriate agency. In other words, complaints involving Title I are to be submitted to the EEOC while complaints involving Title II are to be submitted to the DOJ unless those complaints involve public transportation, in which case they are to be submitted to the Office of Civil Rights of the FTA of the DOT. Remarkably, complaints involving architectural barriers are to be submitted to the U.S. Architectural and Transportation Barriers Compliance Board, not to be confused with DOT. Complaints involving the Individuals with Disabilities Act are to be reported to the DOE, and those involving violations of the Rehabilitation Act are to be submitted to the DOL. Determination as to which act or title is being violated is to be based on the definition and clarifications as set out in the specific sections according to the wording of the ADAA. So, while Title I refers to employers with 15 or more employees and issues of "reasonable access," 504 discusses "reasonable accommodations" as well as program accessibility and communications accommodations. The difference between "access" and "accommodation" will have to be left for philosophers and lawyers to decide, but it is not unforeseeable to imagine that the terms themselves come into conflict. Given the legal quagmire, the idea that the ADAA is intended to open opportunities and to ensure equal treatment for people with differences particularly in the public arena remains dubious. The question as to whether the ADAA fully serves the people or whether the creation of the bureaucracy is such that it serves as a further barrier to equality of access and accommodation remains an issue. Furthermore, it is unclear which office is responsible for complaints that the ADAA itself acts as a barrier to equality.

Added to the above levels of confusion is the issue of ADA/ADAA applicability in Native American communities. The language of the ADA/ADAA creates difficulties in interpreting tribal compliance requirements. The DBTAC Southwest ADA Center 2010) offers a clear and concise discussion of the issues involved. According to the DBTAC Southwest ADA Center, the primary issue involves the "doctrine of sovereign immunity: where in most situations, state and federal courts do not have the jurisdiction to hear private lawsuits brought against Native American tribes" (DBTAC Southwest ADA Center 2010: 1). The article states that upholding of sovereign immunity by The United States Supreme Court is a result of policies designed to uphold self-determination and self-sufficiencies of tribes and to eliminate the problems faced by overtaxed and underfunded tribal governments (DBTAC Southwest ADA Center 2010: 1). The article does however state that immunity is not to be used to avoid federal law; it restricts legal retaliation from individuals but "does not protect against enforcement action by the United States government..." (DBTAC Southwest ADA Center 2010: 1). The relationship is similar to that of state and federal government, in that in most cases federal law trumps state law.

According to the DBTAC bulletin, Title I specifically eliminates "Indian Tribes" from consideration, but Title II and Title III make no specific mention of Tribes. Under Title II, Tribal governments are not specifically defined as "state or local governments" and so are exempt. Title III may be applicable according to the Eleventh Circuit under the auspice of universality, but private lawsuits filed involving either

Title II or III would most likely be dismissed based on immunity. The article goes on to suggest, however, that the Attorney General could file a lawsuit regarding Title III and recommends that tribal businesses consider the potential for such action by designing public plans to comply with Title III (DBTAC Southwest ADA Center 2010: 2). The article also discusses the *504* section of the *Rehabilitation Act* stating that it offers "no explicit language" but does state that "programs or activities" receiving federal funds must comply. While the specific tribal governments may be exempt because they have no language specifically tying them to state governments, they do receive funds for "programs and activities" from the Bureau of Indian Affairs , an agency which is tied to *504* (DBTAC Southwest ADA Center 2010: 2–3). While tribal governments must comply with the Architectural Barriers Act because it is overseen by a federal agency (The Access Board), the issue of immunity again comes into play when considering the Individuals with Disabilities Education Act (DBTAC Southwest ADA Center 2010: 3). As for the Fair Housing Act,

> According to the Department of Housing and Urban Development, the requirements of the FHA do not apply to Indian Tribes and their tribally designated housing agencies (TDHE) for housing funded by the Native American Housing Assistance and Self-Determination Act of 1996 (NAHASDA). However, these funds trigger the accessibility requirements of section 504 of the Rehabilitation Act. It is also HUD's position that the Fair Housing Act does apply to State-recognized Indian tribes and their TDHE's. (DBTAC Southwest ADA Center 2010: 3–4)

State-recognized Indian communities most likely fall under Title II and other titles within the ADAA because the language of those operations contain specific terms and definitions binding them to state affiliation (DBTAC Southwest ADA Center 2010: 4).

The final section of the DBTAC Southwest ADA article discusses the problems with achieving disability access on tribal lands. The article suggests that tribal governments need to establish disability guidelines to ensure access and equality for disabled individuals. However, it is noted that the differences in tribal governments may create obstacles as each government is unique in construction and treaty relationship (DBTAC Southwest ADA Center 2010: 4). With no specific requirement for adoption, tribes have differed in their responses to ADAA. Research done by the BIA in 1999 indicates that the responses varied from a complete acceptance of the letter of ADA to the acceptance of the spirit of ADA. Other tribes adopted only parts of the ADA. The research noted that the responses centered more on the inability to fund the adoption rather than the lack of support for the ADA itself. The research cited extended monetary difficulties because of legal land and water right protection battles as a major obstacle to ADA adoption. These legal battles and the need to protect reservation boundaries often excluded the possibility of funding ADA adoption. The site further notes that no government agency is required to fund the monetary gap necessary for the adoption of the ADA (Kathy Dwyer Center on Disability in Rural Communities 2010).

Furthermore, as reported by Bradford (1992), D. L. Fixico (1986) states that the attempts in the 1950s and 1960s to relocate Native people from the reservations to the cities for jobs placed approximately half of the Native American population in urban communities. Because the jobs did not exist in the numbers promised, most of those who moved to the urban area lived in substandard conditions. Bradford further reports that according to J. C. O'Connell (1987),

> ...the rate at which the State-Federal rehabilitation system provided rehabilitation services to American Indians with disabilities was substantially lower than that for the U.S. population as a whole. Specifically, Rehabilitation Services Administration (RS) data "showed that American Indians who are disabled appear to be underrepresented in the State-Federal system... In the area of sensory disorders (condition of the eye and ear), orthopedic impairments due to accidents, asthma and allergies, diabetes, speech conditions, and skin conditions"...Further, when investigating the use of state agency rehabilitative services by adult Native Americans. Morgan and O'Connell (1987) found that "client output after successful rehabilitation closures for Native Americans did not differ from that of the general population. However, the rate of successful closure among Native American clients was substantially below that of the general population." (Bradford et al. 1992: 1)

IHS

ADA/ADAA requirements focus on governmental statutes regarding disability issues. However, the primary distribution of individual care for Native Americans falls to the IHS. The IHS is located in the governmental division of Health and Human Services. The IHS is responsible for the distribution of "comprehensive health service" for approximately 1.9 million Native Americans and Alaska Natives (AI/AN). The budget for 2009 was set at $4.05 billion with a potential increase in 2010 (Indian Health Services 2010b). According to one stakeholder workgroup, the

IHS provides only 55 percent of the funding necessary to bring AI/AN population equal to the health benefits experienced by "mainstream Americans"(Indian Health Services 2010f).

"The 2005-2007 Current Population Survey revealed that the American Indian and Alaska Native (AI/AN) population has larger families, less health insurance (the number of AI/ANs without health insurance is over double that for U.S. all races), and a poverty level nearly twice that of the rest of the population" (Indian Health Services 2010e). Compounding these issues is the fact that the tribes have various ways in which they interact with IHS including direct service, contract, or compact. IHS service delivery is determined by the tribes based on the tribal considerations of self-determination. (Indian Health Services 2010h).

> Self-Governance Tribes currently control nearly $1.2 billion of the IHS budget of approximately $4.05 billion, or about 30 percent of the total IHS FY2010 budget appropriation. Tribal Self-Governance programs served 550, 646 of the 1,500,044 users (37 percent) of Indian health care programs in 2009. Each year, Tribes assume additional IHS programs under the authority of Title V of the ISDEAA. (Indian Health Services 2010h)

In addition to rural and tribal areas, the IHS also serves urban AI/AN communities. This service was established under the Indian Health Care Improvement Act, which has recently been permanently reauthorized under President Obama. As of 2009, the "IHS provides contracts and grants to thirty-four community-based, nonprofit urban Indian programs providing health care services at forty-one sites throughout the United States" (Indian Health Services 2010i).

One final aspect for consideration under the IHS involves personnel. While active physician employment has increased, there continues to be a vacancy rate of 21 percent. The IHS site explains that this vacancy rate may reflect issues of clinic isolation and the geographically difficult locals involved in AI/AN rural and reservation practices. Dental vacancies are estimated at 24 percent and pharmacy vacancies at 26 percent. The rate that concerns the IHS is in the 26 percent vacancy in the nursing population, which may be exacerbated by estimated future shortages of registered nurses in the general U.S. population (Indian Health Services 2010j).

Given the above budget, responsibility levels, and personnel concerns, the IHS faces challenges in providing sufficient health care without the necessary resources. The requirement for basic health care delivery under these conditions leads to additional workplace stress and the potential inadequate or nontreatment of individuals needing physical and mental health care. When the rehabilitation needs of AI/AN populations are included in the equation, the already stretched budget becomes tissue thin especially given that rehabilitation needs are often chronic or permanent. In addition, many health care workers note that medical equipment for disabilities can be difficult to acquire because the IHS is not authorized to cover certain types of medical equipment.

Taking into consideration the above listed needs in Native American and Alaska Native communities, the complexities of the ADA/ADAA legalities, and the limitations of the IHS, one begins to understand the difficulties for those individuals with different needs in receiving treatment and rehabilitation services. The levels of bureaucracy and legality offer some of the hurdles. Attempting to navigate the various policies and Titles as well as the multitude of agencies keeps many from even attempting to seek help. (It should be noted that social security, Medicare, and Medicaid have been left out of this discussion but offer increasing levels of challenge in terms of interaction with tribal legal considerations.) Given the overwhelming paperwork and the investigation involved in pursuing health care needs, many Native Americans and Alaska Natives prefer to deal with health issues without the involvement of these agencies. However, these are not the only considerations for these populations when attempting to gain access to proper health care.

Barriers of Trust

While the statistics and legal considerations may cause an individual to sink beneath the tar, it is often the social issues that keep that individual from resurfacing. The issues of social despair and distrust that can descend on communities facing the levels of poverty and prejudice as those found in Native American and Alaska Native areas may be the greatest barrier to proper health care service. Many within these communities view U.S. governmental programs with distrust given the historical track record and the failure of the U.S. government to negotiate in a nation-to-nation manner. Furthermore, the legal complexity of the IHS and the ADAA cause many to believe that there is no intention on the part of the U.S. government to truly serve the people because these programs are designed to be inaccessible. A complete discussion concerning the distrust experienced in Native American and Alaska

Native communities will have to be set aside for other texts. However, this section will offer some information that documents the distrust in order to introduce the need for further exploration and consideration. If this obstacle cannot be eliminated, the concern is that many of those attempting to deliver health care services will never emerge, but instead become fossils lost in the tar.

Beyond the more practical difficulties of accessing care from the above agencies, La Fromboise et al. (1997) notes that the manner in which many of these agencies deliver care acts as a barrier for Native Americans and Alaska Natives. La Fromboise cites several sources that mention a lack of cultural competency in health care agencies including the fact that these agencies tend to employ primarily non-Native American and Alaska Native workers. It is not always a matter of these workers intentionally establishing barriers so much as it is a matter of AI/ANs not feeling welcome, respected, and understood that causes many to stop treatment or to not seek assistance at all. For example, the article cites a survey done by A. White (1987) that shows a difference in the perception of administrators and clients as to the importance of language differences as a significant factor in the delivery of health care. The administrators felt there was no significant problem, while the clients felt it was indeed a significant problem (La Fromboise et al. 1997). The need to understand the different Native American and Alaska Native cultures, including languages, is essential in order to fully address the health care and rehabilitation needs in these communities.

Rosenthal et al. (1999) further compiled several sources in an attempt to advance the need for cultural competency in rehabilitation agencies. Rosenthal et al. give a summary discussion of Carol Locust's work in wellness and spirituality as well as a discussion of Joe and Miller's (1987) work describing the differences in Anglo and Native American world-views, which can be found in a discussion elsewhere in this text. The discussion of these works by Rosenthal offers a foundation for requiring cultural competency training for personnel involved in AI/AN health care distribution. The lack of cultural understanding not only creates barriers but also implies a lack of respect and value in Native American and Alaska Native worldviews. In turn, this implied or assumed lack of respect leads to misunderstandings and distrust.

What becomes clear is that language, cultural traditions, and spirituality are factors for consideration in fulfilling health care and rehabilitation needs. Specific cultural information should be gained from trusted members of the communities being served. Administrators and personnel should not assume that differing tribes or communities have the same languages, traditions, or spiritualities. To avoid the alienation of clients, trusted individuals should be sought out for discussion and for education. Assumptions that cultural competency measures are unnecessary or that clinics and centers can be run in a non-Native manner will result in limited success for the administration of health care as well as cause potential negative experiences on the part of the clients. The frustration experienced by both personnel and clients can lead to an environment of antagonism and escalading distrust on both sides.

The unfortunate result, of both the history of health care in Native American and Alaska Native communities and the continued lack of focus on cultural competency, creates a lack of trust in ADA/ADAA and IHS agencies. Many Native Americans and Alaska Natives continue to view agencies that are backed by the federal government with suspicion. These views are compounded by the events of the 1960s and 1970s and continued allegations of governmental attempts of assimilation and termination practices. One of the events that has instilled a great deal of distrust involves the allegations of continued genocidal practices through forced sterilization. Lawrence (2001) discusses the practices, carried out during the 1960s and 1970s under the auspices of IHS that sterilized at least 25 percent of Native American Women without their informed consent. The sterilization practices stemmed from early American ideas of eugenics and definitions of "unfit" individuals. It was understood and accepted that "unfit" individuals could be sterilized for the benefit of society as a whole. Native American women were often classified as "unfit" based on their status as "undesirable" (Lawrence 2001: 402–403). The issue for many Native American women has been one of "voluntary" but coerced sterilization. In many cases, women did indeed sign the consent forms (the federal government viewed these acts as voluntary), but often the terms of informed consent were not met (Native American women viewed these acts as coerced). Some Native American women were led to believe that the sterilization procedures could be reversed when they wanted children while others were not told that sterilization procedures were being performed at all (Lawrence 2001: 400–415). Lawrence discusses practices such as those that used medication during painful deliveries or cesarean sections as examples of failed informed consent. The impairment of cognition because of the medication was often exacerbated by the fact that consent forms were written in English above many of the women's reading levels. These forms, if signed, authorized sterilization (Lawrence 2001: 411–412). According to Lawrence's research, a study done by Dr. Connie Pinkerton-Uri

(1974) "revealed that IHS facilities singled out full-blood Indian women for sterilization procedures" (Lawrence 2001: 411). While the General Accounting Office report in 1976 did not verify the reports of coerced sterilization, it did state that the informed consent did not meet Health, Education and Welfare standards (Lawrence 2001: 406). Lawrence documents that even after Health, Education and Welfare practices and forms, which required specific disclosure of actions of sterilization and the risks involved, were adopted, IHS agencies did not always comply and did not initially revise their manuals (Lawrence 2001: 408).

Guadagnolo et al. (2009) confirm the mistrust levels of Native American clients in their research. This article presents conclusions drawn from a survey designed to measure trust and satisfaction involving health care. The survey was administered to Native American and non-Native American patients. The results indicated "that Native Americas were significantly less likely to trust health care providers, clinics and hospitals than non-Hispanic Whites. Native Americans also expressed lower levels of satisfaction with the health care system than non-Hispanic Whites (Guadagnolo et al. 2009: 220).

While not a complete study of trust issues, the above information indicates severe concerns with the implementation of ADA/ADAA and IHS by Native Americans and Alaskan Natives. These trust issues come from a history of conflict between Native American nations and the American nation and will not be easily put to rest. The hope of raising trust would seem to rest with the different agencies' commitments to cultural competency as a requirement of health care delivery.

Discussion

The above data and information were provided to give voice to those who have been called "Hope Warriors" by Carol Locust and others. These are the people who manage to figure out exactly what agency an individual needs to contact for ADAA issues. These individuals discern how social security impacts IHS benefits and manage to negotiate treatment and rehabilitation services despite the limited funding of the different agencies. These are the people, who, when faced with each agency refusing to supply a wheelchair to a child in need, negotiate to provide the chair. This final section has been offered to the voices of those who wish to give their comments. The informants are individuals who work in the areas of Native American and Alaska Native health care and rehabilitation. They will not be identified in order to provide privacy for both them and the clients. The interviews have been done over time and have occurred both in person and online. The comments given here are approved by the informants and have not been changed in content or structure. It must also be noted that only a few of the comments from the interviews are given here because of the limits of the chapter.

The first set of comments listed below center around the availability of services and how those services are delivered in different communities. The informants referred several times to the differences between rural and urban care availability. In many cases, the rural facilities were distant and created travel challenges. The informants mentioned that some tribes have funded vans or pay for gas to those who can transport individuals to the medical facilities. Even with these forms of transportation, the unfamiliarity of distant clinics, hospitals, and personnel can act as a barrier for those who need care. The following comments come from several informants.

> For many of those who need help, it is frustrating for them to be in pain or feeling sick and have to travel long distances. Many would rather stay at home using what they have to help them feel better. It is hard to travel and hard to keep from embarrassment in some cases. It helps that they know others who can take them, but they feel bad for burdening them and keeping them from other things. We would feel the same.
>
> In the hospital there was a young man sitting alone. It was late and dark. He seemed sad and so I went up to see if there was something he needed. He smiled and said he was visiting family and it was several hours to go home. He had decided to stay and rest that night so he could visit again in the morning. He had not eaten so we went to get something before he returned to the waiting room. He talked about how important it was that his family not be alone so far from home in a strange place and so he wanted to stay.
>
> An individual came into the hospital who did not speak English. We have many interpreters for the tribes in the immediate area, but we did not have anyone who could translate for this individual as she was from quite a distance away. She had come in without family as she had been out shopping. We were concerned not only for her health but for the anxiety she felt in not being able to communicate. It made both diagnosis and treatment more complex. These language differences are not uncommon among our clients and we continue to work to be prepared.

While urban services and clinics may be closer in proximity, one informant talks about how the atmosphere in the clinics and hospitals continues to work as barriers. Cultural differences can work to create a discomfort for those who are unfamiliar, and while language barriers may not exist in urban clinics, it would be a mistake to dismiss cultural differences in these areas.

> As we work with individuals from different cultures, it is important to identify and relate to their particular culture. We work on continuing to gain cultural competency by bringing in knowledgeable individuals from varying cultures to educate the staff. We feel it is our responsibility to make the individual as comfortable as possible so they will be able to tell us what they need. The fact is that health care involves problems of all kinds including those that are delicate or personal. If we do not instill an atmosphere of trust and respect, the individual may not tell us all the information we need to successfully assist in solving the problem.

One of the areas that inspired a great many comments from different informants dealt with how information is presented to individuals seeking assistance. One theme that was repeated involved the use of plain language to explain services available, diagnosis, and treatment. Furthermore, not only are language differences an issue, but cultural cues in conversational style need to be understood in order to ensure understanding and informed consent. The following are some of the comments made by different informants.

> On a daily basis I find myself lost in alphabet soup. Trying to remember what form works with which agency is beyond my skills many days. How in the world could people fight through all the letters and designations along with which agency is responsible for what if they were not in this soup every day? I see their eyes glaze over and their shoulders slump as I try to explain the procedure for obtaining a wheelchair or glasses for their children. The paperwork alone is enough to cause some to despair and quit. So, I have made a joke of the alphabet soup in the hopes that we can smile a bit and wade through the soup together. Many times it seems to help. Other times I worry that it will be overwhelming and they will not come back. But I think we are known for being able to help most of the time.
>
> It is important to understand the culture of the people who come for our services. It is important to know the language, but more so to know the right way to say what needs to be said. We often try to have a member of the patient's culture there to help us explain the diagnosis and procedure. Words must be chosen carefully and different Native American cultures use different language. So, that for some one does not speak of death or directly of the illness. It takes some of our new doctors and staff time to learn how to phrase information correctly, but it does not help the patient's understanding if he shuts down because of the way we

deliver the information. Communication is about more than just dumping facts on a patient; it is about giving the information in a way that he or she will understand. That means we need to work hard not to offend with our language when we explain the situation.

Imagine the difficulty in explaining medical procedures to patients who do not speak English. For many of these patients, their languages do not have words for x-ray or heart-valve replacement and those may be some of the easier ones. Try explaining heart catheterization to someone who does not speak English and does not have a television to watch all the medical shows. In the medical field we have become use to the American patient, who knows medical terminology or at least has a TV frame of reference. It is important to have those to interpret, but even they face a challenge when the languages have no words for such things. At times I have found myself trying to mime what needs to be done and at least that usually gets a smile. If my drawing was better that might work too, but my stick figures don't come close to anatomical drawings.

It is important that staff understand the way they say things is important. In non-Indian cultures language does not carry such weight. But when I first started working here I learned my lesson. And I still think of that person I didn't help. She came in, and I was so busy; the phone was ringing and I had a headache from the day, and everything had gone wrong. When she came to the desk I told her I couldn't help her. What I meant was that I need to finish what I was doing and would help her in a minute, but I said it badly. She left when I wasn't looking. One of the Native women who worked with me explained that in her culture, saying I can't help you is final. I will never say that again. I never saw her again. It is not the same in my culture where the squeaky wheel gets the attention. I am now very careful to smile even when I have a headache and be clear about needing just a minute if you could wait please.

It is important to always put things in the positive and not the negative. It is important for the energy for both the situation and the individual. Use positive words and make your face friendly. Be kind, but do not touch others as it is not polite especially children. A smile and a kind word is enough.

Another area of discussion that received many comments from the informants centered on the need to respect, even if one did not understand, the spirituality of the individuals seeking health care services. Native American and Alaska Native spirituality is often unfamiliar to many in the health care and ADA/ADAA agencies. The lack of understanding can lead to mistaken communication and the mistaken elimination of objects that support the spiritual wellness of the individual. For many in the Native American and Alaska Native communities, spirituality is essential for physical wellness to occur. Gaining a cultural competency in these matters may again require contact with respected individuals within the different Native American and Alaska Native communities that the facility treats.

> Working in the hospital, it is important not to touch items in the person's room or on the bed especially if you do not know what they are. There are many different spiritual beliefs and objects. Just because you do not know what something is does not take away the meaning it holds. It is best to leave things or if they need to be moved to ask the family to move them.
>
> Respect is the most important part of caring for rehabilitation clients and anyone with a health need. We do not have to understand or convert to another religion or spiritual practice. We simply have to respect the right of others to believe as they believe. When in doubt ask a family member or a member of the community for help. But put simply, respect others beliefs as you want yours respected.
>
> Our staff has found that Native Americans seem more comfortable if they are in a quiet atmosphere. Different cultural Elders have indicated that silence and quiet are important for spiritual and physical health. So, we try to enter the room quietly and stand at the door to give the person time to adjust to our being in the room. Then we walk quietly to the bed and speak softly. We have also learned that there is often a family member or person that we should talk to as they speak for the person. It takes some focus to remember, but it is part of patient care. Many of us have started using this with non-Indian patients, and it does seem to create calm. There is often just a better feel to the rooms when this practice of quiet and calm is used.
>
> It is important to allow time after giving information. Native people do not rush. It is important that they think and talk to trusted people before deciding. Rushing stops thinking. Rushing will make people do nothing so not to make a wrong choice. Energy will be wrong if rushed.

A final area to note in this section deals with ways in which some of the informants create positive atmospheres. It is the case that any individual can feel anxious in clinics, hospitals, or agencies. For many of the informants, it is important that they create an environment that promotes healing and wellness. The efforts are often not the grand gestures one might expect, but the small kindnesses that create the greatest results.

> One of our patients was a small girl, who needed a wheel chair, but she was young, and the look of it frightened her. She cried when we brought it into the room. One of our staff had become friends with the girl and

had found out that she loved princesses and unicorns. This same staff member recruited us all in an effort to "trick out" the wheel chair. In the end, the little girl loved the colors and the streamers, but it was all of us that may have had the most fun. Now, we look forward to "tricking out" as much of the equipment as possible for the kids. It is possible that the kids feel healthier than the crazy staff around them.

For patients who have to stay a while, we try to get the family to bring in small blankets and pictures. We try when we can to face the beds to the East even if it is not looking out the window. It isn't always possible, but we try to face them the way they are comfortable. Sometimes we can choose the room if we don't have too many on the floor. Different tribes use different colors for healing and spirituality so we try to have them bring in what will help. It just makes the rooms better for the person, and that makes them happier. In rooms where they are alone or where it will not bother the other, we allow music. Headphones are not comfortable for all of our people. But music that is important to them is another way that helps.

Food is an issue for many. It is not just that they are unfamiliar with the hospital, but the food we prepare is very different for many of our patients. It can upset their systems to have new foods. The hospital has worked in different cases to help with the dietary differences. In some cases it has been allowed for the family to bring in some foods.

We allow ceremonies when we can. The different Elders and community members have worked out with the hospital what can be done. We try our best to accommodate all spiritual practices. In some cases this means allowing smudging of the person. We work with the Elders to allow this so that it will not conflict with surgery areas or the like.

The above comments are only a small portion of the information available to agencies wishing to better serve the Native American and Alaska Native populations. It is understood that the history of nation-to-nation negotiations has created a pit wide enough and deep enough that those standing on opposite sides have difficulty communicating. The divide has grown worse as it has been filled with the endless sticky tar of governmental bureaucracy and legal jargon with which both Congress and the courts struggle. Add to this pit of tar the distrust that occurs when peoples feel that their culture is not respected or valued. It is a wonder that health care and ADA/ADAA services exist at all in Native American and Alaska Native communities. What success these programs have, however, is not because of any agency organization or any brilliantly crafted legislation. The success in assisting individuals within the Native American and Alaska Native communities is largely because of the individuals who have jumped into the tar to help others.

It is true that some of these communities have more of these Hope Warriors than others, but even one can make the difference to an individual in need.

For the readers who have made it through the above discussion, the purpose was not to bore you with endless information or to create numbness with statistical data. The purpose was to drop the reader into the tar of bureaucracy that is the daily existence for those attempting to deliver health care and difference assistance to Native American and Alaska Native people. While all of the above agencies and legal determinations may be necessary for setting up a system, they often do little to assist the individuals the system is designed to serve. The real purpose of this chapter was to bring to light the efforts of those who walk into the tar of bureaucracy to help the individuals in need. Furthermore, the point of the chapter was to give voice to those who have just stepped in and to those who have made it to the other side. It is dedicated to those who are treading neck deep and to those who have recently and long ago slipped beneath the surface, leaving their efforts like fossils of hope for future generations.

References

Americans with Disabilities Act (42 USC 126, 1990).

Americans with Disabilities Act (PL110-325, 2008). Retrieved March 2010 from http//www.ada.gov/pubs/ada.htm

Bradford, B., Marshall, C. A., Johnson, M. J. Martin, W. E., & Saravanabhavan, R. C. (1992). The rehabilitation needs of American Indians with disabilities in an urban setting. *The Journal of Rehabilitation* 58(2), 13–21

Bureau of Indian Affairs. (2006). *Gap Analysis of Police to Service Population Based on the FBI's 2004 Uniform Crime Report and BIA data*. Washington, DC: Bureau of Indian Affairs.

Bureau of Justice Statistics. (2004). *American Indians and Crime, A BJS Statistical Profile, 1992–2002*. Washington, DC: Department of Justice.

Bush, G. W. H. (1991). *Statement Reaffirming the Government-to-Government Relationship between the Federal Government and Indian Tribal Governments*. Retrieved March 2010 from www.csdl.tamu.edu/bushlib/papers/1991/91061402.html

Capriccioso, R. (2009). *Indian Country Today Online*. Retrieved March 2010 fromIndiancountrytodaymedianetwork.com/2011/03/obamas-budget-recieves-mostly-positive-reviews/

Centers for Disease Control and Prevention. (2002). Traumatic brain injury among American Inidans/Alaska Natives—Unites States, 1992-1996. *Morbidity and Mortality Weekly* 51(14), 303–305. Retrieved March 2010 from www.cdc.gov/mmwr/preview/mmwrhtml/mm5114.3.htm*Cherokee Nation v. Georgia* (1831) 30 U.S. 1.

Clay, J., Seekins, T., & Cowie, C. (1994). Secondary disabilities among American Indians in Montana. *Rural Special Education Quarterly 2* (1),20–25.

Cornell, D., Ma, G., Coyle, C., & Wares, D. (1999). Assessment of services to American Indians with disabilities. *The Journal of Rehabilitation 65*, 11–16.

DBTAC Southwest ADA Center. (2010). Retrieved March 2010 from www.dlrp. orgDeloria, Jr., V., & Lytle, C. M. (1983). *American Indians, American Justice.* Austin, TX: University of Texas Press.

Donnelly v. United States (1913) 22 U.S. 243

Fixico, D. (1986). *Termination and Relocation: Federal Indian Policy, 1945–1960.* Albuquerque, NM: University of New Mexico Press.

General Allotment Act (25 U.S.C.A. § 331, 1887).

Guadagnolo, B., Cina, K., Helbig, P., Molloy, K., Reiner, M., Cook, E., & Petereit, D. (2009) Medical mistrust and less satisfaction with health care among Native Americans presenting for cancer treatment. *Journal of Healthcare for the Poor and Underserved 20*, 210–226.

Historical Context of the Americans with Disabilities Act (2008). Retrieved March 2010 from www.adata.org/whatsada-history.aspx

House Concurrent Resolution 108 (1953) HCR108.

Indian Civil Rights Act (25 U.S.C. §§ 1301-03, 1968).

Indian Healthcare Improvement Act (PL 94-437, 1973).

Indian Healthcare Improvement Act (PL 94-438, 1976).

Indian Health Services. (2009a) Retrieved March 2010 from www.ihs.gov/publicaffairs/PressReleases/index.cfm?module

Indian Health Services. (2009b). Retrieved March 2010 from www.ihs.gov/publicaffairs/PressReleases

Indian Health Services. (2010a). Retrieved March 2010 from info.ihs.gov/BasisHlthSvcs.asp.

Indian Health Services. (2010b). Retrieved March 2010 from info.ihs.gov/Disparities.asp

Indian Health Services. (2010c) Retrieved March 2010 from info.ihs.gov/injuries.asp

Indian Health Services. (2010d). Retrieved March 2010 from www.ihs.gov/MedicalPrograms/InjuryPrevention

Indian Health Services. (2010e). Retrieved March 2010 from info.ihs.gov/Population.asp

Indian Health Services. (2010f). Retrieved March 2010 from info.ihs.gov/QuickLook2010.asp

Indian Health Services. (2010g). Retrieved March 2010 from info.ihs.gov/SafeWater.asp

Indian Health Services. (2010h). Retrieved March 2010 from info.ihs.gov/TrblslfGov.asp

Indian Health Services. (2010i). Retrieved March 2010 from info.ihs.gov/Urbninds.asp

Indian Health Services. (2010j). Retrieved March 2010 from info.ihs.gov/Workforce.asp

Indian Reorganization Act (25 U.S.C.A. §461, 1934).

Joe, R. E., & Miller, D. (Eds.). (1987). *American Indian Cultural Perspectives on Disability* (pp. 3–23). Tucson, AZ: Native American Research and Training Center, University of Arizona.

Kathy Dwyer Center on Disability in Rural Communities. (2010). *American Indian Disability Legislation Research: Rural Disability and Rehabilitation Research Progress Report No. 2.* Prepared by Kathy Dwyer Center on Disability in Rural Communities, University of Montana. Retrieved March 2010 from rtc.ruralinstitute.wmt.edu/Indian?AIDLReProgressRpt.htm

La Fromboise, T., Pritchett, E. F., Berven, N. L., & Menz, F. E. (1997). Effects of cultural identification and disability status on perceived community rehabilitation needs of American Indians. *The Journal of Rehabilitation 63*(3), 38–44.

Lawrence, J. (2001). The Indian Health Service and the sterilization of Native America women. *American Indian Quarterly 24* (3), 400–419.

Meriam, L., Brown, R., Cloud, H., Dale, E., Duke, E., Edwards, H., McKenzie, F., Mark., M., Ryan., W., & Spillman, W. (1928). *The Problem of Indian Administration, or Meriam Report.* Washington, DC: Institute for Government Research.

National Congress of American Indians. (2010a). *Census Profile of American Indians.* Retrieved March 2010 from www.ncai.org/ncai/resource/data/docs/Census_Information_Center/AI_AN_Profile_FINAL_1.11.07.pdf National Congress of American Indians. (2010b). *Human Needs in Indian Country.* Retrieved March 2010 from www.ncai.org/Human-Needs-in-Indian-Country.88.0.html*National Survey on Drug Use and Health.* (2003). Washington, DC: Substance Abuse and Mental Health Administration.

Northwest Portland Area Indian Health Board. (2006) *NDAIHB Policy Brief Reauthorization of IHCIA.* Northwest Portland Area Indian Health Board, Issue No. 18, p. 1.

O'Connell, J. (1987). *A Study of the Special Problems and Needs of American Indians with Handicaps Both on and off the Reservation.* Tucson, AZ: Native American Research and Training Center.

Patient Protection and Affordable Care Act (PL111-114, 2010).

Public Law 280 (67 Stat. 588, 1953).

Rehabilitation Act (HR8070, PL 93-112, 1973).

Rosenthal, D., Pichette, E. F. Garrett, M. J., & Kosciulek, J. F. (1999). Cultural identification of American Indians and its impact on rehabilitation services. *The Journal of Rehabilitation 65*(3), 3–11.*Snyder Act* (25 U.S.C. 13, 1921).

The White House, Office of the Press Secretary. Press Release for *Patient Protection and Affordable Care Act,* March 23, 2010. Retrieved March 2010 from http://www.whitehouse.gov/blog/2010/03?page=3

Toubbeh, J. T. (1987). Larks and wounded eagles: A commentary on services to Native Americans with disabilities. *American Rehabilitation13*(10), 2–5.

Toubbeh, J. T. (1990). Virdga over Indian Landscape, A speech delivered at the National Conference on Indians with Disabilities. Albuquerque, NM, October 2–4.

United Nations (2010). Press Briefing, January 14, 2010. Retrieved March 2010 from http://www0.un.org/News/briefings/docs/2010/100114_Indigenous.doc. htm

United States v. Sandoval (1913) 231 U.S. 28.

Wallace, L. (2000). *Injuries among American Indian and Alaska Native children, 1985–1996.* Atlanta, GA: Centers for Disease Control and Prevention.

Wallace, L., Patel, R., & Dellinger, A. (2003). Injury mortality among American Indian and Alaska Native children and youth—United States, 1989–1998. *MMWR 52* (30), 697–701. Retrieved March 2010 from www.cdc.gov/ncipe /factsheet/nativeamericans.htm Washington Post. (2010). Retrieved March 2010 from http://voices.washingtonpost.com/44/2009/11/05/obama_addresses_native _america.html

Additional Readings

Canby, W. C. (1981). *American Indian Law in a Nutshell.* St. Paul, MN: West Publishing Co.

Deer, S., Clairmont, B., Martell, C. A., & White Eagle, M. L. (Eds.). (2008). *Sharing Our Stories of Survival: Native Women Surviving Violence.* Lanham, MD: Altamira Press.

Locust, C. (1988). Wounding the spirit: Discrimination and traditional Indian belief systems. *Harvard Educational Review* 58(3).

Moquin, W., & Van Doren, C. (1995). *Great Documents in American Indian History.* New York, NY: Da Capo Press.

Prucha, F. P. (1994). *American Indian Treaties: The History of a Political Anomaly.* Berkeley, CA: University of California Press.

Smith, A. (2005). *Conquest: Sexual Violence and American Indian Genocide.* Cambridge, MA: South End Press.

SECTION 3

Interreligious and Cross-Cultural Comparisons of Disability

The authors in the final section begin to compare and contrast how distinctive cultural communities and religious traditions conceptualize and respond to disability and chronic illness. The objective of the comparative analysis offered in the following chapters is not meant to assume consensus or to foster a uniform approach to defining or responding to either disability or religion. Rather, the objective is to foster cross-cultural and interreligious dialogue about disability and religion, to balance the particularity of religious identity with availability to learning from our neighbors who are different, and to foster innovative ways of expanding the fields of religious studies and disability studies. Each chapter addresses unique themes, questions, and issues that may open new horizons of discovery; each chapter is limited in perspective and incomplete in understanding; each chapter is more of a beginning than a culmination; and each chapter opens borders on the one hand and creates new boundaries on the other.

Michael Stoltzfus and Darla Schumm open the section on interreligious and cross-cultural comparisons of disability by describing some of the unique personal, medical, social, and religious challenges facing people living with chronic illness and disability, with a focus on the comparative connections between suffering, healing, and disability within Buddhism and Christianity. Two core questions anchor the inquiry. First, why are chronic illness and disability often associated with merited suffering in Buddhism and Christianity? Second, what types of Buddhist and Christian practice can help cultivate spiritual healing in the presence of chronic illness or disability? While recognizing the many differences between Buddhist and Christian tradition and belief, the authors argue that both offer spiritual resources for providing renewal and healing for those who struggle with chronically disabling conditions.

In Chapter 9, Lynne Bejoian, Molly Quinn, and Maysaa Bazna compare broad images and understandings of disability studies within three religious traditions: Buddhism, Christianity, and Islam. Concepts such as ability, availability, relationships, and community are investigated, uncovering discourses around social justice, service, and how human difference is considered and constructed. Dialogue across these three traditions and within a disability studies perspective provides a context for scholars, teachers, and spiritual practitioners to critically reflect upon their own religious practice and to imagine new possibilities for interreligious communication. Writing from within their own religious traditions (Buddhism, Christianity, and Islam), Bejoian, Quinn, and Bazna model a form of interreligious and cross-cultural understanding from which we might all learn.

In the final chapter of the book, Lavonna L. Lovern offers a unique comparative perspective regarding the similarities and differences that exist between Native American and Western cultural concepts, treatments, and acceptance of persons of difference, with a specific focus on considerations of health and ability. Attention to the difference between Native American and Western ontological and epistemological conceptions of reality is not designed to be adversarial, but to address how distinctive perspectives alter the way particular communities might approach healing, balance, and medical treatment. The author highlights how most traditional Native American tribes simply do not recognize the duality structure. There are no words in the languages that indicate normal or abnormal, ability or disability. The Indigenous mind tends to live within the perspective of continuum rather than dichotomy, seeking balance rather than difference. In addition, Lovern addresses issues of community, spirituality, and the role that both the individual and the community play in maintaining health and wellness.

CHAPTER 8

Chronic Illness and Disability: Narratives of Suffering and Healing in Buddhism and Christianity[1]

Darla Schumm and Michael Stoltzfus

Chronic illness and chronic disability are human conditions that millions of people experience, but until recently were seldom prioritized in religious, theological, or philosophical literatures regarding how to live with an able yet vulnerable body in a mutually conditioned world. Our goal in this essay is to explore how religious conceptions of suffering and healing might inform the way we think about what it means to live with chronic illness and disability. Through the use of personal narrative, we situate our discussion within the specific religious traditions of Buddhism and Christianity. We explore Buddhist and Christian teachings on the nature of suffering and healing and demonstrate how these teachings are sometimes misrepresented by well-meaning practitioners in both traditions. We then engage in comparative religious analysis as we offer alternative ways of thinking about, responding to, and living with chronic illness or disability. Buddhism and Christianity have many differences, but both offer rich spiritual resources for providing healing and renewal for those who struggle with chronically disabling conditions.

Chronic conditions do not fit the typical pattern of a health crisis and resolution but last for a long period, often for life. Examples of chronic illness include lupus, multiple sclerosis, rheumatoid arthritis, Crohn's disease, diabetes, mental illness, and others. Examples of chronic disabilities include blindness, paralysis, deafness, cognitive impairments, and others. We include both of these categories of chronic conditions in this essay not because they are similar in diagnosis or symptoms, but because many people make inaccurate assumptions about what it is like to live with a chronic illness or disability, give damaging and oppressive explanations regarding why an individual has a chronic illness or disability, and are confused by the unstable and unpredictable symptoms inherent in chronic illnesses and disabilities (Harris 1995; Stone 1995). Furthermore, those who do not directly experience the challenge of living with a chronic condition often marginalize those who do. Therefore, both chronic illness and disability offer unique personal, social, and religious challenges. It may be possible to recover from a chronic disabling condition if medical science discovers its root cause and a suitable remedy, but, typically, there are no established medical protocols for their cure (Kleinman 1988; Sidell 1997).

Further complicating life with chronic conditions is the fact that many chronic conditions are not obvious to the casual observer. While the chronically disabled body is typically all too visible in its impairment (although certainly not always), the chronically ill body is often all too invisible in its pain and discomfort. Chronic illnesses and their debilitating symptoms are very real but often undetectable to the casual or uncaring eye (Kleinman 1988; Stone 1995). The chronically ill can become opaque mysteries even to those who are closest to them. Most people in our culture can understand and sympathize with episodic sickness or disability in which the afflicted eventually get better (bone mends, pain subsides, scar heals). Folks can then return to life as it was previously. Fatal illnesses are tragic but then the illness ends in death. Chronic conditions are neither episodic nor terminal; they are not exclusively visible or invisible. Therefore, they often do not raise questions about cure or impending death, but how to cultivate moral and spiritual development in the midst of ongoing struggle and difficulty.

People who live with chronic disabilities not only struggle with physical health issues but also often struggle with the cultural exclusion that goes along with having an impaired body. Susan Wendell (1996) convincingly demonstrates how the disabled body is often rejected in our contemporary cultural milieu that is so obsessed with images of the perfect body. Disabled bodies confront people with sickness, pain, and suffering that many would rather remain hidden. Our culture views sickness and pain as bothersome momentary problems to be ignored or quickly overcome, rather than integral elements of the human condition from which we can learn and grow.

Framing the Discussion

As a framework for our discussion of chronic conditions, we will be using a classification of illness narratives developed by Arthur Frank (1995) in *The Wounded Story Teller*. Frank describes three kinds of narrative that people can use when communicating their experience with illness or disability. The chaos narrative emphasizes the disruptions of illness and the loss of control over one's body. In many chronic illnesses, chaos is never far away and may occur at any time. The preceding paragraphs describe some of the personal and social chaos involved in chronic conditions. The restitution narrative, favored by medical discourse, focuses on diagnosis, treatment, and cure. It is told as a progressive sequence involving isolated individuals: "I am sick, I have treatment, and I get better." This narrative does not work well for chronic conditions because it tends to isolate people and sets up unrealistic expectations of recovery that often do not address ongoing issues of healing and renewal in one's everyday life.

In contrast to the restitution approach, Frank's (1995) quest narrative views illness and disability as a part of a person's life journey and as an opportunity for moral and spiritual development. The quest narrative is a moral and spiritual journey because it affects relations with others, shifting from egocentric self-pity to greater responsibility and care. Arthur Kleinman (1988), in *The Illness Narratives*, suggests that chronic illness or disability can make people more aware of the multiple forms of human distress and therefore more inclined to act in ways that acknowledge and reduce that distress.

A central question in the quest journey is: What does physical, moral, and spiritual healing mean when cure is unlikely? A chronic condition requires perpetual healing actively constructed by the person moment to moment, day to day. This kind of healing involves a transformation of the whole person, whose attitude toward life changes from despair and frustration to liveliness and peace in spite of the continuing presence of illness or disability. An important step in understanding how chronically ill or disabled people can cultivate a renewed self is to consider the spiritual and cultural nature of suffering and healing: to discover which myths, stories, or worldviews about suffering and healing help structure personal and cultural experiences of loss and renewal, pain and joy (Charmaz 1991; Kleinman 1988).

Disability studies scholars draw a distinction between a medical model approach and a social model approach to disability that echoes Frank's (1995) classification of illness narratives and provides the theoretical framework for our analysis. The medical model of disability parallels Frank's (1995) restitution narrative and understands the limitations that accompany disability and chronic conditions as something that is internally wrong with the individual body and searches for how the "wrong" can be fixed. The social model of disability is reminiscent of the quest narrative because it considers chronic disabling conditions within the broader cultural and religious milieu and taken-for-granted prejudicial attitudes directed toward bodies that do not fit the socially constructed and defined "normal" body (Goering 2002; Morris 2001). Rosemarie Garland-Thompson (2005) explains the difference between the social and medical models of disability as "...a cultural interpretation of human variation [social model] rather than an inherent inferiority, pathology to cure, or undesirable trait to eliminate [medical model]" (1558). Thus, similar to the quest narrative, the social model approach to disability seeks to affirm cultural constructions of suffering and healing that enable all people—those with and without chronic conditions—to enjoy the fullness of an abundant life.

Problematic Religious Responses to Chronic Illness and Disability

We share two vignettes from Darla Schumm's recent experiences that illustrate oppressive religious responses to chronic illness and disability. Darla is legally blind and the coauthor of this essay:
   Vignette 1:

I am lying comfortably on the cozy table in my acupuncturist's office. Mellow music is playing in the background while my acupuncturist soothingly talks me through the placement of needles for that morning's treatment. I am feeling very relaxed and at ease under the care of this wise woman as we chat casually about the different approaches between eastern and western medicine, when suddenly she sticks a metaphorical needle straight into the heart of my soul. In the same calm soothing tone she has been using all morning, she tells me that "according to Chinese religions, physical illness and disability are a result of mistakes made in a previous life; a disability is an indication of a lesson that one's spirit needs to learn."

Vignette 2:

Approximately a year prior to the morning in my acupuncturist's office, I am traveling with my guide dog, Papaya, and need to catch a connecting flight, in an airport whose name I can no longer remember. An airline employee is assisting me with the transfer and begins to discuss the unending bounties of Jesus' love. In what appears to be her characteristically upbeat and friendly tone, she states, "you know, Jesus heals all sins; if you just pray hard enough Jesus will take away all your sins and heal your blindness."

As these two vignettes demonstrate, people with chronic conditions carry not only some form of physical disability but also often a spiritual burden resulting from a religious and social milieu that is suspicious of their spiritual condition. There is a persistent insinuation that chronic illness and disability somehow involve merited suffering (i.e., lesson to learn or result of sin), and well-meaning people often struggle to offer religious explanations and religious solutions to the "problem." Such thinking regarding chronic illness and disability fits well into Frank's description of the restitution narrative, where religious explanations and solutions replace medical explanations and solutions. Restitution narratives, whether medical or religious, do not fit well with people who struggle with chronic conditions.

Based on the descriptive accounts highlighted above, several questions emerge that form the basis and structure of the rest of our chapter. First, why are chronic illness and disability often equated with merited suffering? Second, are the restitution narrative approaches offered in the two vignettes supported by core religious teachings in the relevant traditions? Third, what types of religious understanding can help cultivate moral and spiritual healing in the midst of chronic disability or illness?

Buddhism: Basic Worldview

In the first vignette, Darla's acupuncturist offered an explanation for disability from the perspective of Chinese religions. It must be noted that as Judith Berling (1997) observes in *A Pilgrim in Chinese Culture: Negotiating Religious Diversity*, Chinese religion generally reflects an intermingling of multiple traditions including Taoism, Confucianism, and Buddhism. While a westerner, Darla's acupuncturist embodies the pluralistic nature of Chinese religion. She relies primarily on Taoist teachings in her medical and acupuncture practice, but her explanation of why one might experience a chronic disability is solidly rooted in Buddhist understandings of suffering, healing, and karma. Thus, we focus first on the relevant elements discovered in a Buddhist worldview.

Buddhism teaches us that we live in an impermanent and interdependent world. All objects and people are dependent for their origination and flourishing upon other factors in perpetual transformation. The chapter that you are now reading is dependent upon the tree from which the paper originated, the logger who felled the tree, the word-processor on which the work was typed, the actions of the authors, the decision making of the publishers, and so on. All of these factors, of course, did not arise from nowhere, free from conditioning. The tree grew from a seed in the ground and was reliant on sunlight, rain, and mineral nutrients in the soil. The logger, author, and publishers are all reliant upon their biological parents for their existence, as were their parents before them. Buddhism sees all beings as mutually connected with one another in a great web of relational interdependence, rather than as isolated or separate selves. For the Buddhist, nothing stands alone and apart, self-defining and self-sufficient. All things support, condition, and are mutually dependent on each other (Aitken 1996). With the Buddhist teaching of interconnectedness, impermanence, and no isolated self in mind, we can now discuss suffering, healing, and karma and their relevance to chronic illness and disability. We will discover that the acupuncturist's comments are not supported by Buddhism.

Buddhist Teachings: Suffering, Healing, and Karma

Buddhism teaches that human life involves the Pali term *dukkha*, usually translated as suffering, dissatisfaction, or turmoil. Suffering is vaguely defined as "what is hard to bear," and includes innumerable conditions such as physical pain, psychological distress, and forms of social suffering such as racism, sexism, or poverty (Hallisey 1998: 37). Simply stated, Buddhism teaches that if you take birth as a human being, then pain and sorrow will be a part of the journey. People we love will die. Things we consider precious and ever-lasting will dissolve, rust, or fall away since impermanence and the inevitability of change are basic elements of the human condition (Rahula 1959).

Suffering is not unique to those who struggle with chronic disability or illness. The point is that even those who are physically healthy and materially wealthy nonetheless experience a chaotic, continually festering dissatisfaction. At the core of human personality is a free-floating anxiety that has no particular object but can be attached to any issue, problem, or condition. In Buddhism, the process of spiritual growth is often compared with the healing of illness. The most basic human illness is affiliated not with particular forms of disease or disability but with a false sense of being a separate self set apart from the world around us and the personal and collective chaos that results from a "thirst" for exclusive possession. Suffering, then, is characterized by selfish attachment—a craving and clutching for something permanent that we can cling to—health, life, wealth, or anything we associate exclusively with "me" or "mine." Spiritual growth, in its most basic Buddhist form, involves a quest for healing that frees people from a sense of isolation binding them to a world of selfish craving and the suffering that results.

Buddhism teaches that pain and turmoil are inevitable but that suffering and healing arise from our conditioned ideas or responses to the pain that we are given. For example, when the chronically ill or disabled crave and become attached to the idea of individual cure, so central to both medical and religious restitution narratives, they may find that such craving increases their suffering and sense of chaos while doing little to decrease their pain. Healing is not necessarily affiliated with the absence of illness or blindness. Indeed, such thinking implies that people with chronic conditions might never experience healing at all. Buddhism suggests that suffering decreases and healing increases when we let go of wanting things to be different from how they are and instead move toward an acceptance of what is available in the present moment. Every situation is a mixture of health and illness, so that even within physical distress a healthy process is occurring. Our perspectives of ourselves and others need not operate from an emphasis on deficits, problems, and weaknesses. The teaching that people have no permanent self means that people are always capable of multidimensional growth and transformation, and should be respected accordingly, rather than dismissed as unhealthy by saying, for example, "Oh, she's blind or she's a cripple."

All human life is marked by pain and joy, sorrow and happiness, and these divergent human experiences are intermingled. The medical system, and the correlative restitution narrative, is driven by a thirst for diagnosis that, generally speaking, says, "There can be no treatment or cure until we diagnose what is wrong with you." The process of labeling someone by what is individually wrong with him or her is intrinsic to the medical system and tends to cultivate personal feelings of deficiency resulting in questions such as "why me?" or "what did I do to deserve this?" And if the restitution narrative is granted a religious legitimacy, then people may feel that they are spiritually defective because of the physical difficulty that they experience. This attitude is manifest in the acupuncturist's and airline employee's response to Darla's blindness. The conditioned idea that illness or blindness is symptomatic of individual spiritual deficiency may be as traumatic, or more traumatic, as the chronic condition itself. Buddhism teaches that "why me?" questions serve to isolate people, which is not conducive to spiritual development and healing but is conducive to selfish attachment and increased suffering.

Buddhism recognizes that being impatient or angry at pain, illness, or disability does not cultivate healing. On the contrary, it adds a little more to one's troubles, and aggravates and exacerbates a situation already disagreeable. Buddhism teaches that hatred, anger, and greed, often referred to as the three poisons, inevitably result in increased human suffering. These poisons do not have physical bodies, but reside in people's minds and cultivate chaos from within. To minimize suffering, these three need to be turned into their healing counterparts: greed into generosity, anger into loving-kindness, and hatred into wisdom. This process is central to the spiritual quest for healing and the cultivation of compassion in Buddhism.

The teaching that no distinct or permanent self exists within a person supports the quest for healing and compassion in several ways. While it does not itself support a positive regard for persons as unique creatures created in the image of God, as do Judaism, Christianity, and Islam, it works in other ways. Most important for our purposes, it challenges selfish attachment by emphasizing that all people are compounds of interconnected factors. In particular, it means that "your" suffering/healing and "my" suffering/healing are not inherently different. Suffering and healing do not really belong to anyone. In his classic description of the *bodhisattva* or compassionate path, the medieval Indian monk Shantideva expresses this line of thinking as follows:

> I should eliminate the suffering of others because it is suffering, just like my own suffering. I should take care of others because they are sentient beings, just as I am a sentient being. When happiness is equally dear to others and myself, then what is so special about me that I strive after happiness for myself alone. (Shantideva 1997: 101)

The crucial importance of the *bodhisattva* quest in Buddhism is that one helps to heal oneself by helping to heal others. The spiritual value of this choice lies in its active involvement in society, in the notion that other people are an extension of one's own existence, and in a willingness to find personal healing in the struggle against spiritual and material suffering in general. Buddhism teaches that healing is not an individual but a relational and interdependent process.

These basic Buddhist teachings of interdependence, impermanence, no-separate-self, and *bodhisattva* practice to cultivate compassion are critical elements in understanding the karmic law of cause and effect. The word karma literally means action. All of our actions are conditioned (causality) and have consequences (effects). Karma is seen as a law inherent in the nature of things, like a law of physics. It is not operated by a God or judge. Therefore, physical health or illness is not seen as a karmic reward or punishment, but as simply the natural results of a multiplicity of interconnected actions. Buddhism teaches that individual lives, including issues of chronic disability and illness, are intimately linked to other human beings, to society, to prior generations, and to the natural environment (Nakasone 1990).

Tracing the genealogy of illness and disability is a good exercise in recognizing how all things are mutually conditioned and interdependent. Some illness and disability, such as heart disease and several forms of blindness, are conditioned, in part, by a genetic propensity or predisposition inherited from one's biological parents and even prior generations involving grandparents. Other forms of illness, such as AIDS or the flu, are conditioned, in part, by a disease-causing agent such as a virus that can be acquired by person-to-person contact. Other forms of illness and disability are conditioned, in part, by environmental poisons or toxins. A child born with congenital defects because their farm worker parents were exposed to high levels of pesticides is one such example. Illness and disability, like all things, do not exist in a vacuum, but are mutually conditioned by innumerable causes and conditions. Indeed, no one can fully account for the entire web of karmic causality. An answer to the specific "why me" eludes us. Scientists agree, and the human genome project bears out, that most chronic conditions have both environmental and biological causality.

An all-pervasive interdependence is part of the karmic law of cause and effect, which directs us toward admitting the impossibility of disassociating self from relationship with and responsibility for other people and the broader phenomenal world. Human beings are a small part of a complex ever-changing web of causality where all things are irrevocably intertwined. There is no separate medical or spiritual pathology that individuals can simply discover, diagnose, treat, and eradicate in oblivious independent isolation. The focus on individualistic causes and cures, so central to both medical and religious restitution narratives, is itself recognized as the primary pathology in the Buddhist quest for healing self through healing others.

Christianity: Sin, Suffering, and Healing

Darla's airport assistant joyfully informs her that "...if you just pray hard enough Jesus will take away all your sins and heal your blindness." This statement appears to be firmly grounded in the religious restitution narrative wherein blindness is associated with sin and not simply sin in general but the specific sinfulness of Darla as the blind individual. Robert Orsi (2005) documents the pervasive Christian suspicion that sickness is somehow merited by sin and that a first step toward healing is the recognition of one's own guilt. We will argue that associating disability or illness with individual sin functions to marginalize people and to distort Christian community grounded in mutual support and hospitality. In Christianity, as in Buddhism, healing is not marked by the absence of physical turmoil, but by the presence of resiliency and the quest to perform embodied acts of loving kindness in the midst of human neediness and vulnerability.

Biblical scholar Daniel Simundson (2001) traces the pervasive Christian understanding of suffering as a result of human sin to particular interpretations of the Hebrew Bible. Many Christians believe that God intended that the world be "good," but the original sin of Adam and Eve in the Garden of Eden introduces both sin and suffering as chronic universal elements of the human condition. Sin and suffering become the perennial symbols of chaos in Christian anthropology. Simundson argues that the universal elements of sin shift to a more particular orientation when the Hebrew prophets connect the collective actions of Israel with reward and punishment from God. Israel engages in the collective sin of idolatry, and God, in turn, causes or allows them to suffer temple destruction and exile or, the reverse scenario, Israel is faithful to their covenant with God and God, in turn, rewards and protects them from suffering. Simundson notes an additional Biblical shift away from collective sin and suffering and toward individual sin and suffering in the worldview of the friends of Job. Job's friends argue that a good God would not allow such horrible individual suffering unless Job had done something sinful to deserve the suffering. Thus, we see the progression in the Hebrew scriptures from understanding suffering as a chronic element of the human condition, to suffering as a result of the collective sin of a particular group, to suffering as a result of individual sin enacted and endured by one particular person (Simundson 2001).

The connections between sin and suffering in general and between sin and disability in particular can also be presented in the teachings of

Jesus according to some interpretations of the Gospel of John (Koosed and Schumm 2005). For example, in the story of the healing of the blind man, Jesus's disciples ask him "Who has sinned to make this man born blind?" (John 9: 2, NRSV). While in this particular story Jesus's response indicates that there is no connection between the disability and sin, in the story of the healing of the paralytic man Jesus does seem to link sin with disability by his statement: "See, you are well! Sin no more, that nothing worse befall you" (John 5: 14, NRSV). Thus, we see limited evidence in the Biblical responses to suffering that can explain why Darla's airport assistant and other contemporary Christians might equate a disabling condition with individual and/or collective sin.

Sin can be discussed in personal, collective, and universal terms, or some combination thereof, but the Christian tradition generally agrees that all people, not just chronically ill or disabled people, are beset by sin. Sin levels the playing field in this context. Simply stated, all people are challenged, corrupted, and needy. We are all vulnerable to disease, disability, and pain in ways that are beyond our self-control, and we are all on a quest to find healing and renewal in our lives. A powerful temptation is to hoard material possessions until we attain a level of security that makes us feel safe or well. The temptation is fed by the illusion that it is possible to become so self-sufficient that we somehow free ourselves from the vulnerability of disease and pain. In an interview, Rebecca Green (2006), a public health nurse who lives with Crohn's disease, discusses how the physical vulnerability associated with chronic illness helps to free people from the illusion of self-sufficiency by connecting the sacrificial love of Jesus with a willingness to accept comfort:

> It is hard for Christians (and harder for non-Christians) to understand and accept the sacrificial love of Jesus. But it is a love that is better understood by those whose condition requires them to accept the comfort of others. Those of us with chronic illness are truly blessed to have the opportunity to comfort those who love us, by allowing them to care for us.

Rebecca Green (2006) reflects further on Jesus and comfort:

> There are few instances in which Jesus is comforted. Most people wanted to be healed or comforted by him. In the few examples when comfort is offered to Jesus, he accepts graciously. When a woman approached him, cleaning his feet with expensive oils and her hair, Jesus berated his disciples for criticizing her; he was gracious and accepting of her lavish attention.

These comments recognize that pain and vulnerability can neither be escaped nor ignored, but they can lead to an increased availability to accept comfort and care from others. Chronic physical conditions may help people to recognize the limits of measuring self-worth in terms of independence and the abundance of discovering self-worth in terms of relational dependency (Charmaz 1983). Human beings are never free from vulnerability and a need for mutual support and guidance. Learning to welcome comfort or aid is a primary form of healing and renewal in human relationships. The quest for individual cause and cure, so central to the medical and religious restitution narratives, makes little sense in the context of relational dependency. Indeed, our cultural quest for self-sufficiency functions to block our capacity to receive spiritual empowerment from God and other people. Rebecca's comments help Christians to view the church, and humanity, as a whole, as a chronically disabled community where God is present in the midst of vulnerability, dependency, and the relational comfort and healing that results.

By recognizing their own vulnerability and need to receive healing and comfort from others, the chronically ill and disabled also become aware of the importance of responding to human neediness by opening out toward others in self-giving love. The Christian tradition is grounded in the story of how Jesus lived out a self-giving love under concrete conditions of vulnerability and suffering. While Jesus is often thought to be without sin, he nonetheless suffered dreadful pain, isolation, betrayal, abandonment, and death, but his identity with self-giving love and healing was not diminished. The perpetual vulnerability associated with chronic disability and illness can make people more aware of other people's suffering and vulnerability and therefore more inclined to act in self-giving ways that help reduce that suffering: to openly take responsibility for each other.

There is a reciprocal relational pattern that becomes evident in the nature of healing. The Christian and Buddhist emphasis on healing the self through comforting others becomes balanced by the reciprocal notion of healing self by allowing others to comfort you. Our inability to accept comfort from others will hinder our ability to comfort others. Perhaps this is part of the wisdom inherent in Jesus's appeal to treat others as you would want to be treated. In this context, sin is that which blocks this fundamental relational reciprocity, that which responds to vulnerability with indifference and hardness of heart rather than hospitality and availability to welcome comfort.

Buddhism and Christianity: From Theodicy Explanation to Compassionate Response

In Christian thought, the classic academic explanation for human suffering (and its conceptual sibling, evil) is known as "theodicy" and treats suffering as a problem because it creates a theological dilemma that goes something like this: If God is all good and powerful, then why is there suffering and evil in the world? In this theological context, the problem of suffering is a why question. In Buddhism, however, suffering is a problem in and of itself, and as such, it seems too obvious even to ask why it is a problem. Why questions are particularly problematic in many cases involving chronic illness. No one knows why the immune system attacks itself in autoimmune diseases, for example. In chronic illness, the primary question is: How do people live full lives in spite of chronic suffering and difficulty—not why does God allow people to suffer in the first place?

Theodicy is obsessed with the diagnosis element of the restitution narrative, the medical and spiritual why of chronic illness and disability. Christian theologian Dorothee Soelle (1980) argues that Jesus's life and ministry does not seek to explain human suffering but does provide an example of how to live an abundant life in the midst of human vulnerability. Indeed, God takes the risk of being misunderstood and unrecognized in the incarnation because Jesus was not the kind of God that was desired and expected: God the all-powerful and sovereign King. It is not power and control but a notion of God's vulnerability that is at the heart of the incarnation. Jesus does not act as an independent self-sufficient agent who eradicates human vulnerability and suffering but instead uses human vulnerability and suffering to seek companionship, friendship, hospitality, healing, and comfort in concrete relationship with human beings. Jesus invites the Christian community to experience God's spirit and God's grace in concrete acts of loving kindness in the midst of human vulnerability and suffering.

Illness and disability are very productive images for reflecting on suffering and vulnerability because our thoughts almost automatically turn to issues of nurture and comfort. Healing and care for the sick were integral parts of both Jesus's ministry and of the early Buddhist community. In the case of Buddhism, the model for care giving is the Buddha himself. On an occasion, the Buddha chanced on a sick, unattended monk wallowing in his own excrement. "O monks, if you do not nurse one another, whoever will nurse you?" Thereupon the Buddha bathed the monk, changed his garments, and laid a bed for his ailing comrade.

This experience led the Buddha to declare, "Anyone who wishes to make offerings to me let him make offerings to the sick" (Demieville 1983: 32; Ratnapala 1993: 99–100). This story demonstrates how Buddhism does not focus on speculative explanations but on compassionate response to human vulnerability in the present moment.

Christian discipleship is also grounded in practical loving-kindness rather than a theoretical response to suffering. Jesus modeled what Christians are to do in response to human neediness: "I was hungry and you gave me something to eat, I was a stranger and you invited me in, I was sick and you looked after me" (Matt. 25: 35–36, NRSV). Jesus states that when you feed the hungry, clothe the naked, visit the prisoner, and care for the sick "you do it to me" (Matt. 25: 40, NRSV). Concrete acts of hospitality and care are recognized as embodied works of the spirit, embodied works of the *Basileia* or Kingdom of god in the midst of human healing (Luke 17: 21, NRSV; Matt. 12: 28, NRSV).

Dorothee Soelle (2001), inspired by the life and practices of Christian mystic Meister Eckhart (1260–1329), affirms a faith grounded in the acceptance that God's love and activity cannot be captured by theodicy explanation. Religious explanations for human suffering mirror the restitution narrative and its pitfalls for those who live with chronic affiliations. For Soelle, Christian faith is never an isolating individual affair but recognizes divine healing in the midst of human healing and thus is grounded in the quest for human relational dependency. Soelle (2001) articulates a Christian faith grounded in the realization that tomorrow may or may not bring new medical treatment and cure but that the Kingdom of God is available nevertheless through concrete acts of loving-kindness experienced in the present moment. Rebecca Green (2006) says something similar when she states:

> An emphasis on hope for the future, for many with chronic illness, may result in disappointment and loss of faith when the longed-for relief (or miracle) doesn't materialize. If instead we could foster the skills of prayer and worship as physical tools for ameliorating suffering; if we could prioritize the practice of comforting one another; if we could transform the selfish aspects of suffering into compassion for fellow sufferers and opportunities for those who comfort us, then perhaps Christians might better understand the present availability of the Kingdom of God.

The ongoing faith quest involves discovering God's beauty and pathos in all areas of life, including chronic disability and illness, and perceives sacred reality pervading everyday reality.

A Buddhist parable says:

> If you take a tablespoon full of salt and put it into a glass of water and stir it and drink it, the water will taste quite bitter because of the salt. But if you take the same tablespoon of salt and stir it into a large, clear, pure mountain lake and then take a handful of water and drink it, you won't taste the salt at all. (Wolin 1999: 126)

One point of the parable is that the suffering is not caused by the salt but by the smallness and separation of the container. Both Christian faith and Buddhist practice can strengthen resiliency in the midst of chronic struggle by helping to make the container larger, so that we can more fully share in the joy and sorrow that life brings. Welcoming care from others and responding to the vulnerability of others comes easily to a person who no longer sees separation between self and other (Buddhism); concrete acts of loving kindness and God's Kingdom (Christianity). The overcoming of separation or the expansion of the container is at the same time the realization of reciprocal dependency and compassion.

Conclusion

As Darla's acupuncturist and airport assistant revealed, both Buddhist and Christian religious practitioners sometimes associate chronic illness and disability with merited suffering resulting from individual sin. We have argued, however, that while these are often popular perceptions, they are misrepresentations of what Buddhism and Christianity actually teach about the nature of suffering and the quest for healing. The idea that illness or blindness is systematic of individual spiritual deficiency tends to increase the suffering, chaos, and isolation of those who struggle with chronic illness and disability. Both religious traditions locate a powerful source for spiritual and human healing in the recognition of and quest for human relational dependency.

To maintain a resilient faith despite ongoing struggle displays appreciation for the inherent value and meaning of life, an assurance that transcends health or illness. Neither the Buddhist nor Christian religious quest requires individual diagnosis, treatment, and cure to sustain itself. Both traditions are able to evoke deep love and joy for all that life brings, whether health or illness, without thirsting for theodicy explanation or restitution remedy. Indeed, Christian faith has much in common with the Buddhist perspective that healing is not something one works for in the future as distinct from grateful thoughts and compassionate actions in the present.

Note

1. This chapter was previously published in 2007 in *The Journal of Religion, Disability and Health 11*(3), 5–21, and is reprinted here with permission.

References

Aitken, R. (1996). The dragon who never sleeps. In A. Kotler (Ed.), *The Engaged Buddhist Reader*. Berkeley, CA: Parallax Press.
Berling, J. (1997). *A Pilgrim in Chinese Culture: Negotiating Religious Diversity*. New York, NY: Orbis Books.
Charmaz, K. (1983). Loss of self: A fundamental form of suffering in the chronically ill. *Sociology of Health and Illness 5*(2), 168–195.
Charmaz, K. (1991) *Good Days, Bad Days: The Self in Chronic Illness and in Time*. New Brunswick, NJ: Rutgers University Press.
Demieville, P. (1983). *Buddhism and Healing*. Lanham, MD: University Press of America.
Frank, A. (1995). *The Wounded Story Teller: Body, Illness, and Ethics*. Chicago, IL: University of Chicago Press.
Garland-Thomson, R. (2005). Feminist disability studies. *Signs: Journal of Women in Culture and Society 30*(2), 1558–1587.
Goering, S. (2002). Beyond the medical model? Disability, formal justice, and the exception for the profoundly impaired. *Kennedy Institute of Ethics Journal 12*(4), 373–388.
Green, R. (2006). Unpublished Interviews: 8-30-06 and 9-4-06.
Hallisey, C. (1998). Buddhism. In Jacob Neusner (Ed.), *Evil and Suffering* (pp. 36–66). Cleveland, OH: Pilgrim Press.
Harris, P. (1995). Who am I? Concepts of disability and their implications for people with learning difficulties. *Disability and Society 10*, 341–351.
Kleinman, A. (1988). *The Illness Narratives*. New York, NY: Basic Books.
Koosed, J. L., & Schumm, D. Y. (2005). Out of the darkness: Examining the rhetoric of blindness in the gospel of John. *Disability Studies Quarterly 25*(1). Retrieved from http://www.dsq-sds.org/index.
Morris, J. (2001). Impairment and disability: Constructing an ethics of care that promotes human rights. *Hypatia 16*(4), 1–16. Nakasone, R. (1990). *The Ethics of Enlightenment: Sermons and Essays in Search of a Buddhist Ethic*. Fremont, CA: Dharma Cloud Publishers.
Orsi, R. (2005). *Between Heaven and Earth: The Religious Worlds People Make and the Scholars Who Study Them*. Princeton, NJ: Princeton University Press.
Rahula, W. (1959). *What the Buddha Taught*. New York, NY: Grove Weidenfeld.
Ratnapala, N. (1993). *Buddhist Sociology*. Delhi, India: Sri Satguru Publications.

Shantideva. (1997). *A Guide to the Bodhisattva Way of Life*. New York, NY: Snow London.

Sidell, N. L. (1997). Adult adjustment to chronic illness: A review of the literature. *Health & Social Work 22*, 5–11.

Simundson, D. J. (2001). *Faith under Fire: How the Bible Speaks to Us in Times of Suffering*. Lima, OH: Academic Renewal Press.

Soelle, D. (1980). *Beyond Mere Obedience*. Minneapolis, MN: Augsburg Press.

Soelle, D. (2001). *The Silent Cry: Mysticism and Resistance*. Minneapolis, MN: Fortress Press.

Stone, S. D. (1995). The myth of bodily perfection. *Disability and Society 10*, 413–424.

Wendell, S. (1996). *The Rejected Body: Feminist Philosophical Reflections on Disability*. New York, NY: Routledge.

Wolin, S. (1999). Three spiritual perspectives on resilience. In F. Walsh (Ed.), *Spiritual Resources in Family Therapy*. New York, NY: Gilford Press.

CHAPTER 9

Disability, Agency, and Engagement: Three Wisdom Traditions' Call to Be Radically Available

Lynne M. Bejoian, Molly Quinn, and
Maysaa S. Bazna

Introduction

We have come together as colleagues, educators whose spiritual perspectives are essential and enduring determinants and lenses from
which we engage in the world, personally and professionally. We
use the term "wisdom traditions" in referencing our three distinctive spiritual traditions—Buddhism, Christianity, and Islam—in
line with Huston Smith's (1991) interpretation that emphasizes the
value and practices of these religions, among others, as essential to
the human pursuit and attainment of wisdom, along with this assertion that these wisdom traditions powerfully influence thought and
practice.

Why Consider Availability to "The Other"?

Our purpose in raising the issue of availability is to explore the concept
within our specific tradition, not for comparison, per se, but rather
for our own critical inquiry and self-reflection. Through our examination, we endeavor to deepen our understanding of our own tradition's
conception of the other and to expand dialogue around a common call
to the other through practice—social and spiritual. Thomas Merton

(1960) posits:

> Our pilgrimage is more than the synthetic happy-making of a vacation cruise. Our journey is from the limitations and routines of "the given"...to the creative freedom of that love which is personal choice and commitment. Paradise symbolizes this freedom and creativity, but in reality this must be worked out in *the human and personal encounter with the stranger seen as our other self* [italics added]. (Merton 1960: 111)

Merton, a revered Catholic monk and prolific writer on issues of contemporary life and spiritual practice, is known for embracing both eastern and western spiritual traditions, affirming the beauty and mystery that they share. He contends that one's spiritual path is intricately and immeasurably framed by the idea and presence of availability to others, whether walked in solitude, relationship, or community. Here we embark on our own distinctive "scriptural journey" to consider and thereby uncover our personal readings of our distinctive traditions and explore together possible shared understandings of the other among them.

Buddhism, Christianity, and Islam are united in placing the responsibility of rectifying the inequitable experience of the other as other on the shoulder of society and those within that society. Thus, these three wisdom traditions share recognition of the experience of the other and of the social imperative to improve his or her condition and status. However, recognition is not sufficient: scriptures in all three traditions support the imperative of action. Thus, agency[1] is posited as an essential aspect of our humanness, with respect to the community as well as the individual, involving the affirmation of social responsibility and call to social action on behalf of all others. Our part is to be in the world, responsible to and for others, transforming ourselves, others, and the world, in the way of uplifting all of humanity.

Finding our experiences of the academy not always comfortable— at best, nonsupportive, and at worst, dismissive of our holding, and expressing our spiritual beliefs as essential to learning, living, and teaching—we have embarked on a shared exploration to provide collegial support as well as generate discussion around how our distinctive spiritual perspectives influence and infuse our scholarship and lives. As a result, in undertaking this project, we have brought our spiritual positionalities into greater focus. As we investigate our three spiritual perspectives, shared values and beliefs about disability, engagement, and agency emerge, as well. By focusing on similarities, we do not intend to ignore the distinctions within each tradition or the diversity across traditions; however, here our consideration principally lies in uncovering the possibility of commonalities and connections among our traditions.[2]

Why Disability Studies?

As educators committed to the philosophy, study, and enactment of inclusion, we have found that Disability Studies provides a critical lens by which to view social, cultural, and political practices and perspectives that create, construct, and reify disability (Charlton 1998; Kudlick 2003; Linton 1998). Disability Studies is capitalized to denote a specific theoretical perspective that challenges traditional medicalized deficit-based assumptions about disability (Davis, 1997; Pfeiffer 2003). The idea of the other within a Disability Studies perspective explores the experience of "othering" that occurs within the context of sociocultural-political marginalization and stigmatization based on assumptions of normalcy and ability. Rosemarie Garland-Thomson (1997) explains the concept of the other drawing from Aristotlian philosophy: "The source of all otherness is the concept of a norm, a 'generic type' against which all physical variation appears as difference, derivative, inferior, and insufficient" (Garland-Thomson 1997: 20).

Our Process

Our scriptural examination of the other entails using our three respective wisdom traditions to determine what might be the ways our traditions discuss and address this "disabled other." The value of using a spiritual perspective in this focus on the other is that it provides a context to think through and go beyond conventional constructs, to imagine different possibilities for living together. Also, taking such a perspective can address the ethical and moral questions central to our own profession and scholarship.

Through our process of exploration we uncover similar themes, although we take different approaches in exploring and discussing the concepts within our specific spiritual contexts. For the section on Buddhism, since the basis of all Mahayana texts is the concept of the self and the other, it was necessary for this process of scriptural inquiry to involve selecting those texts of personal resonance that could exemplify practice and thought around the idea of the other and disability. Similarly, concerning the Christian address of the question—while a systematic search of the scriptures aimed at uncovering its conception of the other in relation to disability, and ethical call concerning this other,[3] was undertaken—an emphasis was placed upon the teachings of Jesus as presented in the New Testament scriptures. For the Islamic section, the Qur'an was searched for references to such terms as *blind, mute, deaf, lame, weak, orphan, destitute/needy*, and *wayfarer*. The attempt to understand the intent of these terms was made by examining the roots of the Arabic words and investigating their possible synonyms, cross-referencing the Qur'anic verses containing the same terms, and confirming the meaning with the teachings of Prophet Mohammad (Hadith).[4]

We acknowledge that our work is the result of our own interpretations, undertaken as personal pursuits in the hopes of reconsidering our scholarship within our spiritual contexts. Therefore, this is meant neither to speak to the work of religious scholars nor to speak for our specific traditions. We consider ourselves students of the texts. In addition, our collaborative process involved impassioned conversations around issues including, but not limited to, the purpose of the piece, the social context of religion, and the role of the spiritual in life. Intent to create neither a monologic voice on our wisdom traditions nor on others defined by disability, we endeavor to present a rich tapestry that shows the beauty and extent of our diversity and our difference—even as we seek points of shared understanding. Accordingly, emphasizing and preserving our individual processes of exploration and the richness of our own spiritual perspectives, we have approached and written our specific sections each through our own "voice" and style. Consequently, Lynne Bejoian considers Buddhism, Molly Quinn explores Christianity, and Maysaa Bazna elucidates Islam.

An Examination of Disability and the Other through Three Wisdom Traditions

Exchanging Self for Others: Buddhist Perspective and Practice

Understanding the concept of the other within a Buddhist context is best achieved through an understanding of Mahayana Buddhist perspective. Tsongkhapa (2004) explains:

> The Mahayana is the origin of all the good of self and others, the medicine that alleviates all troubles; the great path traveled by all knowledgeable persons; nourishment for all beings who see, hear, remember, and come into contact with it; and that which has the great skill-in-means

that engages you in others' welfare and thereby indirectly achieves your own welfare in its entirety. (Tsongkhapa 2004: 15)

Then within the Mahayana path there are specific practices that place the other as "object." Justifiably all the Buddha's teachings could be considered mind training. However:

[in] this special usage, mind training refers to specific approaches for cultivating the altruistic awakening mind, especially through the practice of equalizing and exchanging of self and others as found in Śāntideva's eighth-century classic, A Guide to the Bodhisattva's Way of Life. When used in this sense, the term mind training represents an abbreviation of the fuller expression "mind training in the Mahayana (Great Vehicle)" or "Mahayana mind training." (Jinpa 2005: 2)

Mahayana Buddhist paths are focused on achieving this spiritual goal for the sake of all sentient beings— without distinction, and the manner in which this is done is through the practice of wisdom and compassion that must be imbued with the intentional motivation to benefit all beings regardless of status, condition, and relationship. Also known as the bodhisattva path, the fundamental idea is to reframe the human view of self and others. Basically what is required is shifting one's habitual way of thinking of only of oneself (self-cherishment) to thinking of others (cherishing others). This self-cherishment is held dear to us at the cost of others' welfare. As Śāntideva[5] states:

Whatever joy there is in this world, All comes from desiring others to be happy, And whatever suffering there is in this world, All comes from desiring myself to be happy. (Shantideva 1979: 110)

Training the mind, or as it is called in Tibetan lojong, is the "field of practice" (Tharchin 1999: 5) for achieving this goal: the development of "the spirit of enlightenment" (Tsongkhapa 2004) also known as "the spirit of awakening" (Wallace 2005a,b). There are two main aspects to lojong practice. They are dakshennyamje, or "Equalizing and Exchanging Self and Others," and tonglen, or "Giving and Taking."

Dakshennyamje is actually a compound noun that refers to two stages of practice. The first, dakshennyampa, means to practice thinking of oneself and all beings as the same in the sense of equally wanting happiness and not wanting suffering. The second, dakshenjewa, means to exchange position with others, or to shift the mind's focus from concern for oneself to concern for other beings. (Tharchin 1999: 5)

Thus, all beings, including oneself, share the basic desire for happiness and need to eliminate suffering.[6] All others should be prized and cared about in a precious and loving manner. The steps involved in the equalizing and exchanging of self and others requires one to begin with developing equanimity lojong, a style that embodies "down-to-earth practicality" (Jinpa 2005: 1). In Sāntideva's treatise *Bodhicaryavatara (A Guide to the Bodhisattva's Way of Life)* (1997), the call to action is to aid all beings who are in need of happiness and handicapped due to the human condition that is suffering. "He satisfies with all joys those who are starving for happiness and eliminates all the sorrows of those who are afflicted in many ways" (Sāntideva 1997: 21). Thus, there is no distinction derived between self and other, "although there might be a great diversity and multiplicity but all of them are equal, are one in sharing the fundamental aspiration to be happy and overcome suffering" (*Lama Yeshe wisdom archive* 1999).

What does this perspective imply regarding people with disabilities? Acknowledgment must be made that there are beings that have physical and mental afflictions; however, the distinction involves the experience of suffering. The experience of disability does not necessarily equal suffering, since it is the experience of all beings in *samsara* that is the nature of one's suffering. His Holiness the Fourteenth Dalai Lama is quick to acknowledge "the special case of relating to people who are socially marginalized, perhaps because of their behavior, their appearance, their destitution, or on account of some illness" (Gyatso 2000: 121). Thus, the status and experience of a person is seen as a consequence of social marginalization based on attitudes. Character, not disability, is the determining factor. Serving others can occur regardless of ability and one's "ability" does not limit one's ability to serve and travel the path. Anyone can use whatever abilities he or she possesses to help others. Personal action and responsibility are essential to "develop a genuine sense of connection" (Gyatso 2000: 67) to all others regardless of status, appearance, or ability.

Therefore, the basic tenet is that all beings have the same aspiration for happiness and avoidance of suffering. Giving equal opportunity to this "aspiration" is essential:

Hence I should dispel the misery of others,

> Because it is suffering, just like my own,
> And I should benefit others
> Because they are sentient beings, just like myself. When both
>   myself and others
> Are similar in that we wish to be happy,

What is so special about me?
Why do I strive for my happiness alone?
And when both myself and others
Are similar in that we do not wish to suffer,
What so special about me?
Why do I protect myself and not others? (Shantideva 1979: 104–105)

The basis of spiritual practice is rooted in seeing clearly that all sentient beings exist as an interconnected web of relationship; seeing in this way develops compassion, not pity:

> When we talk of cultivating the thought of holding others as supremely dear, it is important to understand that we are not cultivating the kind of pity that we sometimes feel towards someone who is less fortunate than ourselves. With pity, there can be a tendency to look down upon the object of our compassion, and to feel a sense of superiority. (Gyatso 2000: 116)

The concept of pity, as is often considered to be implicit in traditional "care-taking," charity, and helping models, is transformed. Cherishing others is not about pity or charity: "help others and make them happy. We should offer whatever good and useful things we have to all" (Tharchin 1998: 85). Helping is undertaken without reservation or distinction. All beings regardless of status (including disability) are valuable and necessary to one's spiritual development. There are neither implicit nor explicit hierarchies. Viewing others devoid of prejudice and pity is a principle upheld throughout Sāntideva's treatise (1997). Respect and equanimity, not pity, are essential. Since Buddhism accepts that all beings suffer from change—we are born, we age, we get sick, and we die—there is the understanding that every being will become disabled; disability is a natural element of human experience. In addition, because of this perspective, distinctions between statuses based on ability/disability are irrelevant. Ability and disability, like the Buddha, take many forms, and so "the best thing to do is to respect everyone all the time" (Tharchin 1998: 44).

Broken, Blessed, and Beloved:
The Christian Call to be Bread for One Another

And he took bread, and gave thanks, and brake it, and gave unto them, saying, This is my body which is given for you: this do in remembrance of me.

(Luke 22: 19, *The Holy Bible*, King James Version, 1985)

...Come, ye blessed of my Father...For I was an hungred, and ye gave
me meat: I was thirsty, and ye gave me drink: I was a stranger, and ye
took me in: Naked, and ye clothed me: I was sick, and ye visited me: I
was in prison, and ye came unto me. (Matt. 25: 34–36)

Ancient and contemporary notions of Christian hospitality (Bolchazy
1995; Derrida 1997/2000; Oden 2001; Sutherland 2006; Westfield
2001) both come with the call to welcome the stranger, to provide sustenance and nourishment for the other in our midst. The two scriptural
passages cited above juxtapose portrayals of Jesus as both the bread of
life, given for the other, and as the disabled other, in need of the bread
of kindness and hospitality. Christian discipleship is rooted in the recognition that the stranger is no one other than ourselves. I and the
other, with Jesus, are one.

The apostle Paul writes that "all have sinned and come short of
the Glory of God" (Rom. 3: 23). This view inherently embraces an
emphasis that all people are disadvantaged and disabled and in need
of help. Objections may certainly be raised here in terms of associating sin with disability. In fact, the view that disability or disadvantage is a result of, or reflects a consequence of, sin was commonly held
during Jesus's time, and as such was critiqued by him throughout
his ministry of healing. Alas, this view is, however, still embraced
by some within various strands of Christian thought and practice,
reinforcing a contemporary cultural and societal view of persons with
disability that is dehumanizing, antithetical, in fact, to the vision of
Jesus or Paul.

The point that we are raising is not to equate disability with sin, but
rather to acknowledge the human condition that we all share, the constitutive vulnerability and fragility of our humanness. The sinful human
condition beseeches Christians to give and receive hospitality without
grudging (Rom. 12: 13, 1 Pet. 4: 9, Heb. 13: 2, 2 Cor. 9: 7, Titus 1: 8).
Sin can be viewed as the great equalizer where none are superior and
none inferior.

In addition, there is the praxis of Jesus whose whole life and ministry was oriented around serving others, specifically the disadvantaged,
those deemed least in the eyes of the world:

The Spirit of the Lord is upon me, because he hath anointed me to preach
the gospel to the poor; he hath sent me to heal the brokenhearted, to
preach deliverance to the captives, and recovering of sight to the blind,
to set at liberty them that are bruised...(Luke 14: 18)

The gospels set forth the testimony of Jesus's life as oriented toward hospitality to those who are disabled via stories in which the lame walk, lepers are cleansed, blind see, and the deaf hear. As bread, Jesus literally feeds, from a few loaves and fishes, the multitude of 5,000 (Matt. 14: 13–21, Mark 6: 31–44, Luke 9 :11–17, John 6: 1–13); as drink, he transforms water into wine for the wedding feast (John 2: 1–10). The way of Jesus that we are asked as his followers to take is the way of liberation, healing, blessing, fulfillment, discovered in service to others and in allowing others to serve us. We all are in need of hospitality and care.

In a discussion concerning the greatest commandments of God, when the call to "Love thy neighbor as thyself" from the Hebrew Bible (Lev. 19: 18, Luke 10: 25–28) is reaffirmed in the New Testament, Jesus is asked who is my neighbor? Jesus responds by sharing the story (Luke 10: 29–37) of a man traveling from Jerusalem to Jericho who fell among thieves, and was stripped, wounded, and left for dead. First, a priest sees and passes on the other side; next, a Levite comes upon him and passes by; finally, when a Samaritan comes upon the tragic scene, he attends to the injured man, binds his wounds, sets him on his own beast, and brings him to an inn. Beyond this, Jesus reports that when the time came that the Samaritan must depart, he took out two pence that he gave to the inn's host to take care of the man, instructing the host to bill him for all required. "Who, then, was neighbor unto him that fell among the thieves?" Jesus asks. The answer is simply "The Good Samaritan," the person who showed mercy and acted with kindness. What kind of story is it in which a Samaritan, typically viewed as impure, can be the hero of the story and a Pharisee or Levite, typically viewed as pure, can be pronounced as wanting? Perhaps it is the story of the compassion and grace of God unhindered by conventional beliefs and interpretations of ability and disability.

It is this kind of critique and call to action that Obery Hendricks Jr. (2006), in *The Politics of Jesus: Rediscovering the True Revolutionary Nature of the Teachings of Jesus and How They Have Been Corrupted*, points to as the heart of Jesus's ministry, and the reason for his sentence of death and crucifixion. In delineating the "political strategies" of Jesus, he identifies these among them: "Treat the people's needs as holy; give a voice to the voiceless; expose the workings of oppression; and don't just explain the alternative, show it" (Obery Hendricks 2006: 99–100). In this way, we are brought back to the broken bread that is given, Jesus as the living embodiment of that which he preaches in terms of our relationship to the other, a powerful lived example that threatened the powers of the day.

The words and works of Jesus conjointly undertake a profound critique of the worldview/social order of his time. As such, he calls for his followers, those who choose to present themselves to God as a "living sacrifice," to "be not conformed to this world, but be...transformed..." (Rom. 12: 1–2). As a nonconformist, Jesus inverts the taken-for-granted constructions of the other who is "least," claiming that the first shall be last, and the last shall be first (Mark 9: 35); "he that is greatest among you shall be your servant" (Matt. 23: 11, 20: 26–27), the servant of all. Jesus is called a "friend of publicans and sinners" (Matt. 11: 19). All are invited to the breaking of bread; all are welcome to eating together.

Christopher Kliewer (1998) launches a similar critique on contemporary American society with respect to our conceptualization and treatment of the other who is disabled. Setting forth a history by which individuals with Down syndrome are denied their humanity, he calls for a posture of inclusion, full citizenship, in contrast to the legacy of banishment and segregation that has constructed the disabled other as a burden in U.S. culture. Interestingly, while the significance of this finding is little explored, Kliewer uncovers a legacy in art wherein Jesus is depicted with disabilities as a child (i.e., a series of paintings of the Madonna with Child from the fifteenth century by Andrea Mantegna; and the *Adoration of the Shepherds* of 1618 by Flemish painter, Jacob Jordeans).[7] Kliewer speculates that the portrayal of Christ as a disabled child may have reflected an aesthetic effort to capture innocence and purity, and/or an interest in representing the Renaissance understanding of truth as counter to worldly reason.[8]

Henry Nouwen, the well-known inspirational writer, priest, and theologian, was once asked by a friend for a treatise, drawing upon the heart of the Christian spiritual message, that might speak to nonreligious persons, such as himself, seeking nonetheless to live meaningful and whole lives in contemporary times. Nouwen's response to this request, *Life of the Beloved: Spiritual Living in a Secular World* (1992/2002), echoes this central claim and call of Jesus: "You are the beloved...We are God's chosen ones, even when our world does not choose us, [chosen and called]...We are called to become bread for each other—bread for the world," he says (Nouwen 1992/2002: 59, 120).

Yet, Nouwen further asks us to consider that it is perhaps only broken bread that can be truly given, or at least that which is broken is in fact that which is most truly blessed. In this way, Nouwen, drawing upon the example of Christ, speaks of the gift of our brokenness—which is also perhaps the place of our radical openness and source of our greatest fulfillment, known only in giving ourselves for the other and in opening ourselves to receive the beautiful gift, the "exquisite humanness" (Forsthoefel 2006), of the other, as well.

Whether situated as Samaritan, self, Levite, least, disciple, or disabled, acknowledging our mutual humanity, Nouwen (1992/2002) asserts that "Each human being suffers in a way no other human being suffers" (Nouwen 1992/2002: 88). Also called in his life to work with those identified as disabled at L'Arche, a faith-based community inspired by the "Beatitudes," Nouwen shares that pain or impairment may not be the greatest difficulty experienced by disabled people; rather it is the fear or feeling that one has little to offer, to contribute, to give, to others. Yet, he reminds: "the real question is not 'What can we offer each other?' but 'Who can we be for each other?'" (Nouwen 1992/2002: 113); "Yes, indeed, we are chosen, blessed and broken to be given" (Nouwen 1992/2002:103); and "Isn't that what friendship is all about: giving to each other the gift of our Belovedness?" (Nouwen 1992/2002: 30). From the Christian faith, thus, we affirm that the kingdom of heaven, the manna from heaven, is within—where Christ in "you," in (and as) the other, we are one—beloved. Yet at the same time, acknowledging our irreplaceable uniqueness, we bring and present our irreducible otherness, which is, in fact, our gift to share. We are all called together to the banquet table, to the fellowship of the beloved. In blessed communion, offering the broken bread of ourselves each to the other, we partake of an inexplicably divine, sublime feast.

Serving Others over Self: Islam's Guidance for Approaching the Disadvantaged Other

The Qur'an and Prophet Mohammad's traditions are replete with commands and instructions on how to conduct one's life in relation to others: what to do or not to do in one's relationship with others. Such commands are not only plenty but also quite comprehensive. Since Islam is not just a set of injunctions but rather a comprehensive worldview that relates one's understandings, thoughts, beliefs, actions, and goals in an intricate fabric and a coherent formulation, and since Islam focuses on the use of reason and intellect in reaching whatever understanding or belief that then informs one's action, I decided to attempt to gain a more foundational understanding of these commands. As such, this section addresses what can be termed Islam's conceptual or philosophical framework for approaching the issue of the other, and, consequently, what could be described as the Islamic guidance on the treatment of others, along with some specific examples.

> Central to Islam is the oneness of God[9]—a concept issuing from Abrahamic monotheism—the Creator and Sustainer of the universe: "Say: 'He is the One God: God the Eternal, the Uncaused Cause of All Being'" (*The Qur'an*, Asad Interpretation, 1980, 112: 1–2).[10] Everything in the universe has been created by God according to a design, for a purpose and not in vain:

> And [know that] We have not created the heavens and the earth and all that is between them in mere idle play [for,] had We willed to indulge in a pastime, We would indeed have produced it from within Ourselves—if such had been Our will at all! (21: 16–17)

It then follows that the diversity that characterizes nature is not an anomaly or an accident, but rather a sign of the Creator's power and magnificence. On this subject, the Qur'an says:

> Art thou not aware that God sends the water from the skies whereby We bring forth fruits of many hues—just as in the mountains there are streaks of white and red of various shades, as well as [others] raven-black, and [as] there are in men, and in crawling beasts, and in cattle, too, many hues? (35: 27–28)

To humans, God says in the Qur'an: "O [people!] Behold, We have created you all out of a male and a female, and have made you into nations and tribes, so that you might come to know one another" (49: 13)—implying that this equality of biological origin should be reflected in the equality of the human dignity common to all. And, as to the specific purpose of the creation of humans, God declares, "And [tell them that] I have not created invisible beings and humans to any end other than that they may [know and] worship me" (51: 56). Thus, the deepest purpose of the creation of all human beings is their cognition of the existence of God and, hence, their conscious willingness to conform their own existence to His will and plan (Asad 1980). "It is this twofold concept of cognition and willingness that gives the deepest meaning to what the Qur'an describes as 'worship'" (Asad 1980: 806). It is important to make it clear here that the type or level of the mental faculty through which humans could reason or perceive the existence of God is never specified, stressing the natural inherent variety in humans. Asad further elaborates that this spiritual call seeks to enhance the inner development of the worshipper, wherever it is, who by willfully surrendering to God's will hopes to come closer to an understanding of that will, thus, closer to God.

From all of the above—the oneness of the Creator; the inherent design and purpose of God's creation including the diversity therein; the shared origin of humans; worship as the sole purpose of the creation of humans—it is, then, not surprising that the Qur'an clearly states that "Verily, the noblest of you in the sight of God is the one who is most deeply conscious of Him. Behold, God is all-knowing, all-aware" (49: 13), implying that God's measure of a human being's worth lies not on physical attributes or material achievement, but on spiritual and ethical development, which can only be measured by God, not humans. The Prophet most explicitly communicates this message when saying: "Verily, God does not look at your bodies or your appearances, but looks into your hearts" (*Hadith*, Shah Translation, 1999, Muslim, 2564).[11]

On the basis of this framework, I could not find a logical basis in Islam that would support the practice of "othering" fellow human beings. In fact, a very "sharp Qur'anic rebuke" (Asad 1980: 930) was issued by God to the Prophet for a minor act of discourtesy to a poor and blind man in favor of a group of wealthy, powerful, and influential chiefs of the pagan Meccans (see Qur'an 80: 1–10).

As part of one's worship of God, as defined earlier, Islam establishes three stations along the way of spiritual enhancement: "Islam," "Iman," and "Ihsan": "Islam," signifying the most basic level of spirituality; "Iman," signifying a level where one completely accepts, believes, acknowledges and understands and is secure in God; and "Ihsan" (a term that derives from a root of "beauty"), carrying the connotation of beautifying, perfecting, doing better, and improving. The Qur'an carries God's exhortation to humans to work toward, strive for, and seek the higher stations of spiritual enhancement: "Vie, therefore, with one another for doing good works" (2: 148). In another place, the Qur'an describes the believers as "it is they who vie with one another in doing good works, and it is they who outrun [all others] in attaining to them" (23: 61).

When asked about the definition of a muslim,[12] the Prophet answered that a muslim is one from whose hand and tongue other people are safe (*Hadith*, Shah Translation, 1999, Al-Bukhari, 1.10).[13] This particular example seems to reflect the most basic level of spirituality, that it, *Islam*, which is to desist from causing harm to others. In another tradition, the Prophet declares to his companions that none of them shall attain to *Iman* unless he wishes for his brother that which he wishes for himself (Al-Bukhari, 1.12). It seems that this is an improved level of spiritual enhancement wherein one desires and seeks to share with others that which one desires for oneself or that which one might actually possess. Along the same lines, the Qur'an says:

> O you who have attained to [Iman]! Be ever steadfast in upholding equity, bearing witness to the truth for the sake of God, even though it be against your own selves or your parents and kinsfolk... do not, then, follow your own desires, lest you swerve from justice. (4: 135)

or:

> O you have attained to [Iman]! Be ever steadfast in your devotion to God, bearing witness to the truth in all equity; and never let hatred of anyone lead you into the sin of deviating from justice. Be just: this is the closest to being God-conscious. (5: 8)

At this level, God seems to ask that humans consider others as absolute equals to oneself, even at the risk of hardship and disadvantage to one's own self or loved ones.

The even more advanced level of spiritual enhancement, that is, *Ihsan*, seems to be most obvious in the Qur'anic verse that describes those at this level as ones who "rather give them [others in need] over themselves, even though poverty be their own lot" (59: 9), or "who give food—however great be their own want of it—unto the needy, and the orphan, and the captive" (76: 8). In a well-authenticated tradition, a man came to the Prophet and told him that he was in severe hardship. The Prophet, after finding that his own household had no food, asked his companions who among them would lodge this man for the night. A man said "I would" and took the needy man to his home. He then asked his wife to be generous to their guest. She answered that she had nothing but enough food for their children. The man told his wife to keep the children occupied and to put them to bed when they asked for food. He then told her to dim the lights, to bring the food to the guest, and to pretend that she, along with him, was eating. The guest ate, and the man, his wife, and their children spent the night with no sustenance. In the morning, the man went to the Prophet who told him that "God was pleased with what you did for your guest last night" (Al-Bukhari, 3798). This story is not unique in the history of Islam and reveals a lot about how people worked hard to conform to God's exhortation to vie for doing good deeds in their way to draw closer to God.

The Qur'an is replete with exhortations specifically toward protecting the rights and dignity of those who are viewed by fellow human beings as not measuring up to certain standards that are valued in society at a certain time and place (such as standards based on society's emphasis on family/tribal ties and origins and obsession with social and economic status). From this conception, people identified as belonging to this group—including, but not limited to, the *blind, mute, deaf, lame, weak, orphan, destitute/needy,* and *wayfarer*—are actually taken advantage of, abandoned, ignored, discriminated against, oppressed, and looked down on and then treated as *the disadvantaged*. Since this disadvantage is created by society, it is not surprising that the Qur'an places the responsibility of rectifying this inequiry on the shoulder of society by its constant exhortation to Muslims to recognize the plight of the disadvantaged, to stand up for their rights, and to improve their condition and status.

More specifically, with regard to individuals with a physical or mental condition or difference, the Qur'an addresses how the superstitious society associated these conditions with some divine punishment and proceeded to segregate people with such conditions and discriminate against them. An extensive investigation of the Qur'an's attitude toward individuals with certain physical or mental conditions reveals that the Qur'an views these conditions as morally neutral (Bazna and Hatab 2005), neither a curse nor a blessing; they are simply part of the human condition (Musse 2002). This is consistent with the Qur'an's view that every person is potentially perfect so long as he or she works on developing his or her innate and individual qualities to the limit of his or her individual differentiation. It is said in the Qur'an: "Verily, We create man in the best conformation" (95: 4). But in the same breath the verse continues, "and thereafter We reduce him to the lowest of low—excepting only such as attain to faith and do good works" (95: 5–6). Thus, according to Islam, "we—every one of us—can reach a full measure of perfection by developing the positive, already existing traits of which our individualities are composed" (Asad 1934/1999: 12–13).

The Qur'an removes any stigma and barrier to full inclusion of people with physical or mental conditions. There are also several authentic traditions from Hadith that further elaborate how Islam assures the inclusion of those who are weak. For example, the Prophet said:

> If anyone of you leads people in prayer, he should shorten it for amongst them are the weak, the sick and the old; and if anyone among you

prays alone then he may prolong [the prayer] as much as he wishes. (Al-Bukhari, 1.671)

Consistent with the Qur'anic tenet that "God does not burden any human being with more than he is well able to bear" (2: 286), Islam offers relief from certain commands and requirements so as to address the difficulties that arise from the nature of the specific condition. Despite the permission, the expectation to exert oneself to the best of one's individual ability, both in the spiritual and temporal spheres, remains the same for everyone. The following tradition narrated by one of the Prophet's companions helps illustrate what it means to exert oneself to the best of one's individual ability:

A blind man came to the Apostle of God and said: "Messenger of God, I have no one to guide me to the mosque" [Muslims are required to perform the five daily prayers in the mosque]. He, therefore, asked the Apostle of God permission to say prayer in his house. He [the Prophet] granted him permission. Then when the man turned away he called him and said, "Do you hear the call to prayer?" He said, "Yes." He [the Prophet then] said, "Respond to it." (Muslim, 310)

The implication here is that if the man could hear the call to prayer, then he must be close enough to the mosque, in which case the permission to say prayer at home does not apply. All people are expected to constantly do the best they can within their powers, and people with certain conditions are no exception.

In conclusion, the Islamic view encompasses physical, economic, and social disadvantages; promotes respect and esteem for the disadvantaged; expects personal responsibility and personal development from the disadvantaged; proclaims the right of the disadvantaged to full inclusion and full support; and affirms the responsibility and duty of society toward its disadvantaged members. In general, there is no basis for any "othering" or discrimination among people in the Islamic view; one's relationship with others is part of one's relationship with God such that one must use it as a way of drawing near to God in an ever-increasing act of perfecting, doing better, or, in other words, *Ihsan*. While there are specific exhortations and commands with regard to relating to and treating others, including the socially disadvantaged, I view them only as guidelines that attempt to inform our actions and deeds that should be always for the sake of, and on the way to, God. And God knows best.

Conclusion

Through our collective and individual rethinking of the concept of the disabled other via Buddhism, Christianity, and Islam, we have sought to present supporting narratives and scriptural texts that begin to disrupt assumptions about disability, particularly perhaps in its relationship to spirituality and/or religion. Exploring the images, ideas, and understandings of the disabled other within our three wisdom traditions has revealed themes around social justice, service, and the sacred. An overarching assumption embraced by all three is the assertion of a common humanity, the recognition of a human condition we all share (i.e., the desire for happiness as highlighted in the Buddhist tradition). From this foundational base, three major themes are reflected in all our investigations: agency, responsibility, and engagement. Whether called stranger, wayfarer, foreigner, nomad, or orphan—whether termed the abandoned, ignored, oppressed, disadvantaged, weak, destitute, or needy—clearly the "othering" experience of those who do not belong or do not fit the "norm" is prevalently and persistently examined in the scriptures of our traditions through varied and sundry "sermons" and stories. Critical and creative reconsideration of this other from within and through our spiritual traditions has opened up for us our own assumptions and conceptions of the other and enabled us to explore new understandings in sharing and reflecting on them together.

Agency, Responsibility, and Engagement

A myriad of theoretical traditions have come to define agency. From our professional work as educators committed to inclusion, we hold to a Disability Studies interpretation, grounded in the disability rights movement; a position that counters social oppression, promotes self-advocacy and personal empowerment, and supports the full personhood and participation of the disabled (Charlton 1998; Fleischer and Zames 2001). We affirm the conception that agency is of the essence of our humanity, that all human beings are *agentic*—active players in, and of, their lives, an affirmation that we have found our wisdom traditions mutually share. Collective, mutual, and individual responsibility— indelibly linked to this agency and freedom that is constitutive of our humanness—are valued and promoted in all three traditions. Acting for the benefit and betterment of others without distinction underlies this sense of responsibility to others, including the idea that one's individual relationship and service to the other is vital to one's own spiritual growth and life.

Stories abound within all three traditions of acts and practices of being hospitable, receptive, and open to others—with even particular attention to those who are "othered" via disadvantage or disability. Engagement evolves from this sense of social responsibility, where one *lives* one's spiritual beliefs in this way, being in the world and being socially engaged. As one considers this "spiritual equation" of agency, responsibility, and engagement, one is *called to action*. It is not enough to care for, wish to benefit, and serve others before oneself, but one is expected, obliged, to take clear and conscious action to uplift others, and to address the plight of those in need.

The Call to Criticism and to Action in a Challenging Present

Underlying all these assumptions and themes is the need—via agency, responsibility, and engagement—to critique the social order (which, we might add, necessitates a radical critique of oneself in relation to the social order, and to the other, as well). Subsequently, one creates a radical openness to others, rather than pity for others—in actuality, privileging the other.[14] Bringing to bear the question of service and call to openness toward others in this work permits an interesting and provocative understanding of disability and the experience of the other, specifically evoking ideas of mutual, social responsibility.

In a larger context, the current troubling and inhospitable nature of our national and global condition and the overemphasis on consumerism, corporatization, and commodification pose great challenges to human values, relationships, and rights—to the future of our communities. Now, more than ever, it seems that we must take up the call to address the ethical and moral challenges facing our society. Our wisdom traditions, spiritual/religious thought and practice, provide a forum and framework from which to confront and caringly face these challenges (Smith 2001).

Our traditions here teach that opening oneself to the other is not only a demonstration of faithfulness to that which is holy, holy being(s), but also an active expression of faith and gratitude, as well as service. What is required is generously giving the best offerings to this other in our midst. Therefore, rather than a position of inferiority, primacy is given to the disabled other. By inquiring into our three traditions, we have sought to create a space for others—that is, scholars, wisdom seekers, spiritual practitioners, educators, religious teachers—to reflect upon their wisdom (religious/spiritual) traditions and consider their own assumptions about the other who is disabled, particularly in a present context where the disabled other is still too often the stranger who is not welcome.

For us this has meant clarifying our commitments and at intersections of conflict drawing upon them as a ground from which to respond, whether in the classroom, with colleagues, or in terms of our research. In all our courses we include a social action component that requires students to take theory and academic knowledge into their communities. An example of this directed action research is critiquing city systems and community resources in terms of physical and attitudinal access for persons with disabilities. In addition, in terms of our approaches to pedagogy we explicitly create conditions for genuine community, whether in informal class interactions or formal opportunities for discourse and dissent. This also means creating a welcoming space in the classroom where differences are celebrated and respected and connections are made to our shared humanity. We consider the teacher-student relationship, understanding its potential for "othering"; we are willing to make transparent the power dynamics and endeavor to open these up to negotiation and at times even inversion. For one of us, the presence of a deaf student in class called into question overreliance on auditory learning and shifted the pedagogy toward full access and participation, as well as giving over the role of teaching to the student to challenge the entire class to learn in new ways. Thus, the student's potential position of marginalization was reconsidered and transformed. The rights of students come to the fore; we firmly believe that we must model that which we promote, however imperfectly.

We challenge others, as ourselves, that this other may be no longer unwanted and unwelcome, or made to feel so, but rather be embraced as beloved guest, friend, fellow-sojourner. We also set forth the call not only to act on behalf of others but also to recognize the import of these wisdom traditions in addressing the current cry of society for social reform (public, institutional, educational), ethical living, and personal growth.

Notes

1. Given our focus here on disability in relation to the question of the other, as well as our shared professional experiences working in inclusive education programs, we are grounding our conception of agency in that posited through the field of Disability Studies, which we also address further, more explicitly, later in the Conclusion section of this chapter.

2. For example, it must be noted that two of the traditions, Christianity and Islam, share a theistic perspective, which is not the case for Buddhism.

3. *The New Strong's Exhaustive Concordance of the Bible* (1995) was the principal tool used for this inquiry, in searching references (and cross-references) to myriad terms, since *disabled* or *disability* does not present itself directly in the Christian scriptures: that is, *able, ability, other, blind, deaf, lame, orphan, destitute, poor, stranger,* etc. Based on initial findings and identification of key themes emerging from them, subsequent searches engaged such terms as *least, neighbor, food, bread, drink, broken, welcome,* and *hospitality,* as well. Both Hebrew and Greek origins of the use of such words are provided through this reference text.

4. The sources for this study include the Arabic text of the Qur'an; the two most reliable and thoroughly corroborated compilations of Hadith, which are Bukhari and Muslim (Al-Nawawi 1998; Sabiq 1946/1993; Shah 1999); the stories of the companions of the Prophet (Khaled 1994; Shah 1999); *LisanUl-Arab,* which is an expanded 18-volume-dictionary that contains the root, origin, variations of words and their usage (IbnMandhoor 1986 version); and several Qur'anic exegeses, both classical (Abdu and Reda 2002 version; IbnKathir 1885/1986) and modern (Ali 1996; Asad 1980; Malik 1997; Pickthall 1992).

5. There are two different spellings used for this Indian pandit, Sāntideva and Shantideva. Within the body of this chapter, Sāntideva is used; however, in citations and references, the spelling selected by the translator of the specific text is used.

6. The author of this section has received the teaching on this many times and recently directly from Dagpo Rinpoche (oral teaching, October 20–22, 2006), the reincarnation of Lama Serlingpa.

7. For more on this legacy, see Volpe (1986).

8. Here, Kliewer draws upon the work of Michel Foucault (1965) in his *Madness and Civilization: A History of Insanity in the Age of Reason.*

9. The first pillar of Islam is the acknowledgment that there is no god but God.

10. All translations of Qur'anic verses mentioned here are taken from Asad's (1980) interpretation of the Qur'an. The numbers between parentheses indicate the location of the verse in the Qur'an. The first number is that of the chapter, and the second number refers to the location of the verse within the chapter.

11. The sayings of the Prophet (Hadith) are each referenced by (a) the name of the person who compiled and authenticated the Hadith (either Imam Muslim or Imam Al-Bukhari) and (b) the number of the Hadith as listed in the specific compilation.

12. The word "Muslim" with a capital "M" is typically used to imply subscription to a religious cult, which is not what I refer to here. The word "muslim" with a lower case "m" refers to a person who is in constant pursuit

of surrendering to God (that is the meaning of the word "muslim" in Arabic).

13. See Note number 12.

14. Our Buddhist and Christian traditions, in contrast to Islam, share a similar assumption of the sacredness and divinity of the other—expanding the idea of the other as Christ or Buddha, and thus one's openness to the other as, in fact, welcoming and embracing Christ, or Buddha, himself. In Islamic tradition, too, one's treatment of the other is regarded as way to God. Also, all of our traditions affirm the dignity and value of human life. While we collectively consider "enlightenment" to be of considerable intellectual import, when we bring our specific wisdom traditions to bear on this concept, any attempt to find common ground here is wrought with contradiction and complexity. Only in Buddhism is this concept central to one's spiritual practice and realization; in fact, here one's attainment of enlightenment is predicated upon the necessity to be radically open to and serve others. In addition, the self and other in Buddhist tradition is interchangeable.

References

Abdu, M., & Reda, R. (2002). *Tafsir al-Qur'an al-adhim al-ma'roofbitafsir al-manar* [The exegesis of the glorious Qur'an known as the Manar exegesis]. Beirut, Lebanon: Dar Ehia Al-Tourath Al-Arabi. (Publication date of original work is unknown).

Ali, A. Y. (1996). *The Meaning of the Holy Qur'an*. Beltsville, MD: Amana Publications.

Al-Nawawi, M. A. S. (1998). *Riyad as-saliheen* [The orchards of the righteous]. Damascus, Syria: Dar Al-Khayr. (Publication date of original work is unknown).

Asad, M. (1980). *Message of the Qur'an*. Lahore, Pakistan: Maktaba Jawahar ul uloom.

Asad, M. (1999). *Islam at the Crossroads*. Kuala Lumpur, Malaysia: The Other Press. (Original work published 1934).

Bazna, M. S., & Hatab, T. A. (2005). Disability in the Qur'an: The Islamic alternative to defining, viewing, and relating to disability. *Journal of Religion, Disability, and Health 9* (1), 5–27.

Bolchazy, L. (1995). *Hospitality in Antiquity*. Chicago, IL: Ares Publishers Inc. (Original work published 1977).

Charlton, J. I. (1998). *Nothing About Us Without Us: Disability Oppression and Empowerment*. Berkeley, CA: University of California Press.

Dagpo Rinpoche. (oral teaching, October 20–22, 2006). *The Seven-Point Mind Training of the Great Vehicle*. Northfield, VT: Trijang Buddhist Institute.

Davis, L. J. (1997). Constructing normalcy. In L. J. Davis (Ed.), *The Disability Studies Reader*, 2nd ed. New York, NY: Routledge.

Derrida, J. (2000). Step of hospitality/No hospitality. In A. Dufourmantelle & J. Derrida (Eds.) and R. Bowlby (Trans.), *Of hospitality* (pp. 75–160). Stanford, CA: Stanford University Press. (Original work published 1997).

Fleischer, D. Z., & Zames, F. (2001). *The Disability Rights Movement: From Charity to Confrontation.* Philadelphia: Temple University Press.

Forsthoefel, T. (2006). *Soulsong: Seeking Holiness, Coming Home.* Maryknoll, NY: Orbis Books.

Foucault, M. (1965). *Madness and Civilization: A History of Insanity in the Age of Reason.* New York, NY: Vintage.

Garland-Thomson, R. (1997). *Extraordinary Bodies: Figuring Physical Disability in American Culture and Literature.* New York, NY: Columbia University Press.

Gyatso, T., H. H. Fourteenth Dalai Lama. (2000). In D. Side (Ed.) and Geshe Thupten Jinpa (Trans.), *Transforming the Mind: Teachings on Generating Compassion.* London, England: Thorsons.

Hendricks, O., Jr. (2006). *The Politics of Jesus: Rediscovering the True Revolutionary Nature of the Teachings of Jesus and How They have been Corrupted.* New York, NY: Random House.

Ibn Kathir, I. (1986). *Tafsir al-Qur'an al-adhim* [Exegesis of the glorious Qur'an]. Beirut, Lebanon: Dar El-Marefah. (Original work published 1885).

Ibn Mandhoor, J. (1986). *Lisanul-Arab* [The tongue of the Arabs], Vols. 1–18. Beirut, Lebanon: Dar Ehia Al-Tourath Al-Arabi. (Publication date of original work is unknown).

Jinpa, G. T. (2005). Introduction. In Shonu Gyalchok & Konchok Gyaltsen (Eds.), *Mind Training: The Great Collection.* Somerville, MA: Wisdom Publications.

Khaled, K. M. (1994). *Rijalhawlaar-rasoul* [Men around the Messenger of God]. Cairo, Egypt: Dar Al-Mukattam.

Kliewer, C. (1998). *Schooling Children with Down Syndrome: Toward an Understanding of Possibility.* New York, NY: Teachers College Press.

Kudlick, C. J. (2003). Disability history: Why we need another 'other'. The American Historical Review *108*(3), 50 pars. Retrieved from http://www.historycooperative.org/journals/ahr/108.3/kudlick.html.

Lama Yeshe wisdom archive. (1999, August). *Commentary on Chapter 8 of Shantideva's Bodhicaryvara* (Interview with His Holiness the 14th Dalai Lama). Retrieved August 6, 2003, from http://www.lamayeshe.com/otherteachers/hhdl/ meditation/meditation_6.shtml

Linton, S. (1998). *Claiming Disability: Knowledge and Identity.* New York, NY: New York University Press.

Malik, M. F. (1997). *English Translation of the Meaning of al-Qur'an: The Guidance for mankind.* Houston, TX: Institute of Islamic Knowledge.

Merton, T. (1960). *Mystics and Zen masters.* New York, NY: Delta Books.

Musse, I. A. (2002). *Disability: An Islamic Insight.* Retrieved January 6, 2004, from http://www.icv.org.au/ps20011018.shtml

New Bible Dictionary. (1982). Wheaton, IL: Tyndale House Publishers.

Nouwen, H. (2002). *Life of the Beloved: Spiritual Living in a Secular World.* New York, NY: Crossroad Publishing. (Original work published 1992).

Oden, A. (2001). *And You Welcomed Me: A Sourcebook on Hospitality in Early Christianity.* Nashville, TN: Abingdon Press.

Pfeiffer, D. (2003). The disability studies paradigm. In P. Devliege, F. Rusch, & D. Pfeiffer (Eds.), *Rethinking Disability: The Emergence of New Definitions, Concepts, and Communities* (pp. 94–106). Antwerp, Belgium: Garant.

Pickthall, M. M. (1992). *The Meaning of the Glorious Koran.* London, England: Everyman's Library.

Sabiq, A. (1993). *Fiqh us-Sunnah* [Understanding the Sunnah]. Cairo, Egypt: Dar Al-Fath. (Original work published 1946).

Sāntideva, (1997) *A Guide to the Bodhisattva's Way of Life.* V. A. Wallace & B. A. Wallace (Trans.). Ithaca, NY: Snow Lion.

Shantideva (1979) In S, Batchelor (Trans.), *A Guide to the Bodhisattva's Way of Life.* Dharamsala, India: Library of Tibetan Works and Archives.Shah, S. N. (1999). *Alim: The World's Most Useful Islamic Software* [Computer software]. Baltimore, MD: ISL Software Corporation.

Smith, H. (1991). The *World's Religions: Our Great Wisdom Traditions.* San Francisco, CA: HarperOne.

Smith, H. (2001). *Why Religion Matters: The Fate of the Human Spirit in an Age of Disbelief.* New York, NY: HarperCollins.

Strong, J. (1995). *The New Strong's Exhaustive Concordance of the Bible.* London, England: Thomas Nelson Publishers.

Sutherland, A. (2006). *I was a Stranger: A Christian Theology of Hospitality.* Nashville, TN: Abingdon Press.

Tharchin, Sermey Khensur Lobsang. (1998). *The Essence of Mahayana Lojong Practice.* Howell, NJ: Mahayana Sutra and Tantra Press.

Tharchin, Sermey Khensur Lobsang. (1999). *Achieving Bodhichitta.* Howell, NJ: Mahayana Sutra and Tantra Press.

The Holy Bible. (expanded ed.). (1985). New York, NY: Thomas Nelson.

Tsongkhapa. (2004). *The Great Treatise on the Stages of the Path to Enlightenment: Lam Rim Chen Mo,* Vol. 1. Ithaca, NY: Snow Lion Publications.

Volpe, E. P. (1986). Is Down syndrome a modern disease? *Perspectives in Biology and Medicine* 29 (3), 423–436.

Wallace, B. A. (2005a). *Balancing the Mind: A Tibetan Buddhist Approach to Refining Attention.* Ithaca, NY: Snow Lion.

Wallace, B. A. (2005b). *Genuine Happiness: Meditation as the Path to Fulfillment.* Hoboken, NJ: Wiley & Sons.

Westfield, N.L. (2001). *Dear Sisters: A Womanist Practice of Hospitality.* Cleveland, OH: The Pilgrim Press.

CHAPTER 10

Native American Concepts Involving Human Difference

Lavonna L. Lovern

According to the recent United Nations report, an estimated 370 million Indigenous people exist and inhabit more than 90 countries (United Nations, Department of Economic and Social Affairs 2009: 1). Each Indigenous community represents a unique grouping of human knowledge and an equally unique culture. While historically, the knowledge contained in these communities has been ignored or destroyed, recent years have seen a revitalization of interest in Indigenous knowledge theories. Indeed, throughout the world Indigenous knowledge is being sought, and input solicited, in areas from issues of global warming to healthcare. The difficulty is often to determine exactly what is to count as Indigenous knowledge, especially given the centuries of colonization. Much of the traditional knowledge was lost or hidden because of colonial practices of persecution and destruction. Later difficulties included matters of Indigenous identity. Which cultures are to be identified as Indigenous is often a matter left to European historical determinations, with little involvement of Indigenous or First Nation people. The term "Indigenous," in this chapter, will refer to cultures that were first to inhabit a geographical area; have continued the inhabitation, even in cases of occupation; and exhibit viable and unique knowledge claims such as languages and cultural constructs (Maybury-Lewis 1997: 8).

The diversity of Indigenous cultures does not allow for a single categorization of knowledge claims, beliefs, or traditions. However, the worldwide Indigenous communities do share some similarities, which will be used in this chapter to aid the discussion of Indigenous spirituality as it differs from European and European descent spiritual and ideological claims. To simplify the discussion, the term "Western" will be used to indicate cultures and knowledge claims stemming from European and European descendant cultures. It should also be noted that throughout the world, colonization practices have not been exclusively European, but have been undertaken by other non-European countries and civilizations as well. Again, a disclaimer must be noted that the similarities expressed here do not apply to all Indigenous communities, not even all communities in a specific geographical region and should not be used as a guide to or a litmus test for Indigenous communities or individuals. These theories are abstractions taken primarily from Indigenous scholars and Indigenous community members. There are vast differences between geographical regions, individual communities, and individual tribal members based on issues including rural versus urban, traditional versus assimilated, and even sovereign versus nonsovereign. To the extent that it is possible, this chapter will use the voices of the Indigenous to identify similarities and to explain their own knowledge systems.

The focus of this text on "disability" creates an opportunity to explore important distinctions between Western and Indigenous cultures that are too often overlooked or dismissed. In order to get a better understanding of Indigenous spiritual relations as they impact issues of human difference, this chapter will be broken down into three sections. The first section will deal with knowledge claims as they differ between Indigenous and Western cultures allowing for how these foundational assumptions lead to culturally specific definitions of human difference and disability, respectively. The second section of this chapter will focus on community and spirituality in a discussion of wellness as applied to human difference in Native American ideology. The final section will examine the role of language in the perception of difference and how language use establishes cultural positions of equality and inequality involving human difference. At no point is this chapter intended to create an atmosphere of judgment. The differences to be discussed between Indigenous and Western paradigms do not necessitate a normative interpretation. Indeed, a determination of "better than" or "worse than" is not part of an Indigenous discussion of "different from." Indigenous cultures often enter into lengthy discussions involving differences in knowledge claims or cultural ideologies as a way of gaining understanding without a need to determine "who is right and who is wrong." This is the spirit in which this chapter is offered. The information provided is an attempt to continue the discussion of human difference by offering an alternative perspective. There is no intent to either proselytize or change the knowledge, values, or spirituality of any individual or culture.

Foundational Cultural Concepts

One of the difficulties in undertaking a discussion involving diverse cultures is the translation of knowledge concepts. As beginning language students can attest, translation is challenging and perhaps impossible at times. There are a couple of standard translational practices, which are often employed to assist in the transference of knowledge from one language to another. The first involves a word for word translation that assumes that one can substitute a word or phrase from one language for a word or phrase in another language. As students have often complained, such attempts can prove unsatisfying and unsuccessful as there may not be adequate substitutions. Another translational practice attempts to substitute the meaning perpetrated by a word or phrase in one language for the same meaning in another. The obvious dilemma here lies in determining what the meaning of the word or phrase is, in the first language, and which word or phrase best supports the same meaning in the second language. While there may be other practices of translation, the difficulty in translations seems mired in the same debates involving the legal issues of letter of the law versus spirit of the law. Gadamer's (1977) discussions of translation offer some insight especially in the recent studies of colonization and postcolonization issues. However, the deciphering of human use of language as it pertains to both understanding and to the nature of phenomenological experience remains blocked in terms of how exactly translation is to take place.

The difficulty of translation is further exacerbated when the cultures involved do not share foundational knowledge assumptions or the same logical orientation. In fact, one aspect of translation theory that is absent from hermeneutical discussions is how to translate languages with differing logical foundations. Wittgenstein (1969) may have come close in his discussion of language as a series of overlapping systems of family relations, but he failed to explain what should be done with languages that are not related. Kuhn (1970) explained how knowledge and understanding could shift from one paradigm to another, but he too had no plan for the interaction of two completely different paradigms. The very notion of a "shift" implies a continuation of some knowledge claims. What is faced with Indigenous knowledge claims is an examination of systems that adopted logic systems and knowledge paradigms fundamentally different from those in Western traditions. From those differing paradigms developed vastly different, yet advanced and complex, knowledge claims.

Historically, translations of Indigenous knowledge claims and cultural ideology have suffered from the mistaken belief that, at the most basic level, all languages share a common logical orientation and that all human interaction is founded on a common knowledge paradigm. Such beliefs are often supported by the idea that communication, between people of different cultures and languages, exists. The idea being that if there was not a common base, no communication would be possible. The fact that Indigenous and Western people can communicate is then claimed to "prove" that they share the same basic logic orientation, an argument that fails the test of validity. Such assumptions fail to deal with language and phenomena that cannot be translated from one culture to another, instead relegating any such problems to matters of poor linguistics or a lack of proper terminology. Philosophically, this idea can be linked to theories of supervenience and, while interesting, logical supervenience suffers from the same difficulties as the verifiability principle. While a good proposition, the verifiability principle could itself not be verified. The problem with assuming that all language begins with the same logic base and that all knowledge is based in similar assumptions is that there is no way to independently verify such claims. There may indeed be a way to justify such claims in terms of a coherence theory of knowledge, but justification is not verification and the use of a coherence theory already establishes the parameters of the theory according to a specific logical paradigm, which will ignore or dismiss all other systems that do not accept the established standards of coherence.

At this point, an attempt could be made to bump the discussion up one level and enter the ever-expanding heights of metaphilosophy in an attempt to solve the issue of how to translate Indigenous language and culture according to Western logic patterns. However, such attempts would do nothing more than commit the same mistranslations of past academics. A better approach would be to look at the foundations of cultures from the point of view of those who practice the cultures. The practitioners can then establish their logical system and paradigm according to their own standards. By listening to the Indigenous populations discuss their own knowledge claims, one can begin the sort of communicative action supported by Habermas (1984, 1987). To begin a discourse of this sort, the participants must be understood to be equals. In other words, Indigenous knowledge must not be viewed as savage, underdeveloped, unsophisticated, or childish as it is often portrayed in academia. Ironically, the use of these terms to describe Indigenous knowledge comes from a lack of understanding of the logical foundations of the language systems and the intricate base-knowledge claims. Not so ironically, these terms have been employed historically in colonization to systematically dismiss Indigenous knowledge by identifying it as inherently inferior to Western knowledge systems (Sartre 2001: 30–47).

To begin, one of the primary differences between Indigenous and Western cultures is in the logical orientation. While it can be assumed that language is the expression of culture and culture is the extension of language, which precedes the other is not the task of the current discussion and will be left for lengthier postmodern discussions. It is enough for this discussion to admit that language and culture are interlaced so as to both reflect and support each other. When talking about the logical structure of a language one understands that it further both reflects and supports the phenomena that will be experienced by the practitioners of the language. One of the primary logical structures of Western languages is the use of dichotomous components. This dichotomy is the beginning for most logic students as they start to work with true-false structures. And while overly simplistic, the structure of basic dichotomous thinking is established in Western patterns of good/bad, day/night, light/dark, and positive/negative. Advanced courses in logic begin to investigate the continuum between the extremes and ask the questions about things being both true and false or neither true nor false and whether or not such things exist, but the primary orientation begins with dichotomy.

In contrast, a beginning course in Indigenous logic systems would start with a continuum that does not institute absolutes at either "end," simply put an infinite continuum. This logic system has been described by some as a type of tripartite system or one of logical oneness encasing infinite possibility, but translation of the system in terms of Western language makes an accurate description difficult, which is one reason Cajete (2000) uses the structure of metaphoric language. Metaphoric language is described as language that contains multileveled information and multidimensional understanding. An example of metaphorical language can be understood in Indigenous temporal concepts. To begin, many Indigenous cultures give temporal concepts a secondary importance in human existence. What this means is that place rather than time is the primary mode of orientation for both individual and culture (Cajete 2000; Deloria and Wildcat 2001). Place orientation is based on multiple relationships of which physical place is only one mode, but includes others such as spiritual, emotional, and community relationships (Allen 2002). Temporal orientations are considered to be "sublayers" of differing place orientations. Some anthropologists have referred to Indigenous temporal orientation as circular, and while this may be one "sublevel" it is far from the only manner in which temporal relations are experienced. A more inclusive descriptor would state that the temporal as interlaced in terms of past, present, and future in which the orientation of the individual is present and past-looking with the understanding that the future holds possibilities (Mbiti 2006). The importance of this example of the temporal is not to twist one's mind around the different Indigenous theories of time, but to understand that it is clearly not the Western concept of forward-looking linear temporal theories and that temporal circular descriptions are too simplistic. Another reason for the discussion of temporal differences is to further establish that Indigenous and Western people do not experience the world in the same way. The significance for this discussion is that the different orientations create a different way of "being-the-world," to borrow Heidegger's terminology.

In many Indigenous and Western cases, the reported phenomenological experiences differ. When Indigenous and Western people step out of their respective doors in the morning, they often experience very different phenomenological worlds. In some cases, the phenomenal experiences cannot be translated into the other's language or knowledge system. Western cultures have embraced a long tradition of determining what is "real" and what is "imagined" as well as theories to determine what is to count as truth and scientific fact. Indigenous cultures tend to embrace the infinite possibility of phenomenal experience and focus on differing perspectives (Deloria 1979). Again, it is important to establish one of the reasons for why being-in-the-world is so different. As Cajete (2000) notes, indigenous individuals experience the world in constant flux while Western science allows for some absolute values. If the Indigenous concept requires that all things be in flux, or as Cajete calls it chaos, then there could exist only perspectives of truth (Cajete 2000: 16–19). The idea that there are differing perspectives of truth with equal value is a common occurrence. There does not have to be a true and a false position or a winner and a loser. Many people could be winners and many perspectives could be right, and there may be no losers at all. While postmodern discussions have centered on the concepts of truth and perspective, they are often mired in discussions of relativity laced with a fear of chaos or anarchy. Indigenous discussions often start from an understanding of chaos and work toward a discussion of balance (Cajete 2000: 16–19).

Given the above discussion, the individual and cultural experiences of what counts as reality may be quite distinct for Indigenous and Western people. Moreover, what is experienced by members of a given culture is guided by language and tradition. The phenomenon experienced, by dichotomous cultures such as those found in the West, tends to focus on concepts of truth/illusion, science/religion, and fact/fiction with specific guidelines established to tell one from the other. For Indigenous cultures, truth/illusion, science/religion, and fact/fictions are continuations of each other and may have no clearly delineated features. So, while Western knowledge may follow Merleau-Ponty (1962) in his belief that phenomenology must have facticity as its origin, Indigenous cultures make no such requirement, which leaves the door open to spirituality as a starting point for phenomenology.

So, while Western science and psychology might place the spiritual experiences such as visiting with a long dead relative in the category of dream, delusion, or wish, Indigenous science and psychology would affirm it as credible phenomenal experience. Furthermore, Western culture would classify experiences of ghosts and spirits as illusion, imagination, or hallucination; Indigenous cultures value such experiences as potential real phenomena. As to whether the Indigenous or Western perspective is right/wrong or true/false, a determination need not be made. Indigenous cultures would recognize that not all humans experience the same phenomena even within the same communities. Right/wrong or true/false would have no place in the discussion, but would instead be replaced by terms such as experienced/not experienced phenomena by given individuals. In other words, the Indigenous perspective would see the experience of spirits in the same way as experiences of cold or pain. If an individual claims to be cold or in pain, it would be odd and a bit rude for another individual to say that the first individual was not really experiencing those events. And of course the obvious problem is how one verifies that another is not experiencing a sensation of cold or for that matter a sensation of a spiritual nature.

At times, Western academics have claimed that Indigenous cultures do not differ in foundational knowledge claims from those used in Western cultures, only that Indigenous scholars fail to understand this fact. The implication is often that Indigenous individuals lack the mental or educational sophistication to fully grasp the philosophical concepts of epistemological studies. As a counterargument to such Western assumptions, Cajete (2000) gives a detailed discussion of the Native science of interdependence in which he outlines how a multidimensional and multileveled Indigenous science functions. In the same scholarly vein, Vine Deloria in *The Metaphysics of Modern Existence* (1979) establishes the logical foundations of Indigenous experiences of phenomena. Other than mentioning the distinctions between Indigenous and Western logic and phenomenology, it is not within the limits of this chapter to explore these theories in more detail. Instead, the purpose of mentioning the above distinctions is to establish that Indigenous and Western ways of being-in-the-world are unique and quiet distinct. While the uniqueness does not prevent individuals from either culture the ability to communicate or even experience the other, it establishes the need to fully investigate the differences. Understanding cultural differences is often like understanding computers. Computers can handle many programs, but when you boot them up they default to a specific program. Similarly, when individuals step outside the door in the morning, they tend to default to their own cultural knowledge systems when experiencing phenomena. It may be best to leave the discussion with Wisdom (1992) in his work on the issues of the existence of god. Wisdom gives the image of two people entering a garden. One person looks around and see the organization of flowers among the weeds and claims there must be a gardener and another looks around and see the weeds among the flowers and says there is no gardener. Both individuals can justify the stated position, but neither can verify the truth of his or her position (Wisdom 1992: 316–328). The same can be stated for the difference between Indigenous and Western logic systems and phenomenal experience. Both cultural positions may be justified, but verification as to which is the "right, true, or superior" position is not determinable and, from an Indigenous position, no such determination is necessary.

A final comment must be made here before moving to the next section. It is often the case that when Indigenous scholars attempt to explain Indigenous knowledge theories they are criticized either for lacking proper syntax or for being superstitious, uneducated, or unsophisticated thinkers. The syntax criticism is probably the easiest to dismiss because the criticism itself belies a bias toward Western linear thought processes. When Indigenous scholars attempt to explain their knowledge theories they are forced to use Western language constructions, which requires them to use "balanced" syntax constructs. The difficulty occurs when Indigenous knowledge does not fit within the Western construction. It becomes a matter of fitting an octagonal peg into a rectangular hole. Many of the attempts to explain the nonlinear thought processes in linear terms have caused the criticisms that claim Indigenous knowledge to be superstitious, uneducated, or unsophisticated. The reality of Indigenous knowledge theories is that they are equal to many modern Western expressions of quantum mechanics in both complexity and sophistication (Cajete 2000). However, because the theories are difficult to express given Western knowledge constraints, misunderstandings and misinterpretations have been the result. Furthermore, the dismissal of Indigenous knowledge has also led to a dismissal of much of the Indigenous phenomenal experience, which has led to cases of cultural and individual discrimination.

Communities and Human Difference

For the purposes of the second part of this chapter, the discussion will be limited to Native American communities. By limiting the scope of the research, an attempt will be made to offer a complete picture as to how the above information functions in terms of community and human difference. While the scope of information, even with this limitation remains overly broad, the idea is to offer a generalized model of how human differences function within Native American communities. Many of the elements discussed can later be extrapolated to the larger platform of worldwide Indigenous communities. Again, it should be noted that this discussion represents only abstract generalized patterns and should not be enforced as necessary guidelines on any specific individual or community because of the complexity of individual and community variations.

Historically, the discussion of human difference in Western cultures has been based on the concept of deviations from "normal" human ability. Foucault (1982) offers a description of the historical treatment of the insane. A diagnosis of insanity was attached to any deviant behavior and often included everything from mental and physical disabilities to women who were both unmarried and pregnant. Indeed, the idea that three generations of "imbeciles" was enough to get the third generation of unmarried pregnant women sterilized remained a standard in the United States until recently (Holmes 1927). Treatment of human difference in the Western world remains problematic as is evidenced by the lack of academic research regarding the "underserved disabled population." While human rights have been researched and have been the subject of countless academic conferences in multiple academic fields, the human and civil rights discussions of the "disabled" remain academically marginalized. This text offers one of the few attempts to flesh out some of the issues faced by individuals with differences.

As pointed out by Spector in *Cultural Diversity in Health and Illness* (1979), Western medicine, as well as the general public, takes the definition of terms such as "health," "disease," and "disability" for granted. In reality, the usage of these terms reveals the dualistic and linear concepts that are embedded in Western knowledge patterns. Wendell (2008) fleshes out the inherent duality in the descriptive terms such as "handicapped" and "disabled," which are mere synonyms for the term "abnormal." The term "abnormal" indicates a derivation from that which is designated by the term "normal." Her description of normalcy is based on a standard that is accepted by Western concepts of "ideal, or the perfection of, human form." This rather Platonic notion of normal in reality appears to be a bit illusive, but nonetheless there still exists a general concept of "I know normal when I see it" or perhaps better stated as "I know abnormal when I see it." Western culture has often kept individuals with mental and physical disabilities at a distance because of their status as "other" or "abnormal." In fact, individual Western societies are still moving to a state of inclusion as is demonstrated in the legal cases involving disabled individuals and the ratification of legal disability acts. The implications of the treatment of people of difference are often reflected in acts of discrimination as society continues to see difference as an indicator of "other" (Coates 2005). However, as Wendell points out, "(u)nless we die suddenly, we are all disabled eventually" (Wendell 2008: 828).

As discussed earlier, Native American and Indigenous cultures are organized under a knowledge system that implies a multilayered pattern of inclusion on both an individual level and community levels. Moreover, as Cajete (2000) points out, the Native science of interdependence asserts that all things are in flux, which disallows the concept of a static position of "normalcy." Furthermore, no two people can experience the same ability levels in terms of eyesight, strength, or any other human function, and so no "normal" state could be established. "Able" bodied, or mind, becomes a matter of perspective to be determined by the task at hand. The individual is then identified as being "able" or "not able" to complete the task, but no judgment of abnormality is assigned to an individual unable to complete the task. Finally, if an individual is less able in body it does not imply that he or she is less able in spirit or mind. Locust states that individuals whose bodies are severely compromised are considered to be strong of spirit, as it would take great spiritual strength to remain in a severely damaged body

(Locust 1988: 17). For that reason, Locust states that human differences are often left unnoticed or undiscussed as the individual is considered to be more than his or her physical or mental disability. The individual is the totality of his or her body, mind, and spirit. The harmony for this tripartite concept of self is then a unique and ever-changing intertwining of the three aspects of each individual. The individual is then considered within the community based on his or her fulfillment of responsibilities, which are both unique and in constant flux.

According to Galloway et al. (1999), the major difference between Western and Native American concepts of "health," "disease," and "disability" is the difference between definitions that focus on a reductionist model and those that focus on a holistic model. Western medicine functions from a model that identifies the physical or mental anomaly and works to eliminate or to "cure" that anomaly. Native American medicine models function from an initial determination of why an event occurred and how to assist the individual in obtaining harmony, which may mean living with what has occurred. It is often less important to eliminate or cure the individual, than it is to assist the individual in understanding why he or she is experiencing an event and how to balance the event in himself or herself and her community. In many cases, Native American patients identify illnesses or differences as a matter involving spiritual events. In these cases, Locust points out that the elimination of the bodily symptom is not considered sufficient. A traditional medicine person will often be consulted to assist in the spiritual aspects connected to any unwellness (Locust 1988: 11–12). The terminology used to identify individuals in harmony or balance, according to Locust, is wellness, while those out of harmony may be described as being unwell. As each part of the individual is in flux, the maintenance of harmony remains a constant task.

While it is considered to be each individual's responsibility to maintain a state of wellness, it is not a task that can be achieved without the assistance of the community, as the individual is not considered truly separable from her community. In opposition to Western cultural concepts, where independence is of primary concern, Native American communities are organized in terms of interdependence as pointed out by both Cajete (2000) and Markus and Kitayama (1991). In their paper, Markus and Kitayama (1991) talk about the importance of interdependence and independence in terms of the construction of self. For cultures of interdependence, the self is identified in terms of how one relates to the others within the community, whereas cultures identified as independent define the self by using concepts of individual ego

(Markus and Kitayama 1991: 225). The distinction between the two orientations of self is identified according to action motivations, phenomenal experiences of emotions, and judgments of what is to count as being a "successful" self.

Whereas Markus and Kitayama claim that the independent self is motivated by self-advancement and individual success, the interdependent self tends to be motivated by group achievement and group success (Markus and Kitayama 1991: 225–232). They go on to add that the phenomenal experience of emotions is also different. The emotions expressed by the independently oriented self tend toward those of ego such as anger, pride, and frustration, which are often expressed in public so as to allow others to witness the phenomena. The phenomenal experiences of the interdependent self tend towards nonego-oriented emotions such as cooperation and sympathy (Markus and Kitayama 1991: 236). Interestingly, for the interdependent self, emotions in general are rarely expressed in public out of respect for the others within the community (Markus and Kitayama 1991: 236). Thompson (1997) emphasizes the above distinctions as she adapts this theory to her work in Native American vocational rehabilitation. Locust (1988) confirms the above theory when she points out that it is not considered appropriate to inflict one's own emotions on others because the energy of an individual's emotional outburst may impact another in a negative manner and it is not considered appropriate to harm another even unintentionally.

Locust (1988) discusses the Native American concept of spirit as being pervasive in all existing beings. Cajete (2000) continues this explanation of spirit in his discussion of energy as related to all things. The universal participation in spirit, here identified in terms of the active agent energy, is explained by Deloria in his statement that claims "everything in the natural world has relationships with every other thing and the total set of relationships makes up the natural world as we experience it" (Deloria 1999: 34). Cajete (2000) further explains the interaction as the culmination of the phrase "all my relations" (Cajete 2000: 86). The phrase "all my relations" can be interpreted as implying the above-mentioned multilayered phenomenal experience of responsibility. Each individual is born into a community in a network of reciprocal responsibility. A familiar spiritual guideline can be expressed as the responsibility "to do no harm." Native American ethics accepts this requirement of nonharm, but also employs a further requirement of beneficence. The idea involves a multilayered understanding of reciprocity, which requires that an individual is obligated, to the best of one's abilities, to assist all his or her relations in the achievement of harmony or wellness.

While this requirement can be stated in many contexts, the focus on wellness in this discussion predicates the emphasis of harmony as an achievement of wellness. This requirement of assistance is found stated specifically or implicitly in the works of Locust (1988), Deloria (1979, 1999, 2006), and Grande (2004) among other Native American scholars as they discuss the intertwining of individual and community relationships. Basso (1996) makes the same connection in his interpretation of language.

The intertwining of individuals creates an energy of wellness or unwellness depending on the actions of the individuals. Harm can occur when an individual is thoughtless toward another or when harsh words are spoken. Harm can also occur when an individual intentionally acts against another. Cajete (2000) refers to this as the transference of energies. All agents participate in the universal energy and each action carries with it energies as it interacts with other agents. The responsibility of each agent in the community is to use positive energy in both thought and action. It is important to note that thoughts, just like actions, carry the reality of energy and can harm. For example, thinking negative thoughts toward an individual, or simply in general about life, impacts how one individual interacts with another. Individuals can impact others simply by a gesture, a word, or an action, which may influence that individual to act in a similar positive or negative fashion. Studies have shown that words, gestures, and actions impact, both positively and negatively, the wellness of individuals (Kaye and Raghavan 2002). The energy of harm or the energy of healing can be carried in the word, gesture, or action of any given individual.

Native American communities understand the reciprocity concept of energy in terms of "all my relations" to include not only humans but all existing beings as well as beings involved in multilevel phenomenal experiences such as spiritual beings. Furthermore, an individual's responsibility to past and future generations of all beings exists. The experiences of these relationships and the reciprocal responsibilities must be considered in issues of harmony. A person who has neglected his or her responsibilities will have to balance them. The balancing often requires community assistance. For these reasons, the importance of Native American communities in issues of wellness should not be overlooked. Individuals are considered vital to the community in that each is an important component to the overall wellness of the community (Locust 1988). Furthermore, an individual displaced from her community, or separated for any reason, may find herself in a continued state of unwellness, as the self is unable to exist in the state of interdependence that it desires. The interaction of the community and self as the phenomenal experience of the interaction of energy as the agent of spirit is vital to the Native American concept of harmony.

As can be inferred from this discussion, individual human difference is understood as in some ways vital to the continuation of the community in that a community where everyone had exactly the same abilities would not survive the chaotic flux of existence. At the same time, individual human difference is not the defining factor of an individual. It is the individual interacting within the community, and whether or not he or she observes his or her ever-changing responsibilities to harm none and reciprocal beneficence, that define him or her. Locust (1988) gives the example of a young man, who in Western communities would be considered disabled. While being considered "a bit slow," each day he traveled to his neighbors and ran errands for those who could not. He had the legs that many of them did not have as well as the ability to complete many household chores. Each day he would collect the lists of needed items and travel to town to purchase them. He would chop wood or fix broken steps. A visiting social worker noticed the young man and after determining that he needed a group home situation, removed him from his community. The experience of being removed acted as a catalyst to violence for the young man at which point he was labeled a threat and institutionalized under sedation. The devastation of the removal was not just to the young man, but to those in his community who relied on his assistance. The entire community felt the loss of the young man's spirit, leaving a permanent hole where his being and energies had been.

Language and Human Difference

As can be inferred from the above, spirituality is a constant focus of Native American ways of being. There is no dichotomous distinction between that which is sacred and that which is secular. Since all things participate in the use of energies because they contain spirit, no action either mental or physical, is without spiritual consequence. "Language is more than code; it is a way of participating with each other and the natural world... At the deeper psychological level, language is sensuous, evocative, filled with emotion, meaning, and spirit" (Cajete 2000: 72). For these reasons, the language that is used in Native American communities also carries a component of spiritual energy. What is said and how it is said creates consequences for the initial agent, other agents within the community as well as the community itself. For this reason, it is important to frame human difference in positive language. Moreover, in many Native American communities, difference, disease, and death are not spoken of in front of patients or family as such discussions carry a negative energy (Locust 1988). It is understood that the individual and the community need to maintain a wellness of attitude and spirit, which is done by emphasizing positive information. For Native American ideology, one way to assist an individual who is experiencing a difference or a difficult event, mentally or physically, is to use positive language to create a supportive energy of wellness. For this reason, many Native Americans turn to community members and traditional healers while in hospitals and clinics (Hollow 1999).

Indeed, many Native Americans will not seek out Western medical assistance because of the negative language stemming from the reductionist model. Many may forgo Western medicine entirely because of the negativity in both language and practice. How medical personnel, as well as all community individuals, present information carry energy and creates either a positive or a negative atmosphere. The same aversion to negative language in Western language and institutions can be seen in a general practice of cultural separation. Since the "end game" for Native Americans is balance or harmony, it may be deemed more important to seek balance with the difference rather than "cure" or "resolve" that difference. Wendell also notes a proclivity in Western culture and medicine to see "disability" as an individual event. The measure of the "disabled" person is seen in his or her persistence to "overcome" the "disability" (Wendell 2008: 83). If he or she succeeds in overcoming his or her "disability," he or she is labeled with terms such as "success," "an inspiration," or "hero." If he or she does not overcome his or her "disability," she is given labels such as "failure" or "lazy." Individuals who fail to "lift" themselves above their disability may be seen as not working hard enough to overcome the obstacle that is "disability." Wendell points out that there is an additional expectation that overcoming the obstacle is the responsibility of the individual, and in some cases, the family. The financial, emotional, and spiritual support belongs to the individual, or family, not to the larger community or society (Wendell 2008: 83). Such is the consequence for cultures valuing independence over interdependence. The interdependence of Native American cultures requires the invoking of the ethic of reciprocity. The language used to describe the person of difference requires positive terms and community inclusion so as to avoid situations of prejudice or discrimination. Equality of value does not require that each member be the same or reflect an abstract ideal as to a specific way of being-in-the-world. For Native American ideology, equity is a matter of existence not mental or physical ability. An individual's success is not determined by simple mental or physical activities. An individual's success is inextricably bound to the success of the community and, in turn, the community's success is bound to the success of each individual.

It is the difference in language here that brings the discussion in a full circle to concepts of translation. Native American communities may not use language in a way that establishes ideas of "normal" and "abnormal" as such language would make no sense in the context of the constant flux. Furthermore, the use of language creates reality as it is a form of energy, which impacts "all my relations." Even if the individual being discussed is not present, a negative phrasing of "disabled" impacts the entire community. If a community begins to use terms that distance individuals because of the negative connotations, the community wellness is damaged. The wellness of a community requires that each individual be valued equally, which cannot be done using language that perpetuates the inequality of otherness.

Conclusion

Native American communities do not emphasize the human differences between individuals as it is assumed that each person has or will face challenges at some stage of human development. Instead, the understanding of interdependence implies a reciprocal relationship of responsibility. Every individual within the community is understood to be inherently valuable simply by virtue of participating in universal spirit. No individual is inherently more valuable than another regardless of the gifts or differences with which he or she is born as these too are in constant flux. While a medicine person is of great value to a community, so too is the young man who can run errands for the elderly when they cannot. Each person is defined according to his or her multileveled responsibilities and he or she is judged by how diligent he or she is to those responsibilities. And since all things are in constant flux, relationships and responsibilities will also be in flux. The focus for the Native American individual, as stated by Cajete (2000), is to maintain balance in the ever-changing world.

This chapter offers a theory of the differences between Indigenous and Western cultural treatment of human difference and how that treatment is established in the foundational knowledge assumptions of each cultural group. Dialogues involving the equality and treatment of human difference must begin with an exploration of these foundational assumptions with an eye to what inferences follow from them. Furthermore, exploration of interdependent and independent definitions of self also assists in the determination of language and attitude involving issues of human difference. Languages and attitudes that focus on the categorization of the "other" based on physical or mental differences carry the further consequence of establishing a language and attitude of inequality. By establishing an assumption of interdependence, a culture infers a concept of reciprocity that promotes the understanding of equality regardless of mental or physical difference. Using this concept, Indigenous cultures promote linguistic descriptors that depict the Individual's mental, physical, and spiritual being as it interacts with the community. The phenomenal experience of others is then drawn from the energy created by the language used.

With this understanding, the idea of "disability" as a word can carry negative connotations only if it carries any meaning at all. The emphasis for Native American communities is to build a community of all relations in a state of wellness. Wellness is achieved only when reciprocity of assistance occurs. Each member then, human and nonhuman, assists in establishing and maintaining balance in an ever-changing existence. The Importance of spirituality in this endeavor is paramount as all things participate in spirit. Each individual is, regardless of mental or physical difference, a participant in the spiritual and thus of equal sacred value.

References

Allen, C. (2002). *Blood Narrative: Indigenous Identity in American Indian and Maori Literary and Activist Texts*. Durham, NC: Duke University Press.

Basso, K. H. (1996). *Wisdom Sits in Places: Landscape and Languages Among the Western Apache*. Albuquerque, NM: University of New Mexico.

Cajete, G. (2000). *Native Science: Natural Laws of Interdependence*. Santa Fe, NM: Clearlight.

Coates, K. (2005). Learning from others: Comparative history and the study of indigenous-newcomer relations. *Native Studies Review. 16*(1), 3–14.

Deloria, V., Jr. (1979). *The Metaphysics of Modern Existence*. San Francisco, CA: Harper and Row.

Deloria, V., Jr. (1999). *Spirit and Reason: The Vine Deloria, Jr. Reader*. In Barbara Deloria, Kristen Foehner, & Sam Scinta (Eds.). Golden, CO: Fulcrum.

Deloria, V., Jr. (2006). *The World We Used to Live In: Remembering the Powers of the Medicine Men*. Golden, Co: Fulcrum.

Deloria, V., Jr., & Wildcat, D. (2001). *Power and Place: Indian Education in America*. Golden, CO: Fulcrum.

Foucault, M. (1982). *Madness and Civilization: A History of Insanity in the Age of Reason*. Richard Howard (Trans.). London, England: Tavistock.

Gadamer, H.-G. (1977). *Philosophical Hermeneutics*, 2nd ed. David E. Linge (Trans.). Berkeley, CA: University of California.

Galloway, J. M., Goldberg, B. M., & Alpert, J.S. (Eds.). (1999). *Primary Care of Native American Patients*. London, England: Butterworth-Heinemann Publishing.

Grande, S. (2004). *Red Pedagogy: Native American Social and Political Thought*. Lanham, MA: Rowman & Littlefield.

Habermas, J. (1984). *The Theory of Communicative Action: Reason and the Rationalization of Society*. Thomas McCarthy (Trans.). Boston, MA: Beacon Press.

Habermas, J. (1987). *The Theory of Communicative Action: Lifeworld and System – A Critique of Functionalist Reason*. Thomas McCarthy (Trans.). Boston, MA: Beacon Press.

Hollow, W. B. (1999). Traditional Indian medicine. In James M. Galloway, Bruce W. Goldberg, & Joseph S. Alpert (Eds.), *Primary Care of Native American Patients* (pp. 31–38). Boston, MA: Butterworth Heinemann. Holmes, O. W. (1927). Majority opinion in *Buck v. Bell* (274 US 200). (p. 208).

Kaye, J., & Raghavan, S. K. (2002). Spirituality in disability and illness. *Journal of Religion and Health 41*(3), 231–242.Kuhn, T. S. (1970). *The Structure of Scientific Revolutions*, 2nd ed, Foundations of the Unity of Science Series, Vol. 11, No. 2. Chicago, IL: The University of Chicago Press.

Locust, C. (1988). Wounding the spirit: Discrimination and traditional American Indian belief systems. *Harvard Educational Review 58*(3), 315–320.

Markus, H. R., & Kitayama, S. (1991). Culture and the self: Implications for cognition, emotion and motivation. *Psychological Review 98*(2), 224–253.

Maybury-Lewis, D. (1997). *Indigenous People, Ethnic Groups and the State*. Boston, MA: Allyn and Bacon.

Mbiti, J. (2006). *African Religions and Philosophy*. Oxford, England: Heinemann.

Merleau-Ponty, M. (1962). *Phenomenology of Perception*. Colin Smith (Trans.). London, England: Routledge.

Sartre, J. P. (2001). *Colonialism and Neocolonialism*. Azzedine Haddour, Steve Brewer, & Terry McWilliams (Trans.). London, England: Routledge.

Spector, R. E. (1979). *Cultural Diversity in Health and Illness*. New York, NY: Appleton-Century-Crofts.

Thompson, V. C. (1997). Independent and interdependent views of self: Implications for culturally sensitive vocational services. *Journal of Rehabilitation 63*(4), 16–20.

United Nations, Department of Economic and Social Affairs. (2009). *State of the World's Indigenous People* (No. 09.Vl. 13.St/ESA/328). New York, NY: United Nations.

Wendell, S. (2008). Toward a feminist theory of disability. In A. Bailey & C. Cuomo (Eds.), *The Feminist Philosophy Reader* (pp. 826–741). Boston, MA: McGraw-Hill.

Wisdom, J. (1992). *Gods. To Believe or Not to Believe: Reading in the Philosophy of Religion* (pp. 316–328). E. D. Klemke (Ed). Fort Worth, TX: Harcourt Brace & Jovanovich.

Wittgenstein, L. (1969). *On Certainty.* G. E. M. Anscombe & G. H. von Wright (Eds.). Denis Paul & G. E. M. Anscombe (Trans). New York, NY: Harper Torch Books.

Additional Readings

Alderete, W., Pacaldo, G., Huerta, X., &Whitesell, L. (Eds.). (1992). *Daughters of Abya Yala: Native Women Regaining Control.* Summertown, TN: Book Publishing.

Anderson, T. L. (Ed.). (1992). *Property Rights and Indian Economies: The Political Economy Forum.* Lanham, MA: Rowman & Littlefield.

Borradori, G. (2003). *Philosophy in a Time of Terror: Dialogues with Jurgen Habermas and Jacques Derrida.* Chicago, IL: University of Chicago Press.

Deloria, V., Jr. (1999). *For this Land: Writings on Religion in America.* Golden, CO: Fulcrum.

Deloria, V., Jr. (2003). *God is Red: A Native View of Religion.* Golden, CO: Fulcrum.

Fuller, S. (1991). *Social Epistemology.* Bloomington, IN: University of Indiana Press.

Goldman, A. I. (1986). *Epistemology and Cognition.* Cambridge, MA: Harvard Press.

Habermas, J. (1996). *Between Facts and Norms: Contributions to a Discourse Theory of Law and Democracy.* William Rehg (Trans.). Cambridge, MA: MIT Press.

Harden, M. J. (1999). *Voices of Wisdom: Hawaiian Elders Speak.* Oahu, HI: Booklines Press.

Kilpatrick, J. F., & Kilpatrick, A. G. (1964). Cherokee rituals pertaining to medicinal roots. *Southern Indian Studies XVI.*

Locust, C., & Lang, J. (1996). Walking in two worlds: Native Americans and the vocation rehabilitation (VR) system. *American Rehabilitation 22*(2).

Pappas, G. S., & Swain, M. (Eds.). (1978). *Essays on Knowledge and Justification.* Ithaca, NY: Cornell University.

Schaefer, C. (2006). *Grandmothers Counsel the World: Women Elders Offer their Vision for Our Planet.* Boston, MA: Trumpeter.

Notes on Contributors

Maysaa S. Bazna, EdD, is the Founder and Director of Pono Learning, a democratic school based in New York City. At the time this chapter was written, she was an Assistant Professor of Special Education at the College of Staten Island, City University of New York. Her research focuses on the intersections of spirituality, disability, and postcoloniality in educational studies and on the development of special and inclusive education. She can be reached at maysaa@ponolearning.org.

Lynne M. Bejoian is an experienced disability advocate and services professional. She is a committed educator to the full inclusion of and access for all persons with disabilities in all aspects of human endeavors. Her scholarship is in disability studies in education, and she has taught within the City University of New York.

Priscilla Gilman is a transplant from the Gulf Coast of Texas to the hills of Vermont. Along the way she has lived in Indonesia, studied studio art at Dartmouth College, and earned a Master's in Performance Studies from Northwestern University. She has been very sick for 17 years and symptomatic for 17 years before that. She spends most of her time in the two downstairs rooms of her house, where she writes as much as she is able and draws stick figure cartoons for her blog, http://www.heaveninmyfoot.com.

Erynn Rowan Laurie is a professional madwoman living close to the shores of Puget Sound, under the shadow of the Cascade Mountains. Poet, writer, disabled Navy veteran, and lifelong geek, she is a practitioner of Celtic Reconstructionist Pagan spirituality, exploring the intersections of poetry, mental illness, ecopsychology, and Celtic myth.

Lavonna L. Lovern graduated with a PhD in philosophy from the University of Missouri-Columbia and began teaching at Central Methodist College (University) where she was given tenure and Associate

Professor status in the Department of Philosophy and Religion. Dr. Lovern was also granted the position of Director of Honors for ten years. After 15 years, Dr. Lovern moved to the Valdosta, GA, area and is an Assistant Professor in the Department of Philosophy and Religious studies at Valdosta State University (VSU). Dr. Lovern continues to work with several Native American tribes in Kentucky and Arizona and currently sits on the board for Mantle Rock Native American Education Center in Kentucky and consults with a nonprofit Native American organization in Tucson, AZ. Dr. Lovern, along with several other VSU faculty members, has established a Native American Studies minor.

Jeff McNair, PhD, is Professor of Special Education at California Baptist University (CBU) where he directs the Education Specialist program for students with moderate/severe disabilities. In 2010, he launched the online MA program in Disability Studies at CBU, which is one of the few of its kind at a Christian college. He is also Director of the Christian Institute on Disability's Policy Center, part of the Joni and Friends Organization. He is currently the President of the American Association on Intellectual and Developmental Disability's Religion and Spirituality Division. Jeff and his wife Kathi have personally facilitated inclusion of adults with intellectual disabilities into church settings for over 30 years.

Dr. Jo Pearson is Reader in Theology and Religious Studies at the University of Winchester, UK. Her research engages with Wiccan, Pagan, and magical groups, particularly with regard to disability, mental health, and pain. Recent publications include *Wicca and the Christian Heritage: Ritual, Sex and Magic* (London: Routledge) and "Resisting Rhetorics of Violence: Women, Witches and Wicca," in *Feminist Theology* 18(2), 141–159, 2010. She can be contacted at the Department of Theology and Religious Studies, Faculty of Humanities and Social Sciences, University of Winchester, Sparkford Road, Winchester, SO22 4NR, UK. Email: jo.pearson@winchester.ac.uk.

Molly Quinn is Associate Professor in the Curriculum & Teaching Department at Teachers College, Columbia University. Presently, she enjoys teaching courses in arts-based pedagogies, elementary social studies, and curriculum theory and design—engaging students dialogically, philosophically, autobiographically, aesthetically, experientially, critically, in the study of curriculum and the art of teaching. The author of *Going Out, Not Knowing Whither: Education, the Upward Journey and the Faith of Reason* (2001), much of her scholarship, grounded in the field of curriculum studies, engages "spiritual" and philosophical criticism toward embracing a vision of education that cultivates wholeness, beauty, compassion, and social action.

Abigail Schindler received a Master's of Science in Disability Studies from the University of Illinois at Chicago in May 2010. She currently works as a research project professional in the Department of Developmental and Behavioral Pediatrics at the University of Chicago.

Darla Schumm is an Associate Professor of Religion at Hollins University—a small liberal arts women's college nestled in the midst of the Blue Ridge Mountains. Darla received her BA in interdisciplinary studies with concentrations in history, psychology, and women's studies from Goshen College, her MA in Social Ethics from the Pacific School of Religion in Berkeley, CA, and her PhD in Religion, Ethics, and Society from Vanderbilt University. Darla's current research focuses on intersections between religious studies and disability studies. She has several published articles in this area and is the coeditor of this volume and its companion *Disability in Judaism, Christianity, and Islam: Sacred Texts, Historical Traditions, and Social Analysis*. She enjoys running, knitting, reading, and playing with her son in her free time.

Michael Stoltzfus is Professor of Philosophy and Religious Studies at Valdosta State University in Valdosta, GA. In addition to numerous articles, he is contributing editor of this volume and its companion *Disability in Judaism, Christianity, and Islam: Sacred Texts, Historical Traditions, and Social Analysis* (2011). He teaches courses in the areas of comparative religious ethics, religious pluralism and interreligious dialogue, world religions, and the intersections of religion and popular culture. His PhD in religion, ethics, and society is from Vanderbilt University (1998). Email: mjstoltz@valdosta.edu.

Aimee Burke Valeras, PhD, LICSW, attended Boston College for her undergraduate and Master's of Social Work degrees and Arizona State University for her doctorate in social work. She has presented nationally and internationally on the topic of disability and qualitative research methodology. She currently lives in Concord, NH, working with the Dartmouth Family Medicine Residency, as a social worker in both educational and clinical roles at a community health clinic for uninsured and underinsured people. She enjoys hiking, swimming, reading, and being with family.

Index